Reforming Foreign Aid: Reinvent the World Bank

Lessons in Global Poverty Alleviation from 40 years of adventures (and misadventures) in International Development

Inder Sud

CONTENTS

Preface

Almost every developing country has been the recipient of aid from the World Bank and a plethora of other national and international aid donors. And many countries, notably in Asia, have made dramatic progress in reducing poverty. Yet, what is striking is that the amount of foreign aid received has little or no correlation to which countries are progressing and which ones are not. In 1971, when I first joined the World Bank, Malaysia, Indonesia, and Thailand were not much richer than many countries in sub-Saharan Africa. Korea was still a poor country. But when I left the World Bank in 2001, Korea was already a rich industrialized country, and Malaysia, Indonesia, and Thailand were well on their way to upper middle-income status, while sub-Saharan Africa was still mired in poverty despite the abundance of foreign aid poured into the subcontinent.

The idea of writing a book about the foreign aid had been in my mind for almost ten years. Through thirty years at the World Bank, I witnessed the varying paths to development taken by different countries. After retiring, I became an adjunct professor, teaching development to graduate students at George Washington University and Duke University. My interactions with young, bright students committed to making a difference in alleviating global poverty and eager to learn how to go about doing it helped me hone and reflect upon my own experiences. My students were not hesitant about questioning the prevailing wisdom about development. Most held a somewhat negative view of the official aid agencies, especially the World Bank. Some had even participated in protests at the World Bank annual meetings, something that had become a routine event since the first major protest at the 1992 meeting in Madrid. NGOs, many of them thought, could provide the answer to alleviating global poverty.

I was rather proud of the work I had done in countries like Korea, Thailand, Malaysia, Indonesia, and Chile, that had broken out of poverty within one generation. But the students would rightly question whether the progress was because of foreign aid or despite foreign aid. It was always difficult to separate out cause and effect. The miraculous progress by China would inevitably lead to a discussion about whether democracy was an aid or a hindrance to development. Our discussions

1

of experiences with NGOs highlighted not only their contributions to development, but also about how NGOs can sometimes actually detract from development. Some of my students had spent significant time in some of the poorest countries, working for organizations like Peace Corps, CARE, Save the Children, and others. They had often worked side by side to projects financed by official aid agencies, including the World Bank, and questioned the distortions caused by donor projects.

The rich class discussions, with widely varying perspectives, helped me crystallize my own thinking about development and foreign aid. It reinforced my earlier view that foreign aid can work, but in very limited set of circumstances. First and foremost, there must be leadership in the country committed to improving the well-being of their people and a vision to make it happen. With these preconditions, foreign aid can help. However, foreign aid can never be the driver of development. On the flip side, the way foreign aid is implemented, with its preoccupation with periodical global declarations, push for ever-increasing volume of aid, and discrete projects as the delivery mechanism, can actually deter development.

I first started writing more generally about foreign aid but soon found the story becoming extremely complex when trying to describe the myriad of official foreign aid organizations, each with its own peculiarities. This made for tedious reading; so after a few false starts, I decided to make the World Bank as the focus of my book. Although in today's world the World Bank is only one of many players in the international development arena, it is by far the single largest source of foreign aid and arguably the most influential institution in shaping thinking about development. It is an organization that many people love to hate. It is often a subject of much criticism from all sides of the political spectrum. But it is also the one organization donors call upon to lead aid efforts when faced with a difficult challenge such as post-conflict reconstruction. And of course, it is an organization I know most intimately. However, many of this book's conclusions are applicable to the larger realm of foreign aid more generally.

When I worked at the World Bank, many people genuinely interested in issues of global poverty and foreign aid would often say to me, "I am really impressed with what you do. But do the projects you finance really work?" I felt that this was an entirely reasonable question, whether one came from an aid-donor country or from an aid-recipient country. Yet of the many books written on the subject, few were really accessible for the interested but non-specialist audience. I have written this book in such a way that the average citizen can find it digestible, not just insiders of the foreign aid community. My conclusions stem from personal stories and anecdotes that help to illustrate the complex interactions of development. My hope is that readers from all walks of life will benefit from the provocative ideas put forth here and further their thinking on the role we place on foreign aid generally, and World Bank specifically, in the years ahead.

Introduction

Foreign aid has been a subject of controversy throughout its more than sixty years of existence. The Marshall Plan, which was the precursor to the foreign aid as we know today, itself attracted considerable debate and criticism when it was proposed by the then secretary of state George C. Marshall. The proponents saw it as a moral responsibility to help Europe's war-torn economies and help "end poverty, desperation, and chaos" and to "permit the emergence of political and social conditions in which free institutions can exist."[1] The opponents, mostly from the right wing of the Republican Party, opposed it for their own ideological reasons. They disliked the socialistic tendencies of Europeans, the additional burden on U.S. taxpayers that it would create, and further unwarranted U.S. entanglements. But there were also serious criticisms from several notable economists. Wilhelm Ropke, an influential advisor to the German minister of economy Ludwig Erhard, believed that economic recovery would come from moving from central planning to a free-market economy and not from an injection of outside funds, going as far as to say that the Marshall Plan could actually forestall the transition to a free-market economy. Erhard would later credit Ropke's advice for the postwar German recovery.[2] Henry Hazlitt, a widely read economic journalist in the United States, was another vocal critic and wrote numerous articles in opposition to the Marshall Plan. In his 1947 book *Will Dollars Save the World?* Hazlitt criticized the Marshall Plan, arguing that economic recovery comes through domestic savings, investment, and private enterprise, and not through large subsidies.

The Marshall Plan was short-lived, lasting only four years, partly because the European (and Japanese) recovery was very rapid, and partly because of opposition to further U.S. assistance to countries that were already considered to be back on their feet. But the claimed success of Marshall Plan gave impetus to creating programs to help the growing list of newly independent countries in Asia and Africa.

The approach to foreign aid mirrored the approach of the Marshall Plan, which was to build the economies of the desperately poor newly independent countries by a large injection of external (at the time mostly from the United States) capital. Drawing from the well-known economic theories of the time of growth being driven essentially by the accumulation of capital and labor, the prevailing view among economists was that the newly independent countries—later christened variably as the "third world," the "backward nations," etc., before settling on the more benign and politically correct term of "developing countries"—had ample labor, but what they lacked is the capital. In the second edition of his popular introductory economics textbook (*Economics: An Introductory Analysis*, McGraw Hill, 1951), Paul Samuelson wrote (that) "the backward nations cannot get their heads above water because their production is so low that they can spare nothing for the capital formation by which their standards of living could be raised" (p. 49).

Samuelson's reasoning resonated with the basic instincts of the self-assured American public of helping the less fortunate. But it was reinforced further by also the prevalent cold war attitudes of resisting the expansion of Soviet influence around the world. Communism, it was feared, will find fertile territory in the poor third world. India, one of the earliest newly independent and a large third world country, became one of the first, and perhaps the most important, countries for the launch of foreign aid. India was followed in rapid succession by a host of other countries in Asia and Africa to gain independence from the colonial powers. The short-lived Marshall Plan was replaced by a rapidly growing foreign aid program. The World Bank, the permanent multilateral institution created in 1944 under the Marshal Plan to finance the reconstruction of western Europe and Japan, later also spearheaded the expansion of foreign aid.[3] It made its first loan to a third world country, Chile, in 1948.

The United States also continued with its bilateral aid efforts[4] for a decade after the end of the Marshall Plan under various organizational initiatives and changing focus until 1961 when the U.S. Agency for International Development (USAID) was established by the Kennedy administration with the sole purpose of helping economic development of poor countries. In proposing the new United States foreign assistance program, President Kennedy cited both the security and moral justification, suggesting that the economic collapse of developing countries "would be disastrous to our national security, harmful to our comparative prosperity, and offensive to our conscience."[5] Kennedy went on to suggest that "the 1960s presented an historic opportunity for industrialized nations to move less-developed nations into self-sustained economic growth."

The foreign aid program, however, also invited considerable criticism. Economists Milton Friedman, of the University of Chicago and Peter Bauer of the London School of Economics were two of the most renowned and early critics. Their criticisms mirrored the earlier criticisms by conservative economists of the Marshall Plan that foreign aid represents an unwarranted expansion of government and holds the prospect of actually retarding economic growth. In a 1958 article in the Yale Review ("Foreign Economic Aid: Means and Objectives"), Friedman even went on to argue that "despite the intentions of foreign economic aid, its major effect, insofar as it has an effect at all, will be to speed the Communization of the underdeveloped world." Although Friedman's fears about the expansion of communism proved to be hyperbolic, he did not waver from his fundamental premise. In a lecture at the Smith Center for Private Enterprise Studies on November 1, 1991, contrasting the impressive growth in Hong Kong without foreign aid with India's dismal growth, Friedman noted the following:[6]

> India has been a major recipient (of foreign aid); it got some $55 billion of foreign aid over the past forty years. It is tempting to say that India failed to grow despite foreign aid. I believe it is the other way; in part, India failed to grow because of foreign aid. Foreign aid provided the resources that enabled the government to impose the kind of (interventionist) economic policies it did.
>
> What is true of India is true much more broadly. Foreign aid has done far more harm to the countries we have given it to than it has done good. Why? Because in every case, foreign aid has strengthened governments that were already too powerful. Mozambique, Tanzania, and many other African countries testify to the same effect as India.

Bauer continued to be a persistent critic of foreign aid up to his death in 2002, writing numerous articles and books on the subject. Based on his extensive experience in a number of developing countries, including India, Bauer argued that foreign aid increases the power of the government, leads to corruption, misallocates resources, and erodes civil society.[7]

Some six decades after the launch of foreign aid, there is little agreement among academics and practitioners on the utility of foreign aid. The arguments remain the same, although the protagonists have changed. Jeffrey Sachs of Colombia University is joined by the likes of celebrity stars Bono and Selma Hayek in advocating for more aid. William Easterly of NYU has emerged as a vocal critic, echoing much of Friedman/Bauer arguments based on his own empirical studies and field observation of relationship between aid and development.[8]

The American public finds itself conflicted: their idealistic tendencies that lead them to support foreign aid are countermanded by their even stronger suspicion of the governments of developing countries that they believe to be generally corrupt and inept. Their ability to understand both sides of the argument is limited by the extensive, highly technical and theoretical academic literature on aid effectiveness that unfortunately remains largely inaccessible to them. Overall, American public attitude toward foreign aid can at best be described as ambivalent.

The American politics reflects the public attitudes. The majority in Congress has always been skeptic about the priority for foreign aid, given doubts on its effectiveness and little evidence of it having bought any friends for the United States among the third world. For most of the 1970s and 1980s, foreign aid allocations for both U.S. bilateral aid programs and for the U.S. contributions to multilateral aid agencies like the World Bank and various United Nations aid agencies, could be approved largely through "continuing resolutions," that enabled the legislators to duck from voting for these explicitly. There were few advocates to be found for foreign aid in the halls of Congress.

However, the focus on terrorism in the late 1990s began a shift toward foreign aid. Economic deprivation, it was argued, was at the root cause of terrorism, and thus economic progress must be an integral part of the efforts to counter terrorism. The events of September 11 accelerated the support for this new paradigm. The Bush administration's national security strategy released in 2002 explicitly made the link, noting that "America is now threatened less by conquering states than we are by failing states." It promoted foreign aid as the American "soft power" against terrorism. The debates about aid effectiveness were suddenly forgotten and overshadowed by the newfound alliance between liberals, who previously believed in foreign aid as a moral responsibility, and conservatives, who bought into the potential of foreign aid to fight terrorism. U.S. foreign aid suddenly had new life. A conservative president promised to double foreign aid in five years and launched new aid programs—PEPFAR to fight AIDS around the world and the Millennium Challenge Corporation to provide significant funding to countries that promoted democracy and good governance. President Obama was a strong supporter of relying even further on this American soft power, at least as much, if not more, than military power. He followed up with still larger aid allocation for Pakistan and Afghanistan, two of the potential failing states that pose threat to American security.

It is an open question whether and for how long the renewed support for foreign aid in the era of concern for terrorism will last. There are already many critics of aid programs in fragile and failed states. The critics hold out no hope for foreign aid doing any better in fragile states than in other poor countries, given that the institutions in the former are even weaker, governments with lesser control, and high levels of corruption.[9] An early evaluation by the World Bank of its programs in post-conflict and fragile states does not leave much room for optimism.[10] Reports of widespread fraud and waste from aid programs in Iraq, Afghanistan, Haiti, among others, have reinforced pessimism about the ability of foreign aid to make a difference.

I have been a witness to enormous changes in the developing world in the more than forty years that I have spent in working in the field of development, of which the first thirty years were working at the World Bank. It has been an enormous opportunity to learn about development on the job. I was fortunate enough to start my career working in East Asia where I saw the "East Asian miracle" unfold in front of my eyes. No textbook can ever teach you what you must learn working on the ground. I distinctly remember arriving in Jakarta in 1974 on a rainy afternoon for my first "mission" for the World Bank. There were only two hotels in the city, one of which was hastily put together using makeshift construction methods only recently as the flood of businessmen began to arrive following the boom from the abrupt four-fold increase in oil prices decreed by OPEC. Seoul city in Korea had slums around an open sewer. Malaysia was still an agrarian economy, heavily dependent on palm oil and rubber. And of course, I still have pictures of a dilapidated and overcrowded housing without indoor plumbing in Shanghai when I first visited China in 1980.

These countries have transformed themselves from poverty to significant prosperity within a generation. The World Bank had an active aid program in all these countries, and I developed an optimistic view of the possibilities of foreign aid. But later in my career, my optimism was replaced by pessimism as I worked in other countries in South Asia, Africa, and the Middle East where standards of living were stagnating or, as in many countries in Africa, declining despite large amounts of foreign aid. Looking at the world today, it would be tempting to conclude that East Asians are succeeding because they are more advanced. But I know that forty years back, the East Asian countries did not look terribly different from countries in other parts of the world, including

Africa, a point that has been well documented by Harvard economists David Lindauer and Michael Roemer in their 1994 book *Asia and Africa: Legacies and Opportunities in Development*. I simply cannot accept the view expressed by a subset of aid optimists that I would call "aid apologists" who, having by now seen numerous failures, expound the view that development is an inherently difficult task and that it should be acceptable to have large numbers of failed projects.[11]

After forty years of witnessing firsthand experiences in development in more than fifty countries, I now believe that foreign aid has worked but in a very specific set of circumstances. Sustained good leadership and commitment in the country are critical to success. The contribution of foreign aid is secondary at best. But I have also learned that there are serious issues with the way foreign aid has been delivered that have contributed to its failures. These aid modalities have become even more ineffective in the current world environment where globalization has become a much bigger force for development than foreign aid. This book is an attempt to point to changes in foreign aid that are necessary if it is to be effective and relevant.

There are numerous providers of foreign aid, large and miniscule. The biggest ones individually are the four multilateral development banks—The World Bank that works worldwide, and three regional development banks each for Asia, Latin America and the Caribbean, and Africa. All four of these essentially work on the same lines. Several industrialized countries have their own aid agencies that also finance development, with a special focus on their "spheres of interest" that can be based on history (e.g., French in West Africa), colonial ties (e.g., UK in South Asia and Africa), national foreign policy (e.g., the United States in Egypt and Pakistan), commercial interests (e.g., Japan in East Asia), or, in recent years, concern for major global issues (e.g., HIV/AIDS). Since 2001, controlling terrorism and post-conflict reconstruction and state-building have become a major preoccupation for bilateral foreign aid programs of many western countries, most notably the United States.

The bilateral aid programs also essentially work on the same basis as the programs of multilateral development banks, with twists dictated by national interests or policy. Although the bilateral aid programs can be significant in some developing countries, individually they are generally much smaller than the amount of aid provided by the multilateral development banks.

I have chosen to make the World Bank as the focus of this book with the expectation that my analysis and recommendations can be generalized for foreign aid more broadly. There are a number of reasons for my decision to take this approach. The most obvious reason is that the World Bank is where I spent a bulk of my career and thus an institution I know the best. But the main reason is that it is the single largest and most influential institution financing development. Its policies and programs—unfortunately both good and bad—are generally followed by the other three multilateral development banks, and by and large by most bilateral aid agencies. As an institution with virtually universal worldwide membership,[12] it reflects so to speak the collective wisdom on development. And despite misgivings from time to time, the United States and other industrialized countries turn to the World Bank for leadership when faced with difficult challenges, be it aid to the Palestinians or rebuilding Afghanistan, or providing liquidity to developing countries (along with the IMF) during international financial crises.

This book is not an academic treatise on assessing foreign aid. There are many other books that attempt to do this, although most of such books have been more useful in generating debates among academics rather than enlightening the general public. A significant number of these books deal with fine details of foreign aid and are thus accessible only to foreign aid insiders. My aim is to engage an average educated citizen who has an interest, but not necessarily expertise in the subject, nor a taste for high analytics. Yet she/he wishes to deepen her/his understanding of foreign aid and what can or should be done to reform it.

I have organized the book in three sections. Section I is a firsthand account of my thirty-year journey through the World Bank. I detail the most important assignments that I had in the World Bank, including the key events that shaped my thinking about the way aid works or should have worked. I highlight some memorable moments as well as disappointments. My aim is for the reader to develop through my stories an understanding of the World Bank and how it actually works in practice. In section II, I delve into the topic of aid effectiveness. I present data on performance of World Bank projects and point to circumstances under which projects succeed and when they fail. I conclude that while overall the success rates of projects is within an acceptable range, there is a wide variation among countries, with projects in the poorest countries that are most in need fairing the worst. Moreover, the project mode of delivering aid is increasingly problematic and does not ensure successful development even when they succeed. I conclude that the World Bank needs to adjust its focus and modus operandus to achieve better outcomes in development.

In the last section III, I present proposals for reforms that the World Bank, and by extension other aid agencies, need to make in their way of doing business if their aid is to be effective in the future. I advocate budget support rather than project aid as the principal modality for foreign aid. I also propose a hardheaded approach to foreign aid that rewards country's record of good performance rather than trying to turn around poor performers based on promises of doing better in the future. Contrary to the slogan of stock pickers, for foreign aid, past performance is actually indicative of future performance. Most importantly, I argue for fundamental reforms in the governance of the World Bank that is arcane and ineffective in monitoring and ensuring that World Bank aid actually delivers development.

PART I.

Learning about Development: A Thirty-Year Journey at the World Bank

1. Introduction to Washington DC

I arrived in Washington DC on a hot, humid summer night in August1971. It had been a long drive from Minnesota. My girlfriend, Peg, who was soon to be my wife, had driven with me. We had planned to make a stop on the way but the excitement of reaching Washington to start a new life was too exciting. I had accepted a job offer from the World Bank as a "Young Professional" which was, and continues to this day, as the most sought out point of entry for bright, young recruits to the World Bank. Peg had been a teacher of mathematics the previous year in the San Francisco Bay area, while waiting for me to finish my PhD at Stanford. She did not have a job lined up before the move but was confident that she will have no difficulty finding one. Both the Fairfax County and Montgomery County school systems even then had a national reputation for quality, and she was excited at the prospect of teaching in either one depending on where we decided to find a home. As someone who grew up in the lush suburbs of Minneapolis and who enjoyed being in nature, she would not even consider the possibility of living and working in the district.

It was just getting dark as we entered DC. The streets were mostly deserted even though it was not even nine as yet. With the help of an AAA map, after navigating the confusing roundabouts of Washington, we found our way to the Dupont Plaza Hotel that the World Bank had reserved for me. Parking the car at the entrance, we entered the hotel while keeping a wary eye on our bicycles that we had carried on the trunk-mounted carrier all the way from Minnesota. The travel information we had read about Washington DC all had prominent warnings about muggings and thefts.

"I have a reservation, but I am a day early," I announced to the desk clerk, who had already been not so discreetly sizing us up since we entered the front door. The desk clerk thumbed through a set of index cards until he found one with my name on it and he handed me a registration card. As I was about to start filling in the usual information, he again looked at the index card with my reservation, glanced at Peg, and again at the reservation. "It is for a single room for seven nights?"

I fully knew that the World Bank would have only booked a single room for me since I had not considered it proper to ask my new employer to book a double where my girlfriend could stay with me. I assumed that I could add Peg to my reservation when checking in.

"Yes, I know but there are two of us. So please give us a double," I said, continuing to fill the registration form and trying to exude confidence.

"Sorry, we cannot rent one room to people of opposite sex unless you are married. You must rent two separate rooms if both of you wish to stay here. This is the law," said the clerk, showing firmness and a touch of disdain.

This first introduction to Washington DC was a rude realization that life in a liberal campus in the San Francisco Bay Area is not the microcosm of American life. I also realized that I was in the south and not straight due east of California that I had thought like most geographically challenged Americans.

We drove around for over an hour, looking for an alternative hotel, getting lost in the residential areas of Northwest, Washington DC, and some of the seedy parts of the city, crossing the Potomac River at least twice. The darkness of the night did not help. Suddenly, seeing a lit-up hotel sign, we drove in to enquire if they had a room. Having learnt from the last experience, we confidently strode in and checked in as "Mr. and Mrs. Inder Sud." Only upon waking up in the morning and going downstairs for breakfast, we realized that we had checked into one of the fanciest hotels in Washington. We checked out and settled in the less intimidating surroundings of the White House Motel in suburban Virginia, where we spent the next four weeks while looking for an apartment.

As I write this book, gay marriage is the law of the land – a far cry from the days when unmarried couples could not share the same room. Social change happens, but it takes time – a lesson that applies just as well to development.

2. Welcome to the World Bank

I arrived at the World Bank headquarters the next day. I was a few minutes early for my 10:00 a.m. appointment with my assigned personnel officer. I took a short stroll around the block both to spend the extra time and to catch my bearings in this unfamiliar city.

The World Bank occupied a series of four buildings within a small block bounded by "G" and "H" streets in the north and south sides and 18th Street on the west. The side facing the 19th Street was occupied by the International Monetary Fund. Some of the buildings at one time had belonged to the U.S. government and had been gifted to the World Bank and the IMF after the Bretton Woods convention in New Hampshire that established the two "Bretton Woods sisters" as they were commonly known.

The side of the building facing the "G" street had been constructed later by the World Bank as it expanded its operations by purchasing and consolidating properties from several small shops that were located on that side of the block. The only exception had been one hamburger joint whose owner refused to sell out. He was famously known to have told a committee of the board of the World Bank that was formed to negotiate with him, "I have never dealt with a bank in my life, and I am not about to do so now."

After much negotiation and various offers of sweeteners, including an office paid for by the World Bank for him up the street, he had extracted a nice deal whereby he retained his ownership of the small lot and allowed the World Bank to build a restaurant for him that fitted in with the rest of the building. He promptly named his restaurant "World Buttery" and did a thriving business for a number of years from World Bank staff until finally selling the property to the World Bank some twenty years later at a great premium.

The executive director from India had documented the story for his government back home drawing the lesson: you can be very independent in your actions if you are not dependent on foreign aid! The point was to stay with me for many years to come as I observed firsthand a strong correlation between development success and home-grown policies.

A few minutes before the appointed hour, I took the elevator up to to the floor on the "D" building that housed the entire personnel function. I was greeted warmly by my assigned personnel officer who, after exchanging a few pleasantries, got down to the paperwork. He introduced me to the person specifically assigned to help non-U.S. staff with settling in Washington DC, a function I came to appreciate immensely over the years not only because of its utility but more so because of the excellent person assigned to the task. Lacy Carter was a true legend at the World Bank up until her retirement in the late-1980s.

The young professionals were given two six-month rotational assignments before they were selected for a permanent placement by one of the departments. The rotational assignments were purposely in areas you knew nothing about in line with the goal of giving the young recruits—also widely known, but not always without trepidation by the experienced staff, as "future managers"—as wide an exposure to the bank's work as possible. My first assignment was to be with the Water Supply and Sanitation Division that managed projects worldwide in this sector.

I met Harold Shipman, manager of the division, over lunch. He was a sanitary engineer by training and had vast experience in the sector before he came to the bank a few years earlier. He was friendly and welcoming. But he was not entirely sure how I would fit into his work. Traditionally, project development and appraisal work, particularly in the hard infrastructure sectors, had been the domain of engineers and financial analysts. Economic analysis was seen by project managers as a new requirement imposed on them by President McNamara, and most did not appreciate the need. After some discussion, he assigned me to do the economic analysis for a water and sewerage project for Kingston, Jamaica.

I was to become the third member of the Jamaica project team, the other two being a sanitary engineer and a financial analyst. Both were highly accomplished mid-career professionals. Rajagopalan, or Raj as everyone called him, was the sanitary engineer and the leader of the team. He held an advanced degree from the Johns Hopkins University and had worked for fifteen years in India before joining the World Bank in the late 1960s. He was one of the first specialists from India hired by the World Bank. Bob Smith was a Canadian who, like many of his contemporary English Canadians, spoke with impeccable English accent. He had worked for several years in Canada and in the British colonial administration in Africa before joining the World Bank. Bob was the typical of most project specialists at the time—mostly white men, technically well qualified, highly experienced in their respective fields, and often with developing country experience acquired from working in one of the colonial empires. Raj was atypical but from among the growing ranks of qualified third world professionals that McNamara had decreed must be better represented in the bank. India was one of the few developing countries that produced qualified people in adequate numbers and was soon to become one of the major sources of recruitment for representation from "Part II countries," the term used in the bank for developing countries.

The World Bank only hired experienced professionals in mid-career on the presumption that these are the kinds of staff who would command the respect of our developing country clients and from whom they could learn. The young professionals like me were introduced to infuse young blood and fresh ideas in the organization, but with strict limits on the numbers. The program recruited some fifty persons per year through a highly competitive worldwide process. We were viewed with some trepidation by the mid-career types who feared that the young folks, who were generalists and did not have sufficient experience, would in due course take over the bank. Their fears were well justified. In the first five years since the start of the program, several "graduates" of the young professional program had been promoted to managerial positions, a trend that accelerated all the way into the 1980s. The older professionals were unhappy that the young professionals were often promoted over them, far too prematurely in their view. They attributed this to the report-driven culture of the World Bank that they felt placed a high premium on the young professionals' good writing and presentation skills over solid technical skills and experience. The controversy continues to divide the technical specialists from the generalists even to this day, although it has died down a bit with the graying of the original young professionals!

Raj handed me a big large stack of reports on the project in Jamaica when I met him. He asked me to go through them and come back to him with any questions. He thought that since this was to be my first project assignment, I should consider it mostly as a learning experience. This suited me just fine since I neither knew anything about Jamaica nor about municipal water supply!

3. The Missionaries: World Bank Experts

Within three weeks of my arriving at the World Bank, I was on my first "mission" to Jamaica. The word mission was, and is, used in the World Bank to describe any official travel to a country for meetings of any sort—to review a project, to discuss the program, or even to deliver a lecture. I was intrigued by the usage of the term for its negative connotation among those of us who came from the "less civilized" world. But I did not think much about it beyond this initial intrigue and soon was as fluent in its usage as my colleagues.

Raj had decided that we had enough information in hand from the various reports that had been prepared over the years to now appraise the project, and an essential part of the appraisal was a visit to the country for firsthand discussions. The Jamaican government had welcomed the news since it had received several missions in the last few years to review progress of the preparatory work. The advice from the bank that it was ready to appraise normally meant, barring unforeseen events that finally a firm financing commitment would be forthcoming and project implementation could start. They anxiously awaited the arrival of the mission.

The two weeks we spent in Jamaica were exciting, exhilarating and, yes, very tiring. We were lodged in a comfortable hotel, probably the only western hotel in Kingston at the time. For two weeks, the three of us—Raj, the mission leader, Bob, the financial analysis, and me, a rookie economist—spent most of our waking time together, except for times when we broke up for separate meetings with the people working on our area of concern in the project. Raj and Bob would split up often since they had their distinct areas of expertise and had specific Jamaican specialists—and invariably consultants—working with them. But I did not have a counterpart since no one in Jamaica thought that economic analysis of a water supply project warranted the employment of a dedicated economist. So I spent most of my time tailing Raj, splitting off a few times to join Bob in his discussions on financial matters.

Raj was in true form and clearly the man in-charge. He would ask pointed questions from the staff of the water authority that was responsible for the project and their consultants from the UK, who had been hired to prepare the project. He had prepared himself well and was in full command of the facts. Can you not reduce the height of the dam? What happens if there is a hundred-year flood? Why have you specified steel pipes when pre-stressed pipes would be less expensive? Can the distribution system absorb the additional quantity of water? Are the proposed measures to control water leakage, or "unaccounted for water" in the technical jargon, adequate? Water wastage was, and continues to this day, a major problem in many developing countries.

Accompanied by what seemed like an army of Jamaican counterparts and their consultants, we hiked up to the top of the mountainous site where the dam was to be built. More questions from Raj about the geology, terrain, vegetation, resettlement plans for people living in the proposed reservoir area, etc.

Some questions had straightforward answers. The project consultants were world-renowned in the field and had properly covered the topic in their studies. Sometimes they simply accepted Raj's suggestions. But some questions resulted in a spirited discussion, which generally concluded with an agreement to do more investigation.

Bob had holed himself with the financial managers of the water company and carried out a parallel dialogue on the finances. The principal emphasis seemed to be on the adequacy of tariffs to sustain the investment during operations. Tariffs had not been revised for years, and the water company had to rely on annual subventions from the government to maintain and operate its assets. Of course, given the shortage of government budget resources, generally the government is unable to provide the necessary subsidy that starts the vicious cycle: unwillingness by the government to set adequate tariffs lead to insufficient revenues for the water company, that in turn to need of government financial support to cover operations and maintenance; fiscal constraints of the government means that the financial support does not materialize or falls far short of needs; the water company thus faces a shortage of funds for maintenance; lack of adequate maintenance leads to poor service, that in turn leads to resistance from customers to pay for the service; and back to shortage of funds. This is the vicious cycle that existed in Jamaica and which I was to find in numerous other countries throughout my work in development. Of course, wanting to get World Bank's loan support, the Jamaican water company made promises for tariff increases in the future and better financial performance of the water company, that our experience told us are unlikely to be fulfilled but still we accepted. And the great game continued. All Bob could do is to have a thorough analysis of the issue, discuss it with anyone and everyone in the position of responsibility—the Prime Minister included—and get an agreement on the financial policies to be followed in the future.

We concluded our work in the two weeks that we had planned. Raj declared the project to have been successfully appraised when we had the final meetings with the various ministers concerned. He went over the conclusions of the mission methodically in each meeting. They mostly nodded agreement, pausing to ask a few questions or indicating the difficulty of implementing some of the things we were asking. Raising water tariffs was invariably the agreement that they dwelled on the most. We promised to present the loan for the approval of the World Bank's board of directors as soon as they had satisfied the conditions that we had specified in the long list of actions we left for them. There was satisfaction all around among the Jamaicans that the money will indeed be forthcoming after three years of hard work in preparing the project. The minister hosted a dinner in our honor with toasts to the success of the project.

I was in complete awe of my team, particularly Raj. I was amazed at his knowledge and experience. His mastery of the subject was all too clear. I would notice heads nodding in affirmation whenever he spoke. They took his views seriously, not because he held the purse strings but because they considered him a real expert. The Jamaicans welcomed his probing questions as a way to improve the project design and not as intrusion. This was my first lesson in development: the developing countries of course like the aid money, but what they like even more is the honest advice from seasoned professionals. This was at the core of the World Bank I saw and admired over the years.

I had carved out my work as doing the economic analysis for the project. No one in Jamaica had any real interest in this other than to satisfy the World Bank's requirement. After all, how do you quantify benefits of drinking water? I fell back on the traditional method of using water charges as a proxy for the benefits, although everyone knew that it is an imperfect proxy particularly since the charges tended to be below cost. I added a couple of twists of my own to expand the analysis. Having just come from a renowned university, I was very proficient in the use of computers that were still a novelty for my colleagues. I decided to simulate a range of estimates using alternative assumption and could show that the economic return would be high within a plausible value of benefits. I also prepared computer-generated charts that Raj loved (a picture is worth a thousand words!). It was all fairly straightforward, but earned me a reputation of being very creative. A one-eyed king I was! But maybe that was exactly the point of bringing in young fresh blood to the World Bank.

We had worked very hard. Raj and Bob enjoyed great respect of the Jamaicans. Besides appreciating their expertise, the Jamaicans thought of them as only having the best interest of their country in mind. Their motive was nothing more than searching for solutions to their problems that made the most sense. We had indeed been on a mission: a mission to help the city of Kingston improve its water system so more Jamaicans will have access to safe water. The term took on a new and positive meaning for me, and I wanted to be a "missionary" like Raj. Only later in my career I began to once again question the term as I saw development experiences across a range of countries and better understood the importance of home-grown ideas, even if they are not as good as what the experts can offer.

4. Development is Sometimes Saying "No"

My six months in the Water Supply and Sanitation group passed quickly. The Jamaica assignment was followed by work on a project in Ghana to expand water supply in the Greater Accra-Tema region. Raj was the team leader for this project as well, and again I was asked to handle the economic analysis. The experience was very similar: pouring over reams of project reports, a visit to Ghana to review the project, site visits, a close scrutiny of the various aspects by the team, agreement on various modifications in the project, and agreement on the loan covenants to conclude the appraisal successfully. Having learned from the Jamaica experience, I was much more proactive myself in seeking out the necessary information to complete economic analysis of the project. All in all, I had busy and productive six months.

My next six-month assignment should normally have been in the "Area Department" that was responsible for managing World Bank's relations with the individual borrowing countries. The department was staffed by macroeconomists who kept their finger on the pulse of the country's economy and a number of "loan officers," who handled day-to-day relationships. There was a degree of tension between the staff of the projects and the area departments: the former had the final say on when a project was ready to receive World Bank financing and the latter on which projects would be included in the bank's program for a particular country. The fact that the project staff generally tended to be older and experienced professionals and the area staff younger with not as much practical experience, but still vested with considerable authority and tapped much more frequently for managerial appointments than the project experts, created a degree of tension. But the tension—often thought of as "creative tension"—helped maintain a valuable balance in thinking and served the World Bank well. Most young professionals were expected to be exposed to both sides of the house during their rotational assignments.

I decided, however, to opt for the research side for my second rotational assignment. I had thought of research as my calling having having absolutely loved the four years I spent at Stanford doing my doctoral research. My doctoral thesis had been on modeling an airport airport system, and I considered transportation as my field of interest. I was attracted to the group in the World Bank doing research and policy work on transportation and thought of it as my permanent home upon graduation from the young professional program. I was able to persuade my personnel officer that it made sense for me to join them for my second assignment since I was very sure of my longer-term interests.

I had barely settled into my assignment when my manager, Tony Churchill, walked one day into my office, handed me a manila folder, and left after saying, "Take a look at it and tell me what you think?"

The folder contained a letter in French with an accompanying English translation from President Omar Bongo of Gabon—yes, he was president in 1972—to the World Bank president Robert McNamara. The letter opened with the normal flowery language and long-winded courtesies typical of letters in French and went on to ask for World Bank assistance in financing a railroad to connect the deep hinterland jungle of Gabon with the port city of Owendo. The project, he said, was needed to open up exploitation of timber forests for export of hardwood. He called the project the highest priority for the country. Accompanying Bongo's letter was a separate letter from the then French President Georges Pompidou to McNamara in strong support of Bongo's request. Pompidou indicated that the French were also committed to this important project and would be willing to co-finance the project with the World Bank. Scribbled on top of Bongo's letter was a cryptic note, "David: Please handle. Bob."

David Henderson was the director of the economics department that included transport research as one of the units under it. David had turned the letters over to Tony who, in turn, had assigned me, literally the lowest (and the youngest) person in the hierarchy to pass judgment. The World Bank was a very small organization at the time—some six hundred people as I recall—and the letters were on my desk the day after they had been read by McNamara. I at once felt important and also scared. I knew nothing about railways and even less about Gabon.

I read the letters several times over. They were on impressive presidential letterheads. I recall Bongo's letterhead adorned by lions as looking particularly impressive. I had never in my life seen letters from famous people, much less presidents of two countries. I read the letters over several times, the first couple of times to make sure that I absorbed the contents fully but later mostly out of nervousness for having been handed what looked like an important task.

For the next three weeks, I immersed myself in learning as much as I could about Gabon, the economics of railroads, the world market of timber, and anything else someone would suggest for me to read. I had no difficulty finding experts in each of these areas within the building. I would typically call up one of them, ask him for his views and advice, chase down relevant reports that he would suggest, and often go back with more questions. It was one of the most efficient research processes that I had been through. Just like I had been with Raj and Bob in Jamaica, I was impressed by the depth and breadth of expertise we had within the World Bank. The research took about fifteen days, including most evenings and weekends.

As I analyzed the information I had gathered, it became clear that the project was not viable, either economically or financially. Railways are expensive to build and operate and require significant volumes of freight traffic to justify the large investment. Even under the best of circumstances, timber production in Gabon would be small. Timber was also at the time considered a relatively low-value commodity according to world price projections that a separate unit in the bank maintained for most major commodities. As a sparsely populated hinterland, there would be low volumes of passenger traffic, and in any case, passenger fares can almost never provide adequate revenues. And this is all without having even considered the construction cost estimates by the government of building the railway that our experts considered highly optimistic. So my conclusion was that within any plausible range of estimates of cost and benefits, the railway had a negative return. Moreover, I concluded that the substantial deficits that the project would generate would pose a severe financial burden on the government that it will not be able to bear given its already poor finances.

Tony forwarded my report to McNamara with a short cover note he drafted highlighting my conclusions. The report was returned by McNamara's office with a notation indicating his agreement and asking us to prepare an appropriate response. The next day a letter went out under McNamara's signature to Bongo and another to Pompidou advising them of our decision to not finance the project.

A few days later, a stinging response came from Bongo severely protesting the decision and accusing the bank of all sorts of malfeasance. He concluded by saying, "My soul will rest on coals until this railroad is built." The response found its way to me with an annotation, "no further action needed."

A few days after having finished the Gabon railroad assessment, Tony gave me another challenging task. It too involved a somewhat delicate issue. I did not know whether it was because as a newcomer I did not yet have a full work program and was the only one free to take on new tasks, or because he had gained confidence in my ability to tackle complicated tasks autonomously. But either way, I was happy to have the challenge. The issue this time dealt with shipping.

For several months, developing countries had been agitating that the shipping industry was dominated by the industrialized countries and they, the developing countries, were left out from participating. The issue had been discussed extensively in the various international forums, notably the United Nations Conference on Trade and Development or UNCTAD that nominally had the jurisdiction on the subject. Like other UN organizations, each country had a single vote so the developing countries as a group had the majority. It had passed a resolution asking the World Bank to help developing countries build their international shipping industry. The developing country representatives on the World Bank board—referred to as the executive directors—had taken up the issue. In contrast with the U.N. organizations, votes in the World Bank were (and are) weighted by a complicated formula that includes the size of the country's economy as the predominant consideration. As a result, developing countries as a group held only about 35 percent of the vote.[13] Nevertheless, tradition in the World Bank had been that most decisions are taken by consensus and not through formal voting. However, when an issue became contentious and divided the board, particularly by developed and developing country groups, the president would sometimes try to diffuse the issue by promising a study. Opening World Bank lending for shipping industry was such an issue, and McNamara promised a study in the next three months that will be presented for discussion at a future board meeting.

Again I started by researching the international shipping industry. Since the World Bank had not financed any shipping projects, there was only limited in-house expertise in this field. It instead had a roster of experts it drew on when the issue came up in the context of broader policy advice to the countries. The leading expert was Ezra Benathan, an academic in the United Kingdom. Ezra had written an authoritative book on the economics of shipping that became my first introduction to the subject. I visited him in London and spent some time getting his insights and recent experiences. He also referred me to other experts. While in London, I also interviewed officers of a few shipping companies and the Lloyds of London, the leading insurer of ships.

The picture that emerged from my research was of an industry that was controlled by liner conferences that controlled the major shipping routes and more or less acted as a cartel for the industry. It determined entry conditions, prices, and capacity. As was customary in many industries in those days—for example, airlines—the idea was to maintain an "orderly competition" or in today's terms, a monopoly the cartel. As a result, a number of unregulated operators, termed "tramps" in the industry jargon, had emerged that circumvented the rules and regulations of the liner conferences and were providing unauthorized competition. There was significant excess capacity in the industry that was expected to last several years. Most shipping companies were running losses or at best on very thin profit margins.

My conclusion was that it would be unwise for developing countries to invest scarce resources in an industry that faced bleak prospects for the foreseeable future. Moreover, there was no rationale for the public sector to be involved in a sector that did not have any social benefit and was best left to private sector. A few public sector companies that did exist were making huge losses.

My paper generated a lively discussion at the bank's board. The developing countries' representatives were disappointed in my recommendation but, except for a few who wanted to still make the case on nationalistic grounds, most accepted my conclusions. The World Bank decided to stay out of international shipping, a decision that has held to this day.

The two assignments earned me a solid professional reputation and outstanding performance ratings. My manager made a particularly favorable note of my conceptual and analytical abilities, two skills that were—and still are—valued highly in the World Bank. This reputation was to stay with me for my entire career and shaped several future assignments for me.

On my part, I was greatly impressed by the highly professional decision process in the bank. Contrary to what I had heard, there was no hint of any political considerations entering into the decisions. The only question that was discussed in both cases was, does the investment make sense for the country concerned or for the developing countries generally? As I found out, the best answer was sometimes to say no to popular demand and ignore politics. The World Bank's motto was that it takes only economic considerations in its decisions and is not influenced by politics. My early experiences certainly confirmed this. Later in my career, however, I did begin to see political consideration entering the process more overtly, a development that unfortunately has diminished its effectiveness.

As my six months came to an end, I gladly accepted Tony Churchill's invitation to join the group on a permanent basis. I had happily found my home in transport research and policy work.

Incidentally, on Gabon, Bongo did go ahead and built the railroad on his own with French help but without bank financing. However, I had not followed it, having moved on to other work. Sometime in early 1990, on an airplane from Tokyo to Beijing I came across a story on this project as I was thumbing through the Economist. It described how the project had turned out to be a disaster and had almost bankrupted the country.

5. Elusive Search for the Holy Grail of Development

Peg and I married in the summer of 1972, almost a year after I had joined the World Bank and just before I was to formally start my permanent job in the transport research division. A few weeks before the wedding, I was asked to be a member of a mission to Uruguay to review the country's economy and development needs. My part was to review the policies and programs in the transport sector. Such country reviews were conducted periodically for each developing country to provide a basis for the five-year World Bank assistance programs that had been introduced recently. Unfortunately, the start date of the trip was planned for barely a week after my wedding when I had hoped to be on our honeymoon. Although my boss Tony would have understood if I had begged off this task, I did not want to miss out on an interesting work opportunity. So Peg and I decided instead to celebrate our honeymoon in Uruguay! This was an apt introduction for Peg to our married life to come. There were numerous occasions to come when she saw me take off for faraway places at the most inopportune times. Fortunately, she has been a very understanding and supportive spouse throughout my life.

Within a couple of months of starting my permanent assignment, McNamara announced a major reorganization based on the recommendations of McKinsey consultants. The centralized global projects and area departments were to be broken up into six regionally focused departments with their own projects and area departments, the latter to be now called "program" department. The announcement from McNamara described the rationale for the changes both to accommodate the growing volume of lending (since becoming the president in 1968, McNamara had more than doubled lending and plans for continued further expansion) and to sharpen focus on countries.

I do not recall any internal strife from the reorganization as is common in such instances, and as happened in 1987 when there was a second reorganization—commonly referred to as "The Reorganization"—and which became the historical marker to define all all events. Perhaps I was too new to participate in corridor gossip, and thus oblivious to what was going on around me. But more likely, the rapidly growing staff to deal with the growing volumes of lending meant that there were ample opportunities for growth for everyone in the new structure. In any event, I was not affected personally. Research and policy work remained centralized and was to be strengthened further to provide the common thread across autonomous operational units that were now spread over six regions. My unit now became the central policy coordination and research unit for the all transport work worldwide.

After a few months, I was asked to take on the responsibility for managing a major research project to explore ways in which more labor-intensive techniques could be utilized in civil construction. The project was designed in response to the then prevailing view popularized by German-born British economist E. F. "Fritz" Schumacher that the reliance of capital-intensive technologies often developed for saving labor, were inappropriate for developing countries that had an abundance of labor. Schumacher believed that simple tools and machines, that are significantly cheaper than the technology from the developed world and still capable of improving labor productivity, are more suitable for conditions in "underdeveloped countries."[14] Schumacher coined the term "intermediate technology" for his concept. The Intermediate Technology Development Group (ITDG) that Schumacher founded in 1965 became influential with policy makers in many developing countries. Internationally, the International Labour Office (ILO) was one of its biggest boosters. It had published extensively, extolling the virtues of masonry dams in India that were built by a chain of human hands carrying one stone at a time, and major land leveling projects in China that Chinese peasants had carried out by nothing more than a shovel and a wheelbarrow.[15]

In 1972, the World Bank decided to launch a major research effort to explore further Schumacher's ideas. The impetus for the research was partly in response to the demand from many developing countries. But it was also expected to break the logjam with India, the World Bank's biggest client, that had prevented the World Bank from lending for road construction in India.

With a rapidly growing population and even a large number of new entrants each year to the labor force, the Indian planners were rightly concerned with employment creation, except their response at the time was not liberalization—as has now become synonymous with Indian economic policy—but to rely on government-planned interventions.

Job creation in civil works—roads, dams, irrigation canals—was seen as a major source of employing unskilled labor in large numbers. The planners had virtually banned the use of equipment in most civil works projects. A visitor to India would commonly see road earthworks being constructed with head basket loads, people with hammers breaking up boulders along the side of roads to be used as aggregates, and tar being spread manually by humans using nothing more than watering cans. The only piece of machinery one saw occasionally in road building was a road roller for compaction, but mobilizing the roller at the right time to synchronize with the completion of manually done earthworks or the availability of aggregates was often a challenge. In order to enforce only labor-intensive methods, the Indian government, in addition to making importation of construction equipment difficult, broke up road works into a series of very small contracts for which the mobilization cost of equipment would be prohibitive. The World Bank considered the entire process highly inefficient, with construction lingering on for years, and very poor quality of works. As a result, despite the very large need to build and upgrade the road network, the World Bank could not be involved because of its serious reservations about the Indian approach.[16]

The research project offered the hope of opening up new avenues for World Bank assistance in this important sector. Hence, India was chosen as one of the four initial countries for research—Indonesia, Kenya, and Honduras being the other three. The Indian Planning Commission, that was one of the early proponents of Schumacher's theories, welcomed the World Bank's research effort.

The research project, titled "Substitution of Labor for Capital in Civil Works Construction," received major funding from the World Bank's research budget. In addition, thanks to the intellectual popularity of Schumacher's theory internationally, we were able to mobilize significant funding from several bilateral donors including the United States, Japan, and most of the major European countries. There were few World Bank initiatives that had received such widespread support. I do not recall the exact amount of funding we had, but my recollection is that it totaled several million dollars over the three years that I managed the project.

The research project had been launched about a year before I took over its management, so the research methodology had already been agreed and fieldwork initiated in the four selected countries. The approach was to both study through time and motion studies the efficiency of the traditional methods (such as carrying dirt in baskets loaded on the head or breaking stones manually to produce aggregates) and of "improved" machines (such as a wheel barrow or a crusher or sometimes even an "invention" of one of our engineers that built on a machine that is used in another industry). These studies fed into a model that computed the cost of a given civil works using alternative technologies. There were also some parallel studies done to study related issues such as the market for unskilled labor (to answer doubts raised by some economists whether unskilled labor is indeed as abundant as the central planners assumed) and the extent to which nutrition supplementation improves productivity of labor (it did), and views of contractors about alternative technologies (they were skeptical).

I was very much immersed in managing the project. I enjoyed the responsibility and the exposure it gave me. Regular travel to four countries in three different continents was most educational. Most of our fieldwork sites were located in far-off rural areas and, despite the often primitive and difficult travel conditions to these parts, I loved going to the sites. When visiting India, I would sneak in a long weekend to visit my family in Punjab, and this was a special bonus for me. We organized regular international meetings of all the funders to present progress. I was learning quickly the art of keeping everyone satisfied.

The results of the research were not terribly surprising. We confirmed that better technology did improve productivity in our experimental sites. We also confirmed that the traditional Indian methods of road construction were inefficient, but the real revelation was that they were actually quite capital intensive when one factored in the much higher wear and tear of motor vehicles and considerably longer journey times caused by poor quality roads.[17] But we could not answer the more basic question: if indeed the improved technologies we used were so simple and so widely known, why were the contractors not using them? We had no real answer to this important question, except for some conjectures about tradition or cultural norms or perhaps the development of certain muscles that unskilled people developed over time that reinforced their use of the so-called primitive methods.

Our research was receiving much acclaim (and more money for its expansion into other countries). I was not entirely clear why this was the case. Our research methodology was relatively simple and our findings not that profound. I myself had developed doubts about what we were saying. I could see that our experiments were really nothing but "laboratory experiments" that had little reliability when faced with actual conditions of a construction site. Moreover, I was troubled by the question we could not answer: if these technologies are so good, why they are not adopted? The contractors told us that what matters is the contracting methods, pricing, and reliability of labor supply in determining what method they would select. Why none of our asked us these questions remains a mystery to me to this day. Maybe the contractors were good economists. They apparently understood the functioning of the market better than us!

So while enjoying the heady responsibility and world travels while working on this project, within a couple of years I had also become disillusioned with its approach and relevance. I did not want to continue to oversee research that I felt was not relevant to the practical issues on the ground. I began to think seriously about moving on to some other assignment.

There was also another factor that was making me want to seek a new assignment. In the three years I spent in research, I realized that the more interesting part of the World Bank that was much closer to development was in the operational side that dealt with the evaluation and implementation of projects. I realized that the project work I had done in Jamaica and Ghana during my first rotational assignment was much more rewarding personally and professionally, and was closer to the real development work that I had now come to appreciate. I had also seen my peers who had chosen operational work as their permanent assignments thrive in their work. Rightly or wrongly, most people within the organization saw research as somewhat esoteric and divorced from the realities on the ground, and using up significant resources that should be diverted toward dealing on the ground with the real world issues of development. Deep down I tended to agree, a belief that became even stronger over the years. While some of the World Bank research outputs are truly valuable, a large volume ends up as semi-academic papers that are rarely of any use to development practitioners.

6. Move to Urban Development: Understanding the Realities of Poverty

My opportunity came during a visit to Indonesia in late 1975 with my director, Kim Jaycox, to review our field research. Kim was one of the success stories of a young professional who had moved up at record speed from a young professional to become a department director. Besides professional competence, Kim was also a great manager. He understood that development was a challenging and constantly changing task with no preset answers. He encouraged his staff to think of new and different ways to deal with problems. He supported us but let us get on with our work. I guess he is what we would call an "empowering" manager.

In 1975, McNamara had followed up his widely acclaimed speech in Nairobi in 1973 on rural poverty with another address to the World Bank's board of governors, pointing out the problems of the urban poor, whose condition he described as "unspeakably grim." Following his speech, a new department was created to develop urban development programs. But McNamara was not satisfied with the performance of the department and decided to merge it with the transportation department under Kim's leadership. Not because there was necessarily any synergy between the two functions, but largely because Kim was seen as a more dynamic and innovative manager. The urban agenda needed such leadership.

As a part of his new responsibilities, while in Indonesia, Kim was also visiting a major slum-upgrading project—the Kampung Improvement Program—in Jakarta that the World Bank had financed. Although I had no involvement in the project, Kim invited me to join him on the field visit. We trudged through some of the worst slums I had seen in my life. We were literally walking through muddy paths overflowing with sewage, avoiding human feces and piles of uncollected garbage. The rain in the previous day had made the situation even worse since the slums did not have proper drainage. Yet it was a place full of life with children playing and laughing and adults peeking out at our group through their doorways and greeting us with all sorts of calls in Bahasa Indonesia, the local language, with an occasional "Hello, mister" and "How are you?" My only other exposure to a slum had been fleeting views from a car in cities around the world. This was the first time I had actually been inside of one.

While driving back to our hotel, Kim asked me what I thought about how we were doing. I did not have much to add, except to say that the problem looked overwhelming. Out of the blue, Kim asked me if I wished to shift to work on this and other projects, as if he had read my mind. It took me all of thirty seconds to say yes.

The urban work that I signed up for turned out to be even more interesting and exciting than I had imagined. The World Bank was the pioneer in the 1970s in developing some of the innovative concepts that have since become commonplace in urban policy. To this day, I see this phase as the most exciting time of my career in development.

The developing countries had just begun the process of urbanization. Their populations were still growing rapidly—some 3-4 percent per annum in many cases—but the urban population was growing at almost double the pace. Economists have long known this as an inevitable trend as a country begins to shift from a predominantly agrarian economy toward industrialization. On the other hand, cities in developing countries were—and in many cases still are—totally unprepared to absorb the rapid urban population growth taking place right in front of their eyes. The consequence was a severe strain on already inadequate services. Urban land prices were rising rapidly, partly from the demand by the growing population, but also because of many obstacles to bringing land into the market brought about unwittingly by urban planners. This made even basic housing beyond the reach of a bulk of the population. The poor migrants to the cities were the worst affected. Their only choice was to occupy land illegally on parcels of vacant land—most often owned by the government—that later grew to become a slum. It was not uncommon to have 50-60 percent of the population in some of the major cities like Jakarta, Bombay (now Mumbai), and Manila living in the slums.

So what were the policy makers in developing world doing about it? Dreaming. They dreamed of "orderly" and "beautiful" cities with wide boulevards. Many of them, like me, had studied in the West and had seen the beauty of London, Paris, and San Francisco, and they wanted to emulate these cities. Slums, they believed, were blight on the city that should be wiped out and replaced with "proper" good quality public housing. They declared "shelter" to be a basic right and thus a responsibility of the government to provide. They promulgated building codes and minimum lot sizes, often based on standards left by their erstwhile colonial masters.

Of course, none of this proved feasible. There were simply not the public resources to build housing for the new entrants that came to the city each year much less to destroy the housing stock howsoever dilapidated that existed in the slums. Moreover, the people living in the slums saw them as communities where they lived and worked that could never be replaced by antiseptic public housing blocks. The sporadic attempts at slum clearance invariably backfired on the politicians by generating angry reaction from the slum dwellers that invariably led to electoral defeats.

Thus, policies and programs to deal with slums was a major issue on the minds of developing country policy makers and became an entry point for the World Bank into the sector. The slums housed a bulk of the urban poor living in "unspeakable conditions" that McNamara had spoken about in his address in 1975.

I started my work in urban development in India and Indonesia, two countries I had become quite familiar with through my previous research project. I loved Indonesia for its gentle, soft-spoken people, a very tolerant version of Islam and the great variety of the different islands. India, of course, held a sentimental attachment, and it was a great experience to view it through my new lens of development. I was a part of a highly committed team of people from different disciplines as was the case in my previous assignments. What was different was that my colleagues understood the importance of working with the communities to devise solutions that were unique to them. This was a point of departure from the traditional World Bank infrastructure projects of that time.

We spent considerable time, meeting and talking to people in the slums through formal and informal meetings. People from the community would show up in large numbers to talk to the visitors from the World Bank. Meetings would often last late into the night. They would tell us about their priorities. Some had complaints about past government projects that went nowhere and left a trail of incomplete or dysfunctional facilities. They had tales of woe to share, but also some inspiring accounts of their lives: working multiple jobs to send their children to school, setting up a small business in the slums and making it grow to a point where they were able to employ others, self-help initiatives to bring services to the community, and so on.

We learned a lot from these encounters as did our government counterparts, many of whom themselves had previously never ventured into a slum. First, we learned that while to outsiders slums may be blights on the city, to the people living there, these were communities with strong bonds and relationships. Some of the older and often the biggest slums had existed for years. So clearing and relocating a slum would invariably mean destroying the community. Second, although the houses were dilapidated, often constructed from temporary materials, they represented significant investments by the families over many years. Clearing slums would thus mean destroying large personal investments of the people. With an acute shortage of housing and substantial unmet demand for new housing, it makes no sense to destroy this existing investment and further add to the housing shortage. Indeed, people in the slums are more than anxious to invest more to improve their housing were it not for the insecurity from the constant threat of eviction by public authorities. Third, with land being affordable by only the better off people, the poor on whose shoulders the urban economy rests have no choice but to occupy vacant land. Public policies were not only not helping bring affordable land into the market but often creating obstacles to it through various misguided regulations.

These findings led us to approach the problem of slums in a totally different way. Our approach was to focus on providing slums with essential services like roads, footpaths, drainage and water supply, and sanitation that they lacked while minimizing dislocation. This often meant narrower roads and footpaths than the municipal standards allowed. The roads and footpaths zigzagged around houses so as to not have to tear down a house. And when it was an absolute necessity to move a family, the community decided where they would be accommodated within the community. We kept the standard of services at the minimum essential level for public health that were affordable both by the people and the government. Besides, too high standards posed the risk of rapid gentrification that was not desirable. The decision on what to do within the allocated budget was left to each concerned community to decide. The most important feature of the programs was to give the owners of the houses ownership rights on the plot of land on which they had built the house in return for monthly payments to recover the costs.

The clearance and relocation of slums was only left to extreme cases where people may be squatting on places like drainage systems, railway lines, or other similar situations where they could not safely continue to exist. In such cases, we worked on developing suitable alternatives that were not too far from their place of work.

Even with the policy of preserving and upgrading slums, the cities still faced the need for new housing to accommodate the growing population. Yet it was totally impractical for the government to build houses for them. Here, we promoted the concept of "sites and services" originally developed by the British planner, John Turner, whereby the public sector only developed small plots of land with the basic services and sold them to low-income families. The size of the plots and the level of services were kept to the absolute minimum to make them affordable to the low-income people. It was left to the people to build their own houses incrementally over time through self-help as their resources permitted. This approach recognized that poor themselves rather than the government are better placed to build their own houses. What they lacked is the capacity to assemble land, and this was thus an appropriate role for the public sector.

Selling these ideas, however, to policy makers in developing countries was not easy. Some disliked the "perpetuation of slums." Some city planners could not comprehend the idea of lowering planning standards. The city utilities were invariably hostile since they saw connecting slum dwellers as yet more leakage from their already meager sources of revenues, notwithstanding the fact that people in the slums were willing to pay for services if they got them; indeed, private water vendors did a flourishing business, selling water in these areas by the bucket. Politicians who had routinely promised housing during elections did not want to buy the idea that the government would only provide a very small plot and people will have to pay for it. "This will create planned slums," was something we heard from many of them.

The most naïve view, and that surprisingly still persists among many policy makers, was that the solution to the slums was to stop people coming into the cities. Just keep them on the farm. The misunderstanding about the realities of poverty even among developing country policy makers was truly remarkable. I could see how, like me, most elites in these countries had had little exposure to the poor in their lives.

Our urban group was a very committed and cohesive group. Many of us were graduates of the Young Professional Program, so we were relatively young as a group. We all shared passion for our work; I suspect that this was something Kim Jaycox specifically looked for while putting together the urban department. Most importantly, we knew that we were treading new ground that required flexibility. We subscribed the basic philosophy of our urban work, but we also knew that there were no standard answers. Kim had encouraged us to experiment, learn, and revise. Learning by doing was our working motto.[18]

Most of the larger Asian cities had large slums and an acute shortage of low-income housing. So we found significant demand for for World Bank support in the sector. Within a few years, we had projects in most countries in Asia. Most of them were implemented very successfully, but a few also turned out to be disappointing. Two of my initial project assignments in Jakarta, Indonesia, and in Manila, the Philippines, gave me a taste of both.

In 1976, Jakarta was a burgeoning city of five million people, of which two-thirds lived in Kampungs, which were settlements within the city of large numbers of low-income people. The Kampungs had evolved in the last fifteen to twenty years from small village-like communities in which most Indonesians lived during the Dutch rule to large and densely populated urban slums. Ali Sadikin, then the Governor of Jakarta, had already initiated a program—Kampung Improvement Program or KIP—along the lines of the World Bank's approach. Sadikin wanted to expand the KIP dramatically so he could within a short period of time provide services to all Kampungs and integrate them with the rest of the city. But he also knew that he could not rely on the Indonesian government to finance his effort given other competing priorities, and probably also because he had a deep distrust of the central government that he opposed more openly after leaving office. He invited the World Bank to help him scale-up his efforts. He was willing for the city to borrow and repay the funds, a practice that was quite uncommon at the time when most other cities relied on the national governments for financing.

We developed a program that would provide services to all of Jakarta's slums within ten years. This meant providing services in almost one thousand hectares of Kampung areas annually that housed about five hundred thousand people. This was an unprecedented scale of effort. Most other slum-upgrading efforts we had in other countries covered a fraction of the area in five years that was covered in one year in Jakarta.

The benefit of having as the head of the city someone who had the same vision about slum upgrading as us made for a pleasurable experience. We did not have to go through long and tortuous debates to convince our client about the wisdom of in situ upgrading or minimum dislocation or affordable standards. We instead focused our efforts on improving and systematizing the planning, design, and implementation processes. These were essential if the program were to be expanded several-fold as Sadikin wanted.

Community participation was an important feature of the program even before we got involved. Indonesia had (and continues to have) an organization structure down to the family level. Layers of community leaders represented groups of families, neighborhood clusters, and ultimately the entire Kampung. Although community consultations were held in open meetings, these leaders ultimately had the most influence in deciding how the allocated budgets were to be spent, where the community facilities would be built, the relocation sites within the Kampung to accommodate families whose plots were too small after roads or footpaths were built or whose land had to be acquired for community facilities, and so on.

We hired Janice, a social scientist from the faculty of UC Berkley, to see how these processes worked and whether any changes should be considered. She had an inherent distrust of any system that relied on government-designated leaders and argued for a more democratic system. But whenever she presented her views in meetings, I could see the Indonesians totally befuddled. To them, they had a long tradition that worked well and did not find Janice's ideas workable. In the end, we accepted the Indonesian approach with the requirement that all discussions be open. Janice was most unhappy and subsequently wrote negatively about the Indonesian approach and our unwillingness to impose her views on the officials in Jakarta. For me, it was an early experience that planted in my mind seeds of doubt about the universality of some of the concepts that are propagated by Western social scientists. This is an issue that is even more pertinent today when considering the future of foreign aid.

There were also some other things we learnt from Jakarta. We knew that slum upgrading programs could only be meaningful if they are not seen as one-shot projects but rather a sustained effort over many years. The scale of the problem required this. However, most governments—city or national—lacked adequate resources. Thus, in our approach we emphasized recovering costs from the beneficiaries of improved slums. This meant giving them title to their plots and levying monthly charges to recover costs. Sadikin felt that this approach to cost recovery, while theoretically good, was impractical administratively for a large program like KIP that covered thousands of families per annum. He instead focused on general city revenues that were buoyant and linked these sources to his long-term program. He chose gambling revenues as one important source (In one of our meetings, he remarked only in part in jest, "I hate gambling as a Muslim, but need the money. In any case, it is the Chinese that gamble."). He also felt that the Kampung dwellers enjoyed de facto security of tenure under the customary law in Indonesia, and thus there was little risk of eviction post improvement. These were convincing arguments that we accepted. The Jakarta experience was contributing to our "learning by doing."

Over the years, the program in Jakarta was expanded to other Indonesian cities with World Bank support. After the oil price increase in 1978 that further augmented government of Indonesia's coffers, the program was made a national program.

Much has been written about the success of the Kampung Improvement Program, and there are many that have claimed paternity, including many in the World Bank. As someone who was there at the beginning, I think the credit goes solely to "Bang Ali" or Brother Ali as he was affectionately known to the Indonesian people. He was a visionary leader committed to making a difference in the lives of his people. Sadikin died in 2008 at the age of eighty-two. He left a legacy as one of the early pioneer thinkers of urban development.

Over the years, I have become convinced that home-grown committed leaders are the most significant factors for successful development. Ali Sadikin was just the first of such leaders I encountered.

The Philippines project provided the converse lesson: poor leadership can destroy even the most well-planned efforts. The project involved upgrading of one large slum area, Tondo, located around the port of Manila. Government plans to resettle some 180,000 people living in Tondo some 40-45 km away had created enormous tension with the residents. Imelda Marcos, the first lady, was deeply involved in promoting redevelopment plans for the area. She was reportedly very keen on good urban planning and architecture. With the support of the Catholic Church, the residents had organized themselves into a federation of neighborhood organizations—Zone One Tondo Organization or ZOTO—to resist government efforts to relocate them.

We found ourselves in alliance with ZOTO, and with much effort and dialogue successfully persuaded the government to adopt the in situ upgrading approach. The government also agreed that the few families in the immediate vicinity of the port that had to be relocated to allow the expansion of the port would be relocated in a reclaimed adjacent area.

Tondo had a reputation of being a very tough and violent neighborhood. No outsider, particularly a government official, ventured into the area. But our alliance with ZOTO gave the staff of National Housing Authority of the Philippines (NHA), the implementing agency for the project, implicit protection. We would spend many hours walking through the area or holding meetings with the residents in the community center. We were welcomed warmly since people gave us credit for convincing the Marcos government to change its mind about relocation. The history of community involvement was carried through to the planning and implementation of the project. The residents would often debate different options for upgrading, argue vehemently different views, challenge NHA staff, and take votes. Community involvement was critical to verifying ownership rights after upgrading for existing residents. The meetings were open to everyone. It was an intriguing scene of democracy in action at the grassroots level within a totalitarian state.

The Tondo residents did not want the approach of in situ upgrading with no or minimal relocation. Instead, they wanted, and were willing to pay for replotting their individual lots into more orderly layout. They pitched in to help each other move their houses into the new plots. This was a very labor-intensive and time-consuming process, very different from what we had in Jakarta. The project took ten years to complete compared to the original plan of three to five years, and this is one of its legitimate criticisms. But we were all convinced that this was the right approach in the circumstances of Tondo.

In contrast with the Jakarta project that enjoyed strong support from the governor, the support of the government leaders in Manila was always tenuous. Imelda Marcos was a particularly troublesome actor in the entire process. She would frequently issue instructions that counteracted the upgrading approach. At the time of the Pope's visit to Manila, she ordered the erection of walls along the boundaries of Tondo adjacent to the Pope's route so that he did not see the realities of poverty in the Philippines. She would sometimes order changes in the designs that would add significantly to the cost. The government officials were so afraid of her ire that they never dared question her orders. Sometimes they would feed us information secretly and urge us to challenge her, something we did from time to time but not always successfully.

One incident is particularly memorable. Imelda had ordered that houses along the roads be demolished and replaced by more presentable homes. This was not only a very expensive proposition but it would have also displaced several hundred families unnecessarily. The community was dead against her ideas. The staff of NHA asked me to meet her and try to explain why what she proposed was not workable. I summoned all my diplomatic skills and with my team went to see her in her office in the presidential palace or Malacañang as it is known in the Philippines.

Imelda's office was a long ornate hall with an imperial-looking desk and chair set on top a platform where she sat, with chairs for visitors lining both sides of the hall. Not too dissimilar to what one would expect to see in a medieval court. There were people lined up on both sides, I presume with petitions of one sort or another. She shook our hands and motioned us to sit in chairs in front of her. I had barely started my remarks when she looked to one of the persons on the side and said something. I stopped waiting for her attention and started again a couple of minutes later when I saw her eyes turn back to us. But very soon, she again looked over at someone else and again issued some instructions. This went on for a while, and it was becoming clear to me that it would be near impossible to get her full attention and the futility of trying to carry on a conversation. When she finally did come back to her conversation with us, she went on to narrate a story of her road trip with her friend Christina Ford in the Philippines when at Christina's request they stopped by a roadside village to see a typical Filipino house, and how embarrassed she was that he was so proud to show off his "dilapidated mud house with a tin roof." We all knew then that dealing with her was hopeless. In the end, we had to mobilize my director to see Marcos himself on this issue and subtly ask him to overrule Imelda, which he did. To this day, I do not know if he did this out of fear of the World Bank or, as some Filipino friends speculated, "to let her know from time to time who the boss was."

The entire implementation period of the Tondo project was marred with periodic episodes like this, but surprisingly the team persevered and completed the project albeit with much delay. We developed a healthy appreciation of the difficult conditions under which our Filipino colleagues worked. Whereas I attribute the success of the Jakarta project to a good leader, the Tondo project came close to collapse many times because of bad leadership at the top. Good leadership in Indonesia promoted the expansion of the successful Jakarta program to other cities, and bad leadership in the Philippines was an obstacle to expansion. Leadership matters for successful development.

Ex-post evaluations by independent researchers confirmed that both the Jakarta and Manila projects were successful in achieving their goals of improving the living conditions. In both cases, one not only saw visible improvements in the environment, but also dramatic improvements in housing made by the residents as upgrading proceeded and people had security of tenure. Each day you saw someone replacing the old walls made from cardboard with bricks or mortar, or putting on a new roof, or adding an extra room or another floor. The dynamism of the communities and the pace of change were breathtaking and very satisfying to see. The success of the projects validated our hypothesis about slums and housing.

The two projects opened my eyes to the importance of community participation. These projects directly impacted the lives of the people living in the slums, and it was important to be proactive in seeking people's views. But I also learnt that there is no single approach to community participation and there are also limits to what can be As mentioned earlier, the Jakarta project has been criticized by some as not having given enough room for participation by the common people. I disagree. On the other hand, the Tondo project is sometimes cited as a model, and I disagree with this view also. While it served the Tondo residents well, the very intensive approach requiring enormous time and effort could not be replicated in the numerous other slums in Manila that were also in need of essential services. The lesson is that the approach needs to be thought of in the context of local traditions and culture and the ultimate goal of reaching most of the poor.

Interestingly, in both projects, community participation was not championed by the so-called "social experts" that now populate the bank and other development agencies in large numbers. Ali Sadikin was the champion in Jakarta, and he motivated the approach. In Manila, my colleague David Cook, an old crusty British municipal engineer who had previously been a part of the British colonial service in Africa, was the one who was passionate about it and often told us why we must persevere with it in Tondo when the rest of us thought that the marathon late-night meetings with the community appeared to be going nowhere. In both cases, real-world experience was their frame of reference rather than a textbook approach to social development that many aid agencies, including the bank, now draw from.

7. Country-Driven Development: The East Asian Tigers

Within two years of my joining the urban work in Asia, my division was carved into an East Asia and Pacific Division that covered work from Burma eastward and a second division to handle the work in South Asia. I was appointed the manager of the East Asia and Pacific Division. The division handled not only slum upgrading and housing, but also urban transport, water supply and sewerage, and regional development. I had a staff of twenty-five professionals, a portfolio of ongoing projects of over a billion dollars, and a planned program of $300-500 million of new projects each year. It was an enormous responsibility for me at a relatively young age of thirty-three.

Most of my staff had been involved in the urban work right from the beginning and thus a part of the "learning by doing" approach. They were an energetic and highly committed bunch partly because of having the pioneering spirit and also because they tended to be younger than professional staff in the traditional sectors. We had developed a reputation of work hard and play hard. It was great fun leading such a group. With the splitting of the Asia group, I then had a new director, S. S. Kirmani, an older gentleman from Pakistan, who was a renowned engineer. He had been the chief engineer for the Tarbela Dam in Pakistan[19] before he came to the bank to head one of the projects departments.

Contrary to what many people assumed about Kirmani as a traditionalist, I found him to be a superb manager. He was a very wise man with vast experience on how things actually worked on the ground. He expected results from his managers, but he also encouraged me to maintain the innovative streak and the esprit de corps of the group. His one instruction to me when we met for over lunch after he became my boss, "You must take decisions, even if at times they turn out to be wrong as long as you have done so with good intentions. I will back you fully." Kirmani said that there is nothing worse than a manager who is indecisive and constantly looking over his shoulder for guidance from above. Kirmani was my boss for some six years before he retired, and I moved on to other assignments. I consider him to have been one of my mentors.

In 1987, I moved laterally to become the manager of the energy, industry, and finance group for East Asia, a position I held until 1990 when I moved to South Asia as a senior advisor to the vice president. Thus, in all, I was a manager in East Asia and the Pacific for more than ten years.

My tenure is East Asia coincided with the most exciting period of development in the region. While incomes in most of the developing countries were stagnating or, as in Africa and Latin America, even declining, the East Asian countries were booming. The four major East Asian countries—Korea, Thailand, Malaysia, and Indonesia—had already embarked on their quest to join Taiwan in the elite club that came to be known as the "East Asian Tigers." These countries were experiencing rapid and sustained growth, based in large part from adopting market-friendly economic policies and by investing heavily in education and infrastructure. They had truly transformed their economies within a generation.

Following the lead of Taiwan and Singapore, Korea leapfrogged from a low-income country to a high-income, industrialized country within a generation. When I first visited Korea in 1978, it was still a low-income country with a per capita income of roughly $1,000, not too much higher than Guatemala, Peru, and Jordan, and lower than Mexico and Brazil. There were hardly any private cars on the streets. The government had decided that the country could not at that time afford to have cars and had imposed a stiff tax on ownership. Korea had just started the process of exporting low-cost, labor-intensive goods to the United States and Europe. The shops in Itaewon, the area frequented by foreigners, were full of factory seconds for sale at very cheap prices. There were only two hotels of Western standard in Seoul and none in any of the other cities. Most offices were not heated, which made for meetings during the severe winter months rather uncomfortable. But there were ample signs of a country headed toward a more prosperous future.

Indonesia had been desperately poor in 1970, even poorer than Bangladesh, India, and most African countries. By 1990, its per capita income was 1.5 times that of India and more than double of Bangladesh (table 7.1). Thailand was widely believed to have poor prospect, and Malaysia's prospects were deemed poor because of its reliance on rubber and palm oil as its main sources of income. Both countries had similar levels of income as many African countries when they attained independence. By the end of the century, both had comfortably attained middle-income status.

The results in terms of poverty reduction were equally By 1990, poverty had been virtually eliminated in Korea, Malaysia, Thailand. Even Indonesia saw absolute poverty decline to under 20 percent.

Table 7.1. Income Per Capita Growth of
East Asian Tigers and Selected
Countries (in current US$)

Country	Income per capita				Growth		
	1970	1990	2000	2005	1990/ 1970	2000/ 1970	2005/ 1970
Indonesia	80	590	580	1,170	7.4	7.3	14.6
Korea, Rep.	260	5,660	9,910	16,900	21.8	38.1	65.0
Malaysia	380	2,260	3,450	5,210	5.9	9.1	13.7
Thailand	200	1,410	1,960	2,580	7.1	9.8	12.9
Bangladesh	100	250	350	440	2.5	3.5	4.4
India	110	370	450	740	3.4	4.1	6.7
Egypt	200	700	1,390	1,200	3.5	7.0	6.0
Kenya	120	360	420	520	3.0	3.5	4.3
Nigeria	160	250	270	620	1.6	1.7	3.9
Uganda	100	300	270	300	3.0	2.7	3.0
Mexico	660	2,670	5,110	8,080	4.0	7.7	12.2
Brazil	420	2,540	3,870	3,970	6.0	9.2	9.5

Notes: Data for 1970 for Bangladesh and Uganda are author's estimates
Source: World Development Indicators Database

The bank had an active lending program in all four countries and a very open and cordial relationship. By 1985, Korea had already reached an income level that required it to "graduate" from being a borrower. Malaysia and Thailand had ample resources of their own and were experiencing significant inflows of private capital and thus did not have a need to borrow from the bank. However, all three wanted to maintain a continuing relationship with the bank by borrowing predetermined annual amounts for a few projects in order to have access to bank's technical expertise. This was a testimony to the high level of expertise the bank still had at the time that these countries valued despite the significant advances they themselves had made. However, while they sought our advice on a wide range of issues, it was they who decided the appropriate course of action considering advice from the bank and elsewhere.

Indonesia was the only country among the tigers that had a continuing need for the bank's resources given its large population and still a relatively low income. However, as an oil exporter, it had benefited from the increase in oil prices and was thus in a comfortable fiscal situation. It had done a good job in spending these resources wisely and in the process had become much more confident in its own ability to plan and manage its economy without external resources. One sign of the growing Indonesian confidence was that by mid-1970s, it no longer wanted World Bank staff and USAID-funded advisors from Harvard located in BAPPENAS, the premiere Indonesian planning agency, as they had been heretofore.

Working with clients that did not need our money but wanted to tap our expertise meant that we had to be sure that we provided them with high quality advice. I was fortunate to have high quality staff who were highly respected in their fields. There were many instances where a senior official from one of the countries would call me for advice on some issue or the other. These were either in an area where they wanted the benefit of international experience, or to reconcile differences of view among their experts, or many times to give help them fend off ill-conceived project ideas of their politicians. A report from the World Bank experts was useful at such times.

These requests, while demanding in nature, were professionally very satisfying. In Malaysia, the power company was building coal-fired power plants at the same time while the national oil company was flaring away the abundant gas, just because they could not agree on the right price of gas. This was causing a major economic loss for the country, besides being environmentally more damaging. The issue was settled when our team gave its recommendation on the appropriate formula, which is used to this day. Another time, the head of the Malaysian economic planning unit called me at home to request our team to visit as soon as we could to help decide on the appropriateness of certain power plant technologies that were being pushed on them at the highest political levels by a major industrialized country. His staff knew that the technology was inappropriate but they had been unable to convince the political bosses who were involved in the deal. A review by my colleagues helped them convince Prime Minister Mahatir to not go forward with the proposal. In Korea, the central government asked us for our recommendations on how they should structure urban local governments as they began to experience rapid urbanization. In Thailand, the national planning agency used our study to design their privatization program in infrastructure.

However, there were also instances when a country decided to ignore our advice. Malaysia persisted with its affirmative action policies for "Bumiputras" (sons of the soil) despite our view that it was wasteful and distortionary. The Thais decided to go ahead and build the light rail system in Bangkok when we were advising more modest measures. The Indonesians persisted with their rice subsidy against our advice that it had a negative fiscal impact, but the Indonesians were proven right when this subsidy was instrumental in protecting the poor during the economic crisis of the late 1990s.

The most notable, and often talked about, example of a country going against the bank's advice was in Korea when it decided to go ahead with promoting its car industry while the bank's experts did not think that the Koreans could compete with Japan and the United States! Our Korean friends took great pleasure in reminding us of this instance often after we had all consumed several glasses of "Soju" (whiskey) together. These experiences helped keep us all humble. It also reminded me of the lesson from the "World Buttery" incident I described earlier: you can be very independent if you do not have to depend on foreign aid!

Not being in a position to dictate our views as the bank often did in other countries had a very salutary effect on all of us working in East Asia. We learned to treat the clients with respect and as an equal. We would have a healthy give and take as equal partners. We would often have a meeting of the minds on important issues as we did on most key economic policies. But we also did not consider it an affront when we did not. For most part, however, our advice was welcomed and accepted.

Based on a strong sense of mutual respect, we were able to develop a large lending program. Indeed, lending to competent and well-functioning borrowers in these countries had allowed the bank to maintain both a high level of overall volume of lending, but also acceptable average overall quality of the portfolio since project performance in East Asia has always been significantly better than the other countries, particularly in South Asia and Africa. We had projects in almost every country in the region with the exception of China that was not a member at the time—or more precisely had yet to reclaim its seat on the World Bank Board from Taiwan as the Chinese put it. Soon after rejoining the World Bank in 1980, China became the largest borrower from the World Bank with a program that encompassed virtually every sector including urban development. China's entry to the World Bank was a major event that I discuss in more detail in the next chapter.

Ever since I had joined the World Bank, the mantra I heard often repeated was that our role is first and foremost knowledge transfer and only secondarily to provide funding. A standard question that project proposal had to address was the "rationale for the bank involvement." In practice, however, the preoccupation with lending volumes is much more than the bank likes to admit. The volume of lending was, and continues to be, an important benchmark in assessing the performance of the bank by the board. The bank staff also reveled in doing new projects. After all, this was the most concrete and visible part of development that we could all point to as our success. The client countries also were generally interested in getting funds, although there were few countries like the East Asian tigers that wanted lending as a sure way to get the bank's technical advice. The vast majority of countries were simply hooked on aid, so all incentives were to lend.

Institution building is the most common rationale for the bank's lending cited by the bank's staff in most countries, and included in a perfunctory paragraph in the staff appraisal reports that are presented to the board. I do not remember a single instance where any board member ever questioned it even after they had seen the same rationale repeated in successive projects. In most poor countries, the rationale of institution building was a plausible reason, not that the bank has had much success in this area. However, giving a convincing answer to this question in the case of successful countries like Korea, Malaysia, or Thailand was not easy. Also some board members would ask why we could simply not provide only advice that these clients valued without having to also lend them money that they did not need. The answer, of course, was that these sophisticated countries understood the bank's internal incentive system that rewards staff first and foremost on the basis of the volume of lending they generate, and this is the only sure hook to have competent staff work on their countries. So we would often throw in a study or some training to show the bank's "value added." Most of the times, our advanced clients played along, but sometimes they resisted having unnecessary studies or training that they did not need.

A humorous incident in Korea that I encountered illustrates this point.

The Koreans had asked for help in financing a transport project for Seoul. They had started preparing for the day when car ownership would be inevitably liberalized and forward thinking as they were; they wanted investments in roads and public transport infrastructure to prepare for the day. We had agreed but faced the problem of devising the "rationale" for the loan. This was a particularly difficult challenge in Korea that everyone knew had ample resources of its own to finance the project. As usual, my staff had concocted institution building as a small project component.

I accompanied my team to a meeting with the mayor of Seoul to discuss the project with him. He welcomed us warmly as always and listened to our presentation translated to him by one of his officers. He indicated full agreement and support for the project investments. But when it came to institution building, he did not grasp what we wanted. He asked several questions of us and our answers would be duly translated to him. This would be followed by back and forth in Hangul (the language of Korea) between him and his staff. Then again more questions. I could sense from the body language and the tone of the discussion that there was some confusion. Finally, after some minutes, the mayor said, "Mr. Sud, we are all for this project and like the investment package. But we do not think we need any institution building because my institution already has a building."

My colleagues and I broke up in a quiet laugh knowing that we had failed to sell our fancy ideas to him. I shook my head and simply said, "Never mind."

To this day I have wondered if the Koreans really did not speak English or whether going through translators for everything was their shield against the World Bank's fancy notions of development. My Korean friends assured me that it was the former. But I remain unconvinced!

The 1970s and 1980s were exciting times to be working in East Asia. The success of the countries made us feel good about the work we were doing. It was rewarding to see positive changes happening as if right in front of our eyes. We respected our clients who returned the favor equally. We provided billions of dollars in funding for projects in urban development, housing, slum upgrading, water supply and sanitation, energy, and industrial development. Most of our projects were succeeding, with a much higher success rate than worldwide averages. It would be tempting to say that it was our projects that were fueling the success. But I decided a long time ago that the causality runs the other way: World Bank-funded projects are likely to succeed in countries that are successful and more likely to fail in poorly managed countries. Aid researchers like to call it the "right policy environment" for projects to succeed. I give much more importance to leadership that is willing to accept good ideas from aid donors but only on their terms. They managed to use aid for their purposes rather than let aid donors drive their development agendas.

8. China: The Development Marathoner

In the 1970s, China was still a country closed to most foreigners. It had reclaimed its seat in the United Nations and most of its agencies in 1971, but it did not join the IMF and the World Bank. China considered these Bretton Woods sisters, with their system of voting weighted toward the Western industrial powers, as agents of imperialism. The Chinese economy was centrally planned and based on the concept of collectivism. This was not necessarily something that at the time was looked down upon in development circles. Indeed, many extolled the progress China had made in meeting the basic needs of its people. With the country being largely closed to foreigners, most of the accounts were second hand and probably based on official Chinese propaganda.

In the late 1970s, there were signs of China opening up. After Mao's death, Deng Xiaoping, a reformer, had emerged as the de-facto leader of China and had started making statements that indicated that China was preparing for a change in direction away from collectivism and toward free market.

Kim Jaycox, who as I previously mentioned was the director of the urban department, decided that we should have a small group from the World Bank visit China to learn about its development policies. As the manager of the East Asia urban division, I was invited for the trip. However, at the time Kim did not know that there were also confidential discussions going on between the World Bank management and the Chinese authorities on China joining the bank. So the senior management did not approve of our visit but without telling us the reasons. Several of us, including Kim, nevertheless decided to go by using our earned annual leave and paying our own way.

The visit was planned for February 1979, only a few days after Deng Xiaoping had completed his historical visit to the United States. I don't think this was something the organizers of our trip had deliberately planned for, but it turned out to be fortuitous. We were dubbed by people who would introduce us as "the American group," even though we were not all Americans. This was a common way for the Chinese to designate the groups. More substantively, it was used as a basis for deciding the type of accommodations that would be offered to you and the price to be charged. As the American group, we qualified for the best.

The Chinese people would welcome us warmly, often by standing up and clapping as we would visit a tourist site or enter a restaurant or just be walking down the street. They were full of curiosity about the United States. The odd ones who spoke a little English would pepper members of the group with questions, some very personal (how much salary?). It was clear that most Chinese had never seen a foreigner in their lives, much less met him close-up.

We entered China from Hong Kong. Upon arrival at the border, we walked across the bridge "into" China, carrying our suitcases. China was a mysterious place for all of us, as it was for the rest of the world. So walking "into" is an apt phrase to describe our feelings. As we drove to Guangzhou, we passed through bare countryside. We saw people walking around in their drab blue or grey Mao jackets and loose pajamas. There was no color to be seen anywhere; the overcast days of the Chinese winter seemed to accentuate the dull grey color all around us. The city looked like it could badly use a fresh coat of paint. This was a scene that was repeated in all the other cities that we visited, except that in comparison, Guangzhou was relatively more developed.

We met with city officials in the cities who gave us what seemed like a standard presentations. They would read off from their notes facts and figures about the city to the last digit, not appreciating the incredibility of such precision. They would tell us of their investment needs for roads, subways, water supplies, sewerage systems, although the problems they would describe were not so evident from our visual impressions. A strict control on migration to the cities, the repatriation of many urban dwellers to the countryside during the Cultural Revolution, and a lack of much economic activity had kept the pressures on city services low.

We were also taken to several commune enterprises since we had indicated small-scale industry as another area of interest to us. We would be received by the commune head, who would give us a presentation full of facts and figures as we sat around a table with our hands cupping the glasses filled with hot water to stay warm. The production figures were often impressive, although it was easy to see that they were cooked up to satisfy party bosses. The factories were invariably dilapidated. The factory leaders would present a long list of investments that they felt would cure all problems, with never a hint of collectivism being the issue.

Then there were the obligatory visits to child nurseries in every town and commune to see smiling, happy children who would greet us with patriotic songs. We felt that perhaps these were the few places where the Chinese were depicting the true picture. It is hard to make small children lie.

When we were in Beijing, word came one day that the officials from the Ministry of Finance would meet us. We had asked to meet with government officials, but this was the first real official invitation. As we were to learn later, although our bosses in Washington had firmly decided against an official visit, the Chinese read our visit as an "unofficial official" visit. In diplomatic parlance, this meant that the existence of the visit could be denied if it ever became controversial either in China or in Washington. For the first time, we met with a Chinese government official in his office. We were not told what exactly his position was, but judging from his décor of his office and the higher quality of his grey Mao jacket, I am sure he was a very senior person. He asked a lot of questions from our group leaders about the World Bank. As I was to discover in my subsequent work in China, he was doing his homework before deciding to move forward with joining the World Bank.

We traveled extensively between cities by roads, train, and air. Most of the roads we drove on were single lane and of low quality. The airports were often nothing more than simple sheds. The "soft seat" class in the railways that was reserved for only high officials and foreigners was clean and functional, but the rest of the train had compartments with wooden benches and overcrowding.

We, of course, also took in the conventional tourist sites of Beijing, Shanghai, Xian, Wuhan, etc. They were as enchanting then as they are now, except the fact that we were often the only foreigners visiting them. China was still far from becoming a tourist destination.

It was a remarkable trip over three weeks. China was nothing like any other country any of us had visited. It was hard to form any real impressions. Some of us were very impressed with what was shown to us, while others were skeptical. But for all of us it was a great learning opportunity about a country that we did not know was about to embark on a major transformation.

In the fall of 1979, Robert McNamara visited China to start the process of normalization. This was a controversial move at odds with the view of the U.S. government. As McNamara had done while opening up World Bank lending to Vietnam the previous year over strong U.S. opposition, he did not seek their approval. He sent his personal assistant to simply inform the Treasury, the U.S. government agency responsible for relations with the IMF and the World Bank, of his visit.

McNamara's visit set the stage for China joining—or more accurately as Chinese like to remind, reclaiming its rights in—the World Bank. There were extensive negotiations on legal aspects, particularly the touchy subject of the future role of Taiwan in the World Bank. After all, Taiwan had been a founding member of the Bretton Woods institution, an early borrower of the World Bank, and now as a rich country, a potential donor. It could not simply be kicked out as had been the case in the UN. After much discussion, it was finally agreed that Taiwan would be able to continue to bid on World Bank-financed projects. It was to be referred to as "Taiwan, China" in all official World Bank documents. This showed us the pragmatic side of China. These agreements allowed them to maintain consistency with their long-standing position that Taiwan is no different than any other province of China.

China officially joined the World Bank in April 1980. A number of delegations from China visited us to discuss collaboration. In anticipation of this, my vice president, Shahid Husain, had commissioned a Filipino economist of Chinese descent, Ed Lim, to start preparing background studies on the Chinese economy. Lim, who was to become the principal economist for China and subsequently the director of the entire program, was the only economist who spoke fluent Mandarin. His background work and his language proficiency were to prove invaluable for us. Although sometimes he had to function as a translator for the visiting Chinese delegations in their meetings with the bank officials, his role was much more significant. He had quickly gained the confidence of the Chinese, who looked to him as a bridge to the bank.

Most of the meetings were slow going in part because of the necessity of having to go through translators—often imperfect when Ed was not around to correct the incorrect translation by the Chinese interpreters not accustomed to economic terms and the bank's jargon—and also because of the need to go over the smallest details. The Chinese delegations were invariably well-prepared and copious note takers. For us, China was the new frontier that offered new and exciting opportunities. The entire management group of the East Asia region, from the vice president down, would attend the meetings and take notes.

We agreed to a wide-ranging program of support covering about every sector. It included a large program of lending but also a large program of training. My group was asked to develop a rural water supply project and an urban development project for Shanghai. I fielded teams in the next few months to prepare both projects.

The Chinese asked that the rural water supply project cover five heavily populated provinces with a combined population of over 250 million, or almost a quarter of the country. We tried to persuade them to start with just one or at the most two provinces and expand the program later to other provinces. Our experience with multi-province projects in other large countries like India, Brazil, and Indonesia had not been positive. Such projects generally faced major delays because of the management challenges of coordinating across provinces. The Chinese did not agree. They felt that the needs in the selected provinces were critical, and in the end, we reluctantly agreed with them.

As our teams visited the project provinces, we began to understand why the Chinese wanted to do something in all five. The rural populations in these provinces suffered from skeletal fluorosis, a crippling disease that causes severe deformities in the body. It is caused by excessive fluoride in drinking water. It was shocking to see seriously deformed people in large numbers in the areas we visited. The only cure was to replace the high-fluoride local source of water with water transported from elsewhere.

The Chinese worked hard to prepare the project. A large team was assembled by the Ministry of Health to lead the effort. The Chinese team worked closely with my team in the preparation process. For all of them, this was a new experience. They were unfamiliar with the simplest of economic concepts, but were always keen to learn. Our team would often end up giving seminars in various places that would be attended by dozens of officials. We were impressed with their keenness to learn from the outsiders, a phenomenon we were to observe in all our projects over the years. The World Bank maintains that making funds available for projects is its secondary function. The primary function is to transfer know-how. For the first time in my more than ten years, I saw this actually in practice in a meaningful way.

One of the issues we wanted to raise with the Chinese early on was user charges for water. Our experience with the longer-term sustainability of rural water supply worldwide had not been very good. We often found systems falling in disrepair a few years after construction because of a lack of funds. We thus emphasized that right from the start communities should be actively involved in project design and should be willing to levy charges that are at least sufficient to recover the operations and maintenance costs. Many countries resisted the idea of levying charges, with the usual claim that the communities are too poor to be able to pay anything. The result was water systems falling in disrepair within a few years. We did not know how the communist officials in China would react to our requirement. The team invited me to join them in one of their missions so I could raise the issue at the higher levels. I decided to use the opportunity of a banquet hosted by the Minister of Health in our honor to gently raise the issue.

The banquet was held in the Great Hall of the People located in the heart of the famous (and later to be infamous) Tiananmen Square. It felt a bit heady since we certainly did not think of ourselves to be so important to be worthy of such an honor. Our Chinese colleagues were equally excited. As we were to learn, official banquets were their only source of good eating away from their modest living, but going to the Great Hall of the People was extra special for them also. They told us that the gesture meant that the minister was very pleased with what we had done so far.

There were about forty persons in all in attendance from Beijing and the five provinces benefiting from the project, and our team of five or six. We were seated in groups of eight to ten in round tables underneath magnificent ornate chandeliers. As the head of the team, I was seated at the table next to the minister with an interpreter seated next to me. There was loads of delicious food in numerous courses and Mau Tai and wine flowing freely. By now having attended dozens of official banquets, I had learnt to pace myself and not gorge on every course. There were the usual niceties and small conversation. The minister had lots of questions for me about India, a country about which many Chinese were very curious. At some stage during the dinner, our conversation turned to the rural water project we were preparing. I thought this was the opportunity for me to raise the issue of user charges.

I started by giving the minister an overview of the project and then turning to the outstanding issues we needed to discuss. I asked him his views on cost recovery. His response was immediate. "The villagers will pay." After making sure I had understood correctly, I then asked him what his view was about the poor villages. Again, without any hesitation, the response came, "Then they get a lower level of service, maybe just a stand post instead of a piped house connection, consistent with their ability to pay. If necessary, the villagers have to get together and raise additional funds." Not only that, the Chinese government expected the full cost of the loan, including the foreign exchange risk, to be passed on to the beneficiary village. I was incredulous. The minister could sense my befuddlement and enquired why I looked unconvinced. I was having trouble believing what I was hearing. I was thinking about how many times we had struggled, trying to convince governments about even nominal charges to at least pay for operations and maintenance, and here I was in this communist country where they wanted to have full cost recovery. I thought about how in India politicians invariably stop sensible policies in the name of the poor. I looked at the minister and said, "Mr. Minister, you are lucky you do not have a Socialist Party in China." After my comment had been translated, the minister paused for a few seconds, trying to understand my joke, and burst out in laughter. The incident confirmed the view many of us had developed about the Chinese being communists in name only on economic matters.

Regarding the project for Shanghai, we decided to first launch a study of the city in order to develop an overall perspective of the priorities. The World Bank does such studies, termed as "sector work," when initiating projects in a field it has previously not been involved in and/or in particularly complex situations. Although some countries resist such studies as unnecessary obstacle to moving forward with the project quickly—often for political reasons—the Chinese welcomed them. From day one, they appreciated the broader development knowledge and advice the bank brought. I was able to mobilize some of the most respected people from the bank for the sector study. China held a lot of curiosity for the bank staff, and there were many volunteers for any assignment there. I planned to join the team toward the end of their second three-week visit to Shanghai.

Shanghai had begun to show some signs of change since my first visit three years earlier. There was a little more color in people's clothing. There were more people milling around in streets and parks, slightly more used to having foreigners around. The affect of the one child policy was evident by couples proudly holding in their laps, backs, or bicycles their only child dressed in bright colors. And there were young couples holding hands and kissing in the dark shadows of the park around the bund. In all other respects, the city looked the same.

It was not difficult to identify the city's investment needs. Since Communist China considered cities to be parasites and thus not to be encouraged, little infrastructure investment had taken place in the previous forty years while the population had grown despite on paper a ban on people coming to the cities. There were overcrowded buses, streets clogged with pedestrians, and bicycles that would become dysfunctional quickly if even a fraction of the city residents began to drive cars. There was no sewerage system in this city of ten million (or in any other city except parts of Peking). Instead, the city relied on manual collection of night soil (human excrement) from the public toilets throughout the city. Repulsive as the concept may seem, the entire operation was so well organized that by the time the city showed the signs of life in the morning, tons of night soil had been collected by hundreds of workers moving around the neighborhoods in pedal carts fitted with small tanks. I would often get overwhelmed by the stench when I jogged the streets each morning, but amazed by the efficiency of the operation.

The biggest issue the city faced was a critical shortage of housing. Under the communist system, all housing was owned by the government and allocated to individual enterprises. No new housing had been built for years. So there was no housing to accommodate even the natural growth of population, much less the illegal rural migrants who had found a way to the city. It was not uncommon to see a house meant for one family divided up vertically and horizontally to house up to ten families. There were reportedly thousands of young people waiting for housing in order to get married. The government saw this as a serious social problem.

Shanghai was one of the four cities that had been granted the status of a province in order to give these cities virtually full autonomy. So the Shanghai city government was our interlocutor. A team of city officials, several of them very senior, had been formed to work with us. They would meet us each morning in our hotel where all discussions were held. They would all arrive on their bicycles in the dead of winter, dressed in their customary grey or blue Mao clothing, so it was difficult to judge their status just from their appearance. We never saw the inside of a government office, wondering if that was because of some directive to bar foreigners from going into government buildings. Only later were we to realize that it was because their offices were very cramped and not suitable for greeting visitors.

Extracting any information from the Chinese was a challenge. Obviously, the word had been given that they should cooperate with us fully. But after years of indoctrination and probably fear of giving out "state secrets," it was difficult for them to know how far they could really go. We never got anything on paper. Everything was conveyed to us verbally while we took copious notes. We could never get the full picture of anything, often having to construct it from bits and pieces. Working through interpreters made matters even more difficult. It was tough going.

Having observed the Chinese habit of answering your questions with proverbs, I decided to buy a book of Chinese proverbs and look up some that I could use. At the next meeting when our counterparts were being stingy with information, I said, "You cannot admire the beauty of a garden from a fleeting horse."

A quick retort came, "You do not need to eat a whole bowl of rice to tell its taste."

So while frustrating, the work was at the same time highly rewarding. As all my colleagues working on various projects and studies had discovered the Chinese had an enormous appetite for learning. They knew that decades of isolation from the rest of the world had left them behind, and they were anxious to make up for lost time. Like for the rural water project, our team for Shanghai was also constantly asked to give yet another seminar or send in a relevant expert. Sometimes, the requests were also a result of Chinese experts being isolated not only from the outside world, but also from one another. An incident during the discussions on future transport studies illustrated this.

The Shanghai Bus Company had been diligently carrying out the conventional origin and destination studies each year in order to plan capacity additions. They had read about such studies from textbooks on transport planning. However, the way they did these studies was to hire thousands of university students over two days of their school break to interview each one of the ten million passengers that rode buses daily. Greg Ingram, our very experienced transport specialist, was amazed. He asked why they did not do a sample survey. The response was that a sample survey would not be accurate. Greg then gave them a treatise on how carefully selected small samples can be accurate to a high degree of confidence. But again, the Chinese interlocutors were not convinced and seemed puzzled about how a sample can be accurate. After much discussion, Greg thought for a moment and asked, "How useful do you think a map of Shanghai would be on 1:1 scale?"

After some thought, the Chinese team understood. But then an immediate request for help followed, "Can you send us an expert on sampling to advise us on our next survey?"

Here I was being asked to advise on statistical techniques in a country where mathematics was invented. When I expressed my incredulity at the lack of top-notch statisticians in China who could do this, the response was, "But they are probably in universities and not available for such work." In the event, we managed to find some experts locally and got them to work with the transport team. But we also got an academic from the United States to work with them, primarily to give reassurance to the Chinese. Sometimes our role was just to bring out highly compartmentalized sources of knowledge within the country.

The Chinese were also very anxious to visit other countries to see for themselves how they manage their cities. In almost every other country, such requests for study tours are invariably junkets paid for under the project budgets. Aid agencies are well aware of this but turn a blind eye and see this as a way to buy the support of key officials. Calling it bribery will not be too farfetched. But we found the Chinese to be different. After every study tour, each member produced a detailed report of what she/he saw and learned. I am convinced that the Chinese hunger to learn from whomever and wherever they can has been a critical factor in their success.

The Shanghai sector study provided the basis for a series of sewerage projects that were all implemented successfully. The housing issue, we concluded, required broader policy changes in property ownership and mortgage finance rather than public investment. This was supported through additional advisory work. The Chinese, as is their practice, experimented with changes on a small scale first before adopting them on a larger scale. The revised policy has resulted in major private investments that have now eased the situation completely. It has been gratifying to see that our work has been helpful.

However, we also missed the boat on some of the most significant changes that were to come and that the Chinese had been thinking about even in 1981. We had been invited to Shanghai by the then mayor, Wang Daohan. Wang was a very influential political figure in China. He was the mentor of Jiang Zemin who was to succeed him as mayor in 1985 and later to go on and become the general secretary of the party. One evening, Mayor Wang invited us to the customary lavish banquet held in his palatial office overlooking the Huangpu River. The banquet was preceded by a discussion of our work so far. We talked about possible sewerage project, and he was very supportive. No leader in China wanted the manual night soil collection system to continue. He also agreed with our views on how the housing situation could be improved. When it came to transport, he was not overly enthused about our suggestions for minor improvements through small investments in traffic management. We were only to discover much later why. He was already planning to build a subway system.

After we had finished discussing the findings of our study, he walked us over to a window overlooking the river and pointed to the vast dark area across the river which looked like agricultural land and asked if we could help him develop the area into a new city. I took his request in the same vein as other similar requests from other countries that we generally wrote off as wild dreams of politicians that were not terribly practical. The few new towns that had been developed around the world had generally turned out to be white elephants. So I responded with some polite and noncommittal words. Wang was not upset. He simply nodded his head and motioned us to the lavish banquet table, with Wang starting the dinner with the customary toast ending with *Gambe* (bottoms up).

Pudong today is a bustling city of 5 million and the commercial center of Shanghai. It has an ultramodern airport connected to the city center by a high-speed rail. It is as if Manhattan had been built from scratch in fifteen years. And Shanghai has a very efficient underground metro. Looking back, we clearly had not yet understood fully the Chinese determination to move forward. They were open to all ideas and absorbed them like a sponge. But in the end, they took what suited them and discarded the ones that did not. In my view, this has been the key to China's success.

The World Bank developed a major program in China over the years, and there has always been close cooperation between the bank and China. The relationship has endured despite the hiccup during the Tiananmen events in 1990. The Chinese have grown increasingly competent and confident over the years. They are nevertheless even to this day eager to learn. But they are always in the driving seat when it comes to deciding on a particular course of action. This trait has served China well in its relations with the World Bank. Perhaps along with the East Asian tigers, China is the only country where I can say that their relationship with the bank was truly one of equals.

9. The Environmental Advocates: The New Foes of Development

At 7:00 a.m. on July 1, 1987, I walked into my new office as the newly appointed division chief for energy, telecommunications, industry, and finance for the newly created Country Department II in the Asia region. I had always started my work early in the morning in order to be able to also leave early in the afternoon to be with my young family. This was contrary to the schedule of most other managers. But I always had good bosses who respected my preference and knew not to call me for meetings in the evening unless absolutely essential. As I walked the corridor to my corner office, I could see moving boxes everywhere waiting to be unpacked. July 1, 1987, was the first day when the new organization had taken effect. The new organization had placed every single one of some seven thousand plus staff members into a new unit that required everyone to be moving offices.

I began by unpacking my boxes and putting books and files away. Fortunately, I have never been a hoarder of paper. Early on, I had discovered that the chances are very slim of my coming back to something I put away for later reading. So my unpacking did not take very long. I looked remarkably settled by the time my colleagues began to trickle in. I began thumbing through the briefing papers about my new responsibilities that had been sent to me by various colleagues. Soon, my assistant walked in and put a telex in front of me, saying that it looked urgent and I may want to take a look at it right away. It was a copy of a short telex by the general manager of the Electricity Generating Authority of Thailand (EGAT) to the general manager of Electricité du Laos (EdL) announcing that as of July 1, EGAT has shut off the import of power from EdL. I did not understand the import of the message and waited for my colleague who had worked on our projects with EGAT to arrive in the office.

The reorganization was ordered by the then president Barber Conable, a retired Republican member of U.S. Congress from upstate New York, who had been nominated by President Reagan. Conable had no executive experience and little development experience, but he had been a passionate advocate for the poor during his tenure in the

Congress. He also brought with him the possibility of mending World Bank's relations with the Republican U.S. administration and the perennially hostile (to the bank) U.S. Congress. The reorganization was one of Conable's first actions upon assuming office. It was in response to the growing criticism of the major shareholders—a euphemism used in the bank for United States and other industrialized countries—of the bank's administrative budget, which they saw as a bloated, overgrown bureaucracy. Conable brought in external consultants to recommend changes to improve efficiency and cut costs.

In 1987, Conable implemented a major reorganization. The most prominent feature of the new structure was to organize all operational activities around some twenty-two self-contained country departments, each responsible for all aspects of operations in one or more countries. The country directors were expected to enjoy a high degree of autonomy and empowered to take most major decisions. The decentralization of decision-making was generally welcomed by most people in the bank, who had felt that the decision-making had been too centralized in the office of a single person, Ernie Stern, the vice president in command for all operations. In the new structure, Conable moved Ernie out of operations to head the finance function. Moeen Qureshi, previously the head of finance, took over as the head of operations. The two men had been legendary rivals for many years. Both were highly respected in different ways, but could not be more different in their managerial style. Ernie, a protégé of McNamara, was extremely sharp, quick-witted, and decisive. He did not suffer fools lightly. Moeen was a thorough gentleman, but somewhat indecisive. People who knew Ernie knew that it was only a matter of time that his decisive leadership will be missed and he will be back to his own job. This is precisely what happened when Lew Preston succeeded Conable as president in 1991.

The reorganization was widely criticized both within and outside the bank. Some worried about the dilution of technical quality as the six previous individual sector-focused divisions were fragmented into twenty-two country department-based divisions. They argued that this would dilute limited technical expertise that was already becoming more and more difficult to find. The biggest criticism was of the very clumsy manner in which managers and staff were appointed. The rapid and substantial change caused personal stress, organizational tension, and major disruptions in the work process. Four hundred staff positions were cut; the entire staff had to reapply for the newly created positions. The reorganization was criticized for the disruption it caused, the costs associated with it, and the demoralization of staff. The highly disruptive managerial and staff election process designed to only retain the high performers was in practice taken over by selection by word of mouth, personal contacts and, for certain targeted nationalities, through pressure from the executive directors. The designers of the process had been carried away by theoretical elegance of their proposals and shown little understanding of practical realities of implementation. This trait is deeply ingrained in the culture of the bank and is evident in its project work as well. It is a serious weakness that has persisted to this day. In the ultimate irony, the major goal of achieving administrative efficiencies by staff reduction was also thwarted. Within a few years, the bank was again on an expansion binge. Its staff has grown to over twelve thousand today compared to some seven thousand then! The Harvard Business School was subsequently to write up a case study of this reorganization as an illustration of how not to restructure an organization.

I decided to use the opportunity of the reorganization shuffle to move to a different sector. I had worked in the urban sector for some twelve years and thought it would be interesting to broaden my horizons. I accepted the position as head of the division responsible for energy, telecommunications, industry, and finance for a group of East Asian countries (Korea, Thailand, The Philippines, Malaysia, Laos PDR, Vietnam, and Burma). Besides wanting to learn about some other sectors, I was attracted to this department for two reasons: First, I did not want to work in a department like China or India that dealt with only one country. I liked the diversity of countries this department provided: from upper middle-income (Korea, Malaysia) to low-income (Laos and Cambodia), from free market to transition (Vietnam), and from large (the Philippines) to small (Cambodia). Working in these countries was highly coveted, and it was easy to attract staff of high caliber. Second, and probably more importantly, the department was headed by one of the most respected managers in the bank, Gautam Kaji, who subsequently rose to become the vice president for East Asia and later a managing director. He has been my mentor and has been friend ever since.

Turning to the telex on my desk on July 1, 1987, my colleague, who was familiar with our work in the power sector in Thailand, finally arrived and told me what he thought was the story. Both EGAT and EdL had been long-standing borrowers from the World Bank, and we enjoyed good relations with both. Electricity generated from hydroelectric projects funded by the World Bank and others was the principal export from Laos to Thailand. The quantity of 100 MW was a big deal for the small Lao economy, but an insignificant part of Thailand's electricity production. The price was mutually agreed periodically. For the last year, there had been a disagreement on the price, and Laos had been holding out for a significantly higher price. Apparently, the abrupt turning off the switch was EGAT's way of sending a message to Laos.

I called a senior EGAT manager my staff knew to express my concern about the situation and the hope that the issue will be settled amicably. He gave me the Thai official line about the unreasonable demands by Laos, but then he told me informally to not worry. The action had been taken with full prior knowledge and support of EdL. It was the government of Laos that had been pressing EdL to extract a higher price, even though EdL knew that to be unreasonable. So the action was really intended to shake up the bureaucrats in the Laotian government. He told me that he expected the imports to resume within the next day or so, and sure enough, they did.

EGAT had been a major borrower from the World Bank in the 1970s and the early part of 1980s. In the process, it had developed into a well-managed power utility, with a strong technical and financial capability. Like other East Asian tigers, Thailand had recognized early on the importance of reliable power supply (and transport) for industrialization and subscribed to the bank's view about the need for autonomy and commercialization of the power entities as critical to their ability to meet the challenge of rapidly growing demand. Thus, Thailand (and other East Asian tigers) never faced the power shortages that we see in countries like India. EGAT was strong enough to mobilize financing from the market to finance its investment program. Indeed, foreign suppliers were competing vigorously to sell EGAT their equipment with very favorable credit terms. So it did not really need the bank financing.

Contrary to the impression the World Bank sometimes likes to covey, the volume of lending was, and continues to be, the most important metric of success within the organization and its shareholders. As I will discuss in Section II, it is also a major cause of failure of so many projects put together hurriedly to meet lending quotas. The power sector is normally a sector in which one can make large loans that help balance out the small loans that the bank has to make for sectors like agriculture and human resources, and to pay for the free non-lending advisory services that our clients wanted. One of the East Asian tigers in my department, Korea, now having become almost an upper-income country, was on the verge of graduation[20] as a World Bank borrower, knowing that without any borrowing it will also lose the free advisory services that it valued highly. It had resisted this for several years, but now the board was insisting on it. Malaysia and Thailand, the two other tigers in our department, were becoming increasingly reluctant to borrow from the World Bank given that both were experiencing significant inflows of private capital. However, both showed interest in maintaining a continuing relationship with the bank for advisory service. We thought that we should explore with them the approach of having a predetermined level of lending as a condition for our advisory services, as we had previously done with Korea. His would satisfy internal bank pressures for volume of lending while also meeting client needs.

I visited Thailand with two of my senior energy specialists to start the dialogue with EGAT and the Thai government. The National Economic and Social Development Board (NESDB), the Thai agency for economic planning and policy making, was the agency responsible for donor relationship. The officials of NESDB were receptive to working with us in the energy sector. They had been planning a major restructuring of the power sector, wanting to break up EGAT's monopoly and to open up the sector to competition from private producers. This was the worldwide trend at the time, very much following the model in the United States, the rationale being that competition would improve efficiency. NESDB, like economic planning agencies in other Asian countries, was a very powerful organization. It carried a lot of sway with policy makers. But it was powerless before EGAT, who as a competent and financially rich utility had its own powerbase. Indeed, some people used to suggest in jest that Thailand would be better off if the country were run by EGAT! NESDB sought our help in crafting the sector restructuring strategy, both to tap our expertise but I suspect also as a way to influence EGAT.

The officials from EGAT were cordial, but did not show any interest in borrowing from the bank. They explained that they had valued the bank's assistance over the years but had found the bank to be increasingly bureaucratic and slow. They had a major investment program and could not jeopardize its timely implementation by involving the bank. This had become a common complaint of our clients, except that it was the more successful countries that had started voting with their feet. I told them that I was aware of the problems, but one of our goals in the new structure was to improve client responsiveness. I assured them that with a fully empowered country director as my boss, we will not need multiple approvals before we took decisions. I knew that what I was promising was a tall order. The bank had indeed become a much more cumbersome institution than it previously had been. However, I had been able to assemble a very good energy team that I knew was capable of working at a fast pace, and I had the good fortune of having a decisive and supportive director. As if to put us to test, EGAT officials finally agreed to borrow from the bank for a combined cycle power plant at an estimated cost of $250 million that was already under tender, provided we could process it without causing delay. I looked at my colleagues and saw them nodding to me. I agreed.

My team immediately got to work. EGAT, they knew, had a very good environment department. They reviewed the environmental assessment and found it to be satisfactory with a few minor changes that EGAT accepted. The tendering had been done openly and competitively, although not to the letter of the bank rules. They convinced our chief procurement officer, who had to approve large contracts of this size that EGAT's process complied with the spirit of World Bank guidelines. We had appraised the project within three months and prepared the necessary documentation for seeking approval from our board. My team had delivered on my promise. EGAT management was duly impressed. It was the start of a very productive, renewed relationship. EGAT agreed to a regular pipeline of projects that we would finance. Concurrently, we began working with NESDB on studies of sector restructuring and privatization.

The next project EGAT presented to us for financing was a much more difficult one and on which they were keen to get our advice. It involved rehabilitation and expansion of a very large mine mouth power plant at Mae Moh in the northeast of Thailand. As a plant burning low quality lignite available in abundance in the area, there were issues with the quality of emissions and the ambient air quality. The high sulfur content in the coal caused excessive sulfur dioxide emission that was damaging to the nearby forest. So the project faced major environmental challenges, and EGAT was anxious to tap the bank's expertise in carrying out the environmental impact assessment and in the design and implantation of an environmental mitigation plan.

EGAT and the bank had also been working concurrently on a very small 50 MW hydroelectric project called Pak Mun project that involved a small run of the river dam on the Mun River. The project was too small to process as a separate bank loan, and we agreed to include it in the larger Mae Moh project.[21] I did not know at the time what an ominous decision it was to be.

In the 1980s, the World Bank had faced growing criticism from activist groups, mostly in the United States but also in Europe and Japan, about its neglect of the environmental impacts in its projects. Two major projects had drawn particular attention: the Polonoroeste settlement program in Brazil that was criticized on grounds of ignoring the adverse impacts on forests and indigenous people by construction of roads in the northeast part of Brazil and the Sardar Sarovar dam on the Narmada river in India that would cause hundreds of villages in three states to be submerged, resulting in the forced displacement of thousands of people. The criticisms were well justified. The bank had on paper prescribed policies for environmental safeguards, but these were weak and not always followed. In addition, while the bank would normally agree with the borrower on suitable mitigation measures, implementation was left largely to the borrowers. When the bank teams found deficiencies during implantation, follow-up corrective actions were not always taken diligently by the borrowers. Both Polonoroeste and Narmada projects suffered from all these deficiencies.

In response to the protests, the bank had made its policies much more explicit and prescribed clear obligations for its staff to ensure that the environmental and resettlement aspects were prepared thoroughly and supervised closely during implementation. The most stringent part of the policy was a codification of the requirement that people facing involuntary resettlement must have their livelihoods at minimum restored to their original level and wherever possible enhanced. Simple cash compensation that was (and to some extent still is) prevalent in many developing countries was not an acceptable mechanism. At the time of the 1987 reorganization, a new Environment Department was created to oversee this work. A task force, of which I was a member, set out operational policy that classified projects at inception into three categories depending on the degree and seriousness of impacts: Category "A" being the highest impact, for example for roads and dams, and Category "C" for no or negligible impact for projects such as schools. The Category "A" projects were to receive the most thorough attention. The policy was subjected to public comment and inputs before it was adopted. The environmental activists deserve credit for having highlighted the issue and brought about the necessary changes in the bank's policy.

We were fully aware of the newly codified policies while preparing the Mae Moh and Pak Mun projects. EGAT had already established its own environment and resettlement department and staffed it with well-qualified people. In addition, it sought assistance from external experts, domestic and foreign, to help with the assessments and the implementation of the environmental management plan. We thus had a willing and able counterpart to work with. The Mae Moh assessment was very complicated since it involved having to accept some less than ideal solutions. The cost of having all sulfur removed from coal was prohibitive, so the selected design was the one that still caused some damage to the vegetation, although much reduced from status quo. The Pak Mun work was much more straightforward. The main issues were the resettlement of a hundred or so families and mitigating the adverse impact of the dam on migrating fish. EGAT was able to provide an alternative site for resettlement in the vicinity of the dam and provide them with suitable alternative employment opportunities. The small number of families affected, and EGAT's ability to do this satisfactorily in other projects made the task manageable. For fisheries, EGAT hired specialized consultants with similar experiences in the western United States to prepare a mitigation plan that included a fish ladder and some restocking measures. Our specialists reviewed the plans throughout, made suggestions, and ultimately approved them as being consistent with the bank's policy.

I asked my team to be open and transparent about all the work. A few years back, when I headed the urban division, a barrage we were financing at the Nakdong River in Korea to provide drinking water supply to Busan City had run into opposition from ornithologists. Their concern was the adverse impact the dam could have on the rare migrating birds that frequented the Nakdong estuary. The environmental impact assessment had actually dealt with this issue but we had not consulted enough with the advocacy groups. In the end, the discussion with them resulted in a few changes that improved the plan, and the issue was settled amicably. The lesson for me was that early consultations would have forestalled the problems. Hence we ensured that EGAT formalized consultations with the local environmental groups. On our part, we invited for briefings those in the United States and other countries with an interest. Probe International, a Canadian NGO, was one group that showed most interest. They sent their staff to our offices to study the extensive reports on the project and ask our staff questions.

Contrary to my expectations, the consultations did not result in professional give and take. Instead, Probe was intrinsically opposed to the project. Its focus was on the Pak Mun project. They did not think that any amount of mitigation to protect the fish would be satisfactory. Our experts had actually said this much in their reports, but pointed out that the proposed measures were adequate and consistent with best practice, although one could never have zero impact. There were trade-offs in real life, whether it is a project in the United States or Thailand. Probe staff were not satisfied and began mobilizing opposition among their allies in the advocacy community and with the members of U.S. Congress. They wrote stuff that bore no relationship to reality or facts as we had presented them. A letter-writing campaign followed. As is the common practice among such groups, no one bothered to read what we had presented. They were simply following Probe's lead.

Members of Congress were even worse. Quite cynically, even members who had huge dams in their own districts that they had supported, would write to Conable accusing the bank of negligence and threatening all sorts of retaliatory actions if it decided to proceed with the project. They could care less what the Thais or we thought. Supporting the grievance of one of their constituents sitting thousands of miles from the project and with no stake in it was much more important to them than trying to find facts. We had to attend many meetings with congressional staffers who were invariably rude and condescending.

Probe had also stirred things up in Thailand. A few local NGOs, some funded by Probe or its allies, also began to protest. They would mobilize some villagers to say that the resettlement plan was unacceptable or people purporting to be fishermen, who claimed a loss of livelihood from the depletion of fish. EGAT doubted whether the witnesses being produced were really from among the affected people and whether they had been given financial incentives for their statements. But it was difficult to know. I called a meeting in Bangkok with the key local NGOs so our team could go over the project with them and understand their concerns. As I started the meeting with a few introductory remarks and before my team had even said a word, the head of the NGO delegations declared, "No need. We are going to stop this project." I did not know at the time how close he came to actually doing so.

The government of Thailand was adamant in its support for the project. It dismissed the agitations as the work of a few and told us that we must proceed with the approval process.

The protests found their way to the bank's executive directors through their capitals. The developed country directors quickly began to express opposition. There was even talk about the bank withdrawing from the project. The World Bank annual meetings were to be held in Bangkok that year in the coming fall. The executive directors did not wish bad publicity surrounding this project to infect the meeting.

The representatives of the developing countries were appalled, wondering if this reflected the shape of things to come. They were powerless as minority shareholders and being at the receiving end. However, the representative of Thailand at the board let it be known that he would insist on the project being voted on even if it were to be turned down, a prospect that did not appeal to the rich countries. Many eyed Thailand as a good business prospect and did not wish to see this incident sour their countries' relationship with Thailand. It would have also exposed the flaws in the "consensus system" of decision-making in the board that the bank touted but which in practice meant that the views of the industrialized countries prevailed when they clashed with those of the developing countries. I think they wished that the issue would go away somehow.

My director, Gautam Kaji, refused to buckle. It is customary for many managers in the bank when faced with such a situation to find an excuse to drop the project. They prefer to avoid controversy, lest it somehow reflects on them, but not Gautam. He had personally gone over the details with me and my team and had full confidence in my team's professionalism. He decided to hold an informal briefing meeting for the board where we would lay out before them all the facts and details. Gautam knew that they would find it difficult to oppose the project on a factual basis and will have to confront the fact that their opposition was largely in response to domestic political pressures in their countries. Gautam's stance lifted the spirits of my hardworking team that had been sagging.

The briefing was attended by virtually every executive director or alternate (a deputy to the executive director) and many of their office staff. Gautam asked the team to make a presentation and then opened up the meetings to questions. Many were asked, some prompted by the advocacy groups who had been pressuring the directors from their countries. My team was well prepared, and their answers showed aptly their mastery of all aspects of the project. It was difficult to poke holes in their explanations. After the meeting, the Japanese executive director told us, informally of course, that Japan would support the project but asked that we delay bringing it to the board until after the annual meeting that was to be held in Bangkok that year. Other industrialized countries also signed on with the same request. The project was approved shortly after the Bangkok meeting ended.

My team and I finally heaved a sigh of relief. We were really puzzled by all the attention the project had received and stunned by the misrepresentations. We had gone the extra mile to make sure that the environmental and resettlements aspects had been prepared to the highest standards. The claims of damage seemed wildly exaggerated, particularly considering how small the dam was. A dam that produces 50 MW of electricity is miniscule. Moreover, as a run of the river dam, it does not have much of a reservoir. We were probably paying the price of being the test case for the bank's new policy.

I understood that in formulating the policy on environment, our assumption of "reasonable application" by "reasonable people" was not to turn out to be a good assumption. I then realized that the world of advocacy groups is not pro development. Anything that even hints of a trade-off is an anathema for them. Their interest lies in stopping development at any cost. The Pak Mun protests were just the start. The impact of the Pak Mun controversy had a much wider impact, with the bank staff becoming increasingly risk averse to taking on projects that had any potential of controversy. Some of the major World Bank borrower began to shun the bank financing for major infrastructure projects, sometimes to the chagrin of advocacy groups who felt that they had no leverage without the bank being involved. For much of the 1990s, major infrastructure projects all but dried up. Wolfensohn, who had become president in 1995, initially fuelled the problem by trying to placate the advocacy groups. It was much later that he came to the realization that these groups have "no off switch," a phrase coined aptly by Sebastian Mallaby, a reporter for the Washington Post, in an article he wrote in Foreign Policy magazine based on extensive fieldwork he did talking to people in Uganda who, as alleged by NGOs, were ostensibly being hurt by a dam project.[22]

After initially embracing the NGO view wholeheartedly and requiring all sorts of hurdles for projects to cross, Wolfensohn subsequently reversed course faced with declining volume of lending and growing client dissatisfaction, but only after having secured his second term from the U.S. president. He overruled the recommendation of a commission he himself had constituted that recommended that the bank cease financing dams altogether. But it may already be too late to mend the damage. I doubt that the bank will ever enjoy the reputation of years past when one could say convincingly that our requirements are those that are in the best interest of developing countries and devoid of politics.

I should mention that the environmental issues of Mae Moh's coal-fired plant were much more serious. One could legitimately question our decisions about the trade-offs we made between cost and environmental safeguards. Interestingly, there was nothing said during all the debates about Mae Moh, and instead the focus was much more on the more benign Pak Mun. This reflected the mission of the particular advocacy groups: an opposition to any dam irrespective of the facts and not to safeguarding the environment. To this day, these groups continue to have their "independent researchers" write about the "disaster" of Pak Mun, no matter what the serious ex-post evaluations have concluded.

As an aside, during our informal briefing on the project to the executive directors, I saw a tall, lanky person walk into the meeting a few minutes late and sat quietly at the back, listening to the presentation and the questions and answers. He would occasionally look above his reading glasses sagging on his nose to peer at us sitting up front. I later came to know that it was Lew Preston, who had just taken over as president before the annual meetings. Some speculated that both Gautam and I were in trouble for having put the bank management in this awkward situation. By the end of 1990, Preston had restructured the bank and appointed Gautam Kaji the vice president for East Asia.

His action showed his independence. This was the advantage of having a bank president who had not sought out the job and did not care if he lost it while doing something he thought right. Alas, this tradition came to an end with the untimely death of Preston from cancer three years later and the appointment of Jim Wolfensohn as his successor.

Ever since the Wolfensohn era, the decision-making in the World Bank has been virtually captured by northern NGOs as documented so well by Sebastian Mallaby[23] to the point that it has severely circumscribed its ability to help developing countries in difficult projects where they really need help. The increasingly political appointments of the bank presidents beholden to the U.S. administration have made the situation even worse. The bank staff now shy away from any project where there is the slightest hint of potential controversy. The bank has to find ways to gain back its professional independence if it is to continue to be a leader in development as it was at one time.

10. South Asia: Overabundance of Aid

My next appointment came in 1990 with a promotion. I was appointed senior advisor for operations to the vice president for South Asia, Joe Wood. My responsibility was to advise and assist the vice president in managing all lending operational matters. Ensuring quality of lending was the most important part of my job, but as is typical of such staff positions, the actual responsibilities depended on the preferences and working styles of the particular vice president. I was very fortunate to have Joe as my boss. Besides being a thorough gentleman, he was also a man who knew what he did not know. He had spent most of his career on the financial side of the bank, not in operations, and had selected me for the positions specifically so that he could rely on my counsel on any and all operational matters. Being "close to the throne," it was a position of considerable influence. The best case in such positions is always when the influence comes from the added value one is able to provide. I relished the idea of working for Joe.

The position gave me a valuable perch from which to see the big picture at a regional level and a broader perspective of the bank's work. This was thus an attractive opportunity for me to grow. I was also attracted to the position for another more personal reason. The work brought me closer to my roots. While working in East Asia, I had always wondered why the South Asian countries generally, and India more specifically, could not emulate their success. There is nothing in East Asia I saw that the South Asians could not replicate. I could never convince my countrymen of this whenever I would engage with them. Indian policy makers always had ready excuses: Singapore is too small; Korea and Taiwan benefit from their alliance with the United States; these countries are dictatorships so they do not need to worry about politics; the Chinese can issue orders that the local cadres have to obey; and many more. I thought having now a formal senior position in South Asia would provide me a better platform for pushing reforms.

South Asian countries were the biggest beneficiaries of the IDA (International Development Association), the soft loan window of the

World Bank.[24] IDA loans were made on highly concessionary terms (interest free and fifty years repayment period) provided to the poorest countries, most of which were in Africa and South Asia. While funding for the World Bank loans comes from borrowing in the world capital markets, IDA funds are provided by the rich countries in three-year cycles. The share of the United States in the IDA funding at the time was about 30 percent (now reduced to about 20 percent). Having IDA funds appropriated by the U.S. Congress was always a challenge for the bank management. The bank critics, largely the conservatives, would ask awkward questions each time the administration requested appropriation for IDA. Some questions were simply tactical to vote against the funding. But some were legitimate questions for the providers of the funds to ask: how have the funds provided been utilized. Here, the bank was not on solid ground. Performance of the bank portfolio had been declining steadily in the past twenty years as measured by the assessment by the independent operations evaluation department (OED) that had been set up by McNamara in early 1970s to preempt the demands for GAO audits by some members of Congress. The evaluations showed that about 70 percent of the projects were rated as having successful outcomes in the 1980s, and only about 48 percent if success if measured by the yardstick of "sustainability," i.e., will the project continuing to perform in the longer term. Projects in South Asia and Africa performed the worst, with only 33-45 percent of project assessed sustainable. An internal task force chaired by a respected retired World Bank vice president, Willi Wapenhans, to examine the issue had concluded that pressure to lend had increased over the years and loans were often made prematurely at the expense of quality.

As one of my first tasks, Joe asked me to conduct an internal review of the South Asia portfolio to understand the reasons for poor portfolio performance and identify corrective actions. My findings confirmed the conclusions of the Wapenhans report. Many loans in South Asia were being made without having the necessary technical work in hand just to meet lending quotas. The implementation arrangements were often unclear and only firmed up well after loan approval. As a result, most of our projects were taking around ten years to complete as compared with the typical plan of five years.

The bank policy required that projects should be ready for implementation before they are presented to the board for approval. This meant that designs for at least the first year of the program should have been completed and be ready for tendering soon after the board's approval. For the larger infrastructure projects such as major roads, dams, power plants, etc., the policy requirement was even more stringent: the tenders should have been received for the major works.

This was intended to avoid cost overrun surprises that had been common in the high inflation periods of 1970s and early 1980s. So why was staff in South Asia continuing to take projects for approval prematurely?

The answer I found in my review was something we had known all along: the pressure to lend to meet ever larger annual lending targets. Although the conclusion did not surprise anyone, my review was the first time we had documented the problem. Moreover, the countries considered IDA to be an entitlement and not something they had to earn. Thus, they felt no compulsion to work diligently with the bank staff to prepare projects to acceptable standards.

The problem existed by and large in all countries in the region, but Bangladesh was particularly problematic. There were a large number of donors representing just about every industrialized country and several multilateral agencies, including IDA, anxious to fund projects. The aid funds available far exceeded the country's absorptive capacity. The result was a situation where donors were funding half-baked projects that ran into difficulties the day after approval. We were in the same predicament. Three in four of our projects in Bangladesh were at any given time labeled as "problem projects" in the bank's portfolio management vernacular. Not too surprisingly, Bangladesh also had a large number of projects rated as having unsatisfactory outcomes. Staff told us about how it was impossible to have any leverage with the Bangladeshi government to compel them to comply with the bank's requirements or to keep agreements during implementation.

So here we had a country that was the recipient of large amounts of highly concessionary IDA funds that acted as if it were doing us a favor each time we approved a project! Joe decided that the situation was untenable and decided that time had come to be more serious in implementing our requirements. We discussed the problem with the visiting Bangladeshi minister of finance and the need to deal with the issue both on their side and ours. He listened and nodded. But I was not optimistic that much will change. He had heard all this before.

That year, we decided to not go forward with a number of projects in the pipeline until after they were better prepared. The IDA commitments thus plummeted to a fraction of Bangladesh's quota. There was a lot of protest from the country but we held firm. It had been a salutary lesson that we hoped would be noticed by other countries as well.

India presented a different challenge. It was the largest recipient of IDA funds—some 40 percent of total. But its project outcomes were not much better than those in Bangladesh. In its federal structure, most of our projects were with the state governments with a wide variation in outcomes. My review found that Indian states that were led by chief ministers who had been implementing serious structural reforms had much better project outcomes than other states. We decided that in the future we would lend only to states that had a record of implementing economic and administrative reforms. The central government welcomed the approach because it too was dependent on the states for development and saw the bank's approach giving it political cover.

Within a short time, we began to see small changes in the attitudes of our government counterparts as they realized that we were serious. I began to look forward to pursuing my goal of transferring some of the lessons I had learnt in East Asia to South Asia. Besides, Joe Wood had been a fabulous vice president to work with. Unfortunately, my stay in South Asia was cut short before I had completed my first year on the job. I was appointed the director of a troubled department. I preferred to stay in my current job and forego the promotion. But I was prevailed upon to accept the change by the managing directors in the interest of institutional priorities. So I was only able to watch the situation in South Asia from the outside.

I regret to say that the discipline we had instituted did not last long. We once again succumbed to lending pressures and went back to the old ways. The lending pressures were made worse by some new conditions imposed by the IDA contributors that, while well intentioned, had the unintended consequences of forcing commitments of funds to predetermined sectors even if there were not sufficiently prepared projects. The requirement that a predefined portion of IDA funds must go to education and health gave an increased leverage to the large IDA beneficiaries such as India and Bangladesh since this target could not be met without making large loans to them in these sectors. In subsequent years, IDA donors also insisted that funds not allocated in one year to a particular country revert back to the overall pool, thus incentivizing the bank staff and countries to again cut corners before the year ended. Successive World Bank presidents have embraced the size of lending as the main yardstick of the bank's effectiveness, and perhaps their personal success. Today, quality of the bank projects in poor countries is once again as much a matter of concern as it was in the early-1990s.

Starting in the early-1990, India began to grow beyond its traditional "Hindu rate of growth"[25] of the previous three decades, thanks to the economic reforms. However, the Indian bureaucracy remains as self-serving and ineffective now as it was in 1990. The bank projects still continue to be implemented poorly in several states and have poor outcomes. It has been the dynamic Indian private sector that has saved the day. Bangladesh remains as much of a poor performer today as it was in 1990. It still has multiple donors tripping over each other to "help the country." An overabundance of aid, in my view, has been the enemy of progress in the country.

11. The Discovery of Private Sector

I was visiting my ancestral home in the mountainous region of Himachal Pradesh in India over the Christmas holidays in 1990 when I received a message that a Jim Dyck from the World Bank had been trying to call me at my parents' home in Punjab. This was before the telecommunication revolution in India. Reaching states like Himachal Pradesh by telephone was still patchy. The message from Jim was that I should call him back as soon as possible.

I had known Jim for a long time. He was the personnel officer who originally recruited me from Stanford in 1971. He had since risen up to become the personnel officer for the executive office with responsibility for managerial appointments. I did not know why Jim had called me on vacation, but I knew that it must be important. The message conveyed a sense of urgency.

I reached Jim two days later when I drove down to my home town in Punjab. He had been waiting for my return call. He told me that my name was being put on a short list for the position of a director for Cofinancing and Financial Advisory Service (CFS) and hoped that I would agree. It was to be a promotion to a senior management position, so one does not normally refuse such an offer. But there was a convoluted background to CFS that made me demur for a moment. Jim somehow sensed my unease, and before I could say anything, he said, "I know this sounds strange. You have to say yes for now. It is important to senior management (a euphemism the bank staff uses for the president). I will give you the full background when you are back in town. Meanwhile, enjoy your holidays."

CFS had been a problematic department. It had limited functions that were also not central to the bank's mission. The "cofinancing" part was a remnant from the 1970s when the bank actively sought out other donors to supplement its limited financing of a specific project. However, times had changed with each donor having more than ample aid resources, and there was little compelling reason for them to try to complicate the financing plan of a project with multiple actors. In fact, there was often competition among the major donors, strange as it may seem to someone not versed in the aid business. Nevertheless, as we know bureaucracies almost never die. So the bank kept a group engaged in holding "consultation meetings" with individual visiting donors to tell them about forthcoming projects. By 1990, it had become largely a ceremonial exercise that no one wanted to abandon. The "financial advisory" part was something that had evolved from the "Brady Plan"[26] days when the bank needed a handful of people familiar with commercial banks to help them restructure their debts (mostly in Latin America) with the bank providing additional financing and guarantees. The debt crisis had passed, and the group had been expanded and transformed into a group to offer advice on privatization to developing countries. Once again, it was the case of a bureaucracy not wanting to disappear after a job had been done. The result was a number of staff running around aimlessly, creating work for themselves.

The bank management had tried to abolish the vice presidency but ran into a complication that it should have foreseen. The vice president was of the department at the time was a Japanese national nominated by the Japanese Ministry of Finance. Japan (and a few European countries) had always complained about a lack of adequate representation of their nationals in the ranks of the bank's senior management. Japan, with its surpluses, had become an increasingly large donor to IDA, and the Japanese government often used this leverage to insist on the bank hiring more Japanese in senior positions. Typically, they would nominate one or two Japanese from their government who were not necessarily qualified, or more accurately able to adapt to the "American culture" of the bank. The bank management would try to put them in harmless positions where they would stay for two to three years, enjoy the ample golf facilities of the Washington DC area, and go back to their parent ministries. The CFS vice president was such a Japanese nominee. But in contrast with his brethren in the past, Koji Kashiwaya, the vice president in 1990, was an activist who wanted to energize his vice presidency. He had been the force behind expanding CFS into areas far beyond its mandate and capability that did not find favor with "senior management." Kashiwaya had already picked one of his protégés, another controversial individual widely considered to be a loose cannon, to be the director under him.

Kashiwaya mobilized the Japanese ministry of finance who, in the typical Japanese understatement, told Lew Preston that they would find it difficult to come to Washington for the next meeting to discuss IDA until the issue of CFS, and by implication Koji's job, had been "clarified." Their message was clear and Preston had to reverse the decision. But Preston wanted to make sure that suitable arrangements were in place to restrain Kashiwaya. He vetoed Kashiwaya's handpicked nominee for the director position and instructed Jim Dyck to find someone who would be have stature in the organization and who would be strong enough to restrain Kashiwaya.

When I returned to Washington, I had an urgent message waiting for me from Kashiwaya asking me to see him as soon as possible for an interview. When I saw him, he was cordial, but it was clear to me that he was interviewing me under duress. He spoke circuitously in a somewhat incoherent manner. I had to listen hard to understand what he was saying. He was effusive about my background and experiences in the bank. He also noted approvingly that in contrast with the other candidates on the short list, I also had private sector experience in my previous position as the chief of industry and finance for East Asia, but then agonizingly mentioned his concern that I did not have any "market" (meaning Wall Street) experience that he thought was necessary for the job. The conversation, if it could be termed as such, went on for over an hour. I left wondering about the purpose of the interview since Koji essentially repeated what was already in my CV.

At the same time, I was not inclined to take the job despite the promotion. Joe Wood, my boss at the time in South Asia, was kind and told me that I am too good to have to sacrifice my time in institutional interest for such a lousy and untenable job. The view was shared by other colleagues. I decided to take myself out of the running, not knowing that Koji had already rejected me.

I was to learn later that I was one of three persons whose names were given to him by the president as the short list from which he was instructed to select. But Koji, like many Japanese I have known over the years, was not the one to give in easily. He was an adamant man. His tactic was to dutifully interview the three people on the list, find some fault with each of us, and continue to persist until Lew finally relented and let him have his own pick. The Japanese have a well-known trait of persistence. As many frustrated Western negotiators know, the Japanese can repeat the same answer hundred times during negotiations without blinking. Koji excelled at this game.

Lew Preston, however, was not about to be snookered a second time. When I met him, he motioned me to the sofa chair next to him and remarked, "Sit down, kid." Lew had a way of putting you at ease. "Time has come for your military service."

Lew was a leader I greatly admired, and all I could utter is, "Thanks, Lew." We talked for a few minutes. He reassured me that I will have his support for whatever I did to keep things under control. Managing the Japanese vice president seemed to be the only expectation from me. I was glad to see that Lew understood the situation very well and knew that he will look after me after I have "served my time" in CFS.

I had a reputation in the bank of being a doer who welcomed new challenges, but managing CFS and the Japanese vice president seemed like a daunting task. However, I did not just want to sit around idly, even though comfortably, and pass my time until my next assignment. It is not in my DNA. I decided to look for ways in which CFS could be turned around and its significant number of staff - some of whom were actually very well qualified - could be utilized to contribute to the bank's mission. To my pleasant surprise, I found Koji a willing ally in this effort. Even though his reputation for incoherence and strangeness was fully justified, deep down he was a very committed person who was anxious to find a niche for himself and his vice presidency. Besides, with his Japanese government connections he had the ability to mobilize funding from Japan that we could use in our work. This was an irresistible carrot in a constantly budget-starved operational complex of the bank.

It was a time when there was broad agreement on the importance of private sector in development. The debt crisis of the 1980s, and the influence of President Reagan and Prime Minister Thatcher, had moved the developing world to this consensus. Strapped for resources, many developing country governments wanted the state-owned enterprises that had been a drain on their resources to be privatized. The governments also looked to the private sector to invest in infrastructure, an area that had previously been considered primarily to be the government responsibility. The bank was looking for ways to support these efforts but there was little appetite for funds borrowed from the bank with the guarantee of the government to be channeled to the private sector. In 1990, while I was the chief for industry and finance for East Asia, I had been appointed to head a task force to recommend how the bank could support the private sector. We recommended that the bank have a limited, but important, role in three ways: first, to provide technical advice to the governments in setting up appropriate regulatory environment for the private sector to grow and flourish. Second, to provide technical assistance for privatization that was still a new field with lot of controversy because of the possibilities of private rent seeking in the process. And third, to promote public-private partnerships in infrastructure with the use of guarantees from the World Bank to the private investors for government performance of its obligations and other unforeseen political events. The economists in the bank had picked up quickly on our first recommendation since it was very much within their area of expertise. But there was much foundering on the two other recommendations: privatization support because of a lack of critical mass of expertise in this still new field, and on guarantees, the ambivalent attitude of the bank because of strong opposition from the risk managers who considered guarantees to be too risky (for reasons that were in reality quite flimsy). I decided to make these two areas as the area of focus for CFS and started the process of building up the necessary expertise.

With financing from the Japanese, thanks to Kashiwaya's connections, we created two units responsible for privatization support and private project finance. I sought out two able and respected old colleagues to manage these units. We assigned the ritualistic cofinancing function to a separate unit headed by a manager from the outside who had been hired prior to my arrival in CFS, who I found lacking much substance.

There was a lot of demand for privatization support worldwide. The newly independent countries of the former Soviet Union and Eastern Europe all had an aggressive privatization agenda. Many countries in Latin America were anxious to shed their inefficient and loss-making public enterprises. Most countries in Africa and the Middle East had also jumped on the bandwagon, although as became evident later, many did so to satisfy World Bank/IMF conditionality rather than from any real commitment. This presented an opportunity for my department to step in and create a niche. Based on my experience in privatization in East Asia, notably in Malaysia and Thailand, I knew that what the countries need is not more academic studies for which the bank is notorious. Rather, what they needed was on-the-spot advice from people who had experience in implementing the programs. We recruited some top-notch experts from countries that had launched or implemented successful privatization programs in various countries. They were to focus only on advisory work of finite duration and not get bogged down with lending or long gestation studies. I also decided that we will only work in countries that showed a real commitment to privatization and were not asking for our services just to satisfy some conditionality on privatization imposed by the bank. There was quickly a high demand for their services both from our operational colleagues and from many counties. Within a short period of time, CFS became known for its expertise in this area and assumed the role of the bank's central focal point for privatization. The key ingredients to the success of the privatization unit were: 1) we created it at a time when there was genuine demand from the clients for its services, 2) we were able to recruit some highly qualified experts externally rather than staffing it from within the bank, 3) we did not encumber these experts with internal bureaucratic paperwork and other encumbrances, and 4) we kept it small to maintain quality. These all sound like common sense ideas, but these are not common features of most units in the World Bank.

The private project finance work proved much more difficult and took longer to get off the ground. Once again, there was significant demand from the clients for the bank support for private sector financing of infrastructure. However, having been burnt by ostensibly private projects they had promoted in the past, many developing country governments had appropriately become very cautious about any public support for private investors. The growing volume of private financing that had begun to flow to a few selected developing countries had reinforced this attitude. Yet infrastructure investments can never be done purely through private initiative since the government has the critical regulatory function which, if not exercised appropriately, could kill an investment. Infrastructure investments required a partnership between the public and private sector with appropriate risk sharing. The challenge was to devise mechanisms that limit government liability to only those elements that it can control—mostly regulatory and political risks—and for the private investors to take the full commercial risk.

The traditional bank loans were the wrong instruments to support public-private partnerships in infrastructure since these would in essence pass on the entire financial obligations (and thus commercial risks) to the government that has to be the guarantor of any World Bank loans. However, the use of the bank guarantees provided some interesting possibilities. Although the bank's articles of agreement had envisaged it to be in the business of providing guarantees for debt obligations of developing countries in the capital markets, in practice it had found that it can borrow itself from financial markets around the world—the bank has always enjoyed a "AAA" rating and is able to borrow at rates only marginally higher than the U.S. government obligations—and on-lend it on very favorable terms to developing countries. Also the bank's risk managers had convinced senior management that the use of a guarantee implied mixing the bank's credit with that of the borrowing developing country and has the danger of diluting the bank's excellent credit rating by creating confusion in the market. The assistant secretary in the U.S. Treasury at the time responsible for World Bank relations, David Mulford, was also reportedly adamantly opposed to World Bank guarantees and probably had influenced the views of senior bank management. Koji Kashiwaya, on the other hand, was a big proponent of guarantees apparently with the support of the Japanese government. He had been persistently pushing for them, in part because the few guarantees that the bank had provided as a part of the Brady Plan to resolve the Latin American debt crisis had been managed by CFS. The World Bank typically guaranteed only the late-year maturities and were thus for less than the full value of the underlying loan. Koji had been arguing that such "partial" guarantees are a good way to leverage the bank's support. But I also suspect that Koji saw in the expansion of the guarantees as an opportunity to expand CFS' role, something for which Koji valiantly fought senior management.

The logic of our risk managers or of Mulford was never clear to me but this had been their position when I arrived in CFS. I thought that guarantees were no different than loans in terms of risk to the bank but indeed offered some benefits of leverage, although perhaps not as large as the proponents in CFS claimed. It seemed like a classical bureaucratic turf battle that had simmered on for years without a clear decision. I decided to be agnostic until I could learn more. There was another use of guarantees that CFS had been working on. It was in the context of a large ($1.2 billion) thermal power project in Pakistan—the Hub River Project—where the bank guarantee was designed in a way that it would trigger not in the event the project faced defaults from commercial risks but because of the failure of the government to keep its part of the regulatory agreements or for unforeseen political events in the country. I thought that this was indeed an interesting innovation that should not get tainted by the overall poor reputation of CFS. I decided that with better management, this may well be an idea I could sell to senior management.

The guarantee for the Hub River Project was finalized during my tenure at CFS. I had to spend considerable time and effort trying to manage the process. The person who originated the project and was now assigned to manage its preparation was the same person Kashiwaya had earlier selected for my position but whose selection was vetoed by senior management. He was truly the innovator in this case, but someone who had to be managed closely to safeguard against his free-wheeling tendencies. Some people also suspected his integrity, although I personally had no reason to think so. He had formally resigned when not appointed as the director, but was kept on for a few months (that later turned into two years) to bring the Hub project to financial closure. I would have accepted his resignation and turned over the task of managing project preparation to someone else. But he had even before my arrival worked with Koji to be transferred out of CFS to the Pakistan country department while keeping the project under his control. I thus had a difficult management challenge.

The Hub project reached financial closure in 1993. It continued to be a controversial venture both within and outside the bank. Some people felt that the final terms that Pakistan and the bank agreed were too favorable for the investor. Some in the bank criticized the very high cost incurred in developing the guarantee (several millions of dollars compared with less than half a million dollars for a typical project). In addition, as mentioned above, there were continuing rumblings of possible corruption. I think these criticisms are largely justified but, when taking into account the new path this project broke for the bank, the ultimate judgment in my view should be more charitable.

Lew Preston himself liked the concept of the bank guarantees for regulatory and political risks in large infrastructure projects. He had been the chairman and CEO of JP Morgan before becoming president of the World Bank and understood private sector better than any of us. He asked his senior managing director, Ernie Stern, to see how this instrument can be mainstreamed and used more widely. Ernie gave me the responsibility of developing the proposal for the board. There was still much opposition within the bank to the instrument by the risk managers and also by our sister institutions of IFC and MIGA, who felt that this was treading on their turf.[27] Fortunately, I had the support of Ernie and Lew. After six months of effort, I prepared a proposal that was approved by the board in 1994. The board too was split, but a significant majority of the directors, including all of the directors representing developing countries, supported the proposal. My paper titled "Mainstreaming of Guarantees in World Bank Operations" became my legacy in CFS.

The development of guarantees continued to be a slow process. The bank staff was much more comfortable with using the traditional loans. Most did not understand the private sector and were not the best people to discuss the concept with the clients. In addition, throughout the 1990s, the bank had ample capital that did not give staff or management incentive to find ways to leverage it. On the demand side, some of the better performing developing countries were resistant to the idea, believing that they had sufficient credibility to attract private investment without the comfort of the bank guarantee. Over time, however, the instrument has been used on several important projects. But it still remains relatively small compared with loans. I suspect that if Lew Preston had not died a premature death and led the bank longer, guarantees may well have been a mainstream instrument. Such is the nature of bureaucracies.

I left CFS in March 1995 after having spent three years on the job. I managed to fulfill my mandate of keeping the Japanese vice president in check, but fortunately I could do so by not having to restrain him from pursuing wild ideas but by channeling his and the department's energies to some useful areas. The experience, however, left me dismayed by the posture of some of the industrialized countries whose most important agenda with the bank seemed to be to make sure that their nationals received high level appointments in the bank. Japan was not the only country that pursued this objective (and continues to do so to this day). Several European countries have been equally aggressive, using their contributions to IDA as a lever on the bank management. Several recent bank presidents have exacerbated the situation by themselves pushing overtly political appointments to gain favor with important constituencies. Interestingly, most such appointments have ended badly with the incumbents leaving after a few years, but not before causing harm to the bank's reputation.

Nevertheless, the assignment was most enriching for me professionally. I gained a deep appreciation of the importance of private sector as the engine of development and how instruments of foreign aid can be used to support it.

12. A New President: The Man Who Broke the Bank

The 1994 annual meeting of the World Bank and the IMF were held in Madrid, Spain, in the fall of 1994. This annual event is held in Washington, DC for two years and rotated to a different world capital in the third year. The meetings bring together finance and economic ministers, senior officers of financial industry, important opinion makers from every country in the world, and senior managers from the World Bank and the IMF. Everyone wants to meet anyone important. The president of the bank has a busy schedule as he tries to meet delegations from industrialized and the most significant developing countries. A few other developing country delegations are also scheduled for a meeting with the president based on the recommendations of the bank managers as deserving of such a meeting. Most developing country delegations also meet with the country director and vice president responsible for them.

There are also lots of social events. The host country organizes a couple of entertainment events such as a concert. There are also numerous receptions by country delegations, banks, and others. These are great networking and schmoozing opportunities. I had to pick and choose the events I attended based on their relevance for me, or if they otherwise looked interesting, or in some cases, the hospitality reputation of the host (the receptions by investment banks were generally most lavish and sought after!). These events were generally a good respite from the ritualistic official meetings.

The only bad note for me was on the evening of the concert when I was the random victim of a paintball thrown by a protestor while I was entering the concert hall that ruined my best dark suit; Madrid was the start of the tradition of protestors showing up at all subsequent annual meetings. Fortunately, the bank's insurance policy reimbursed me although they took some time in dealing with my claim not having ever encountered such a claim in the past!

Despite the hectic pace and the busy schedule, bank managers also find themselves with significant spare time between meetings. Sitting in cubicles under one roof is an opportunity to catch up with colleagues one is much too busy to see when in Washington. On one such occasion, Shahid Husain, the then vice president for human resources, invited me for coffee.

We had barely sat down when Shahid, in his legendry curt style, got to the point. "You have done what we asked you to do. Your next job will be as a country director. So be thinking about transitioning out of your current job in the next few months. The most likely place is the Middle East, once we find another position for the incumbent." I was both pleased and surprised. Pleased because a country director was precisely the job I had wanted, and surprised because I had expected an appointment either in Asia or Latin America, where I had the most experience. I also had expressed an interest to work in the transition economies, mostly as a matter of intellectual intrigue and challenge. I knew nothing about the Middle East, and moreover, the Middle East region in the bank enjoyed a reputation of being the "backwater" of the World Bank. Shahid sensed my reservation and went on to reassure me: "I have discussed it with Lew, and he agrees that you are the best choice. You know development as well as anyone else. The issues are the same. Only the context is different. Besides, we need some fresh perspectives in the Middle East. As you have heard me say, 'Everything is learnable except for basic intelligence.' I am sure you will do just fine."

Shahid was one of the most experienced and seasoned vice presidents. He had previously been vice president for East Asia and Latin America in the bank and a cabinet member in Pakistan. He had a reputation for being ruthless, although some of it to me came from his direct and sometimes abrupt manner of communication. Many feared him. I had been a manager under him in East Asia and had gotten along very well with him. I had appreciated his intellect and found his directness and decisiveness refreshing. I trusted his instincts.

This brief conversation sealed my fate for the next six years and started what turned out to be for me yet another wonderful stint in my World Bank career. I will discuss my experience in the Middle East in the next chapter. I digress here to discuss the sudden change in leadership at the bank at the same time that was to have a major impact on the way the bank operated.

In late 1994, Lew Preston was diagnosed with terminal cancer and died a few months later. It was a sad occasion. I had gotten to know him some during my work on guarantees. Like his predecessors, he had not come to the bank with any background in development. What he brought was strong and decisive leadership. He was a delegator and a keen judge of people. He could be tough, but combined his toughness with a great sense of humanity. He understood that making mistakes is a part of any difficult job as long as one learnt from them and did not repeat them. In my assessment, other than McNamara, no one brought better leadership skills. In the tradition of all previous bank presidents, he had not sought the job. Rather, he had taken it on as a sense of duty, leaving his highly lucrative position as the head of one of the leading banks. I was one of his great admirers and felt his untimely death as a real loss for the bank. Following his death in early 1995, a search for his successor was initiated by the Clinton administration. The United States has by tradition always had the right to appoint the president, subject to perfunctory approval by the bank's board.

I was in Israel in March 1995 as my first visit to the region as the Country Director for the Middle East, in the company of my boss, Caio Koch-Weser. We were to attend a meeting of an advisory group of prominent persons from the region that Koch-Weser had set up to provide us with their insights. The meeting was being held in the beautiful ski resort, Fakrah, in Lebanon. Caio was visiting the Palestinian territories on the way and thought it would be a good chance to introduce me as the new director. The Oslo accords had been signed the previous year, and the World Bank had moved quickly to establish an office in Jerusalem to help with the economic development of the Palestinian territories as one of the steps toward the future establishment of a Palestinian state.

In Tel Aviv, we were hosted for a small, intimate dinner by a prominent Israeli businessman that was attended by three prominent members of the Likud Party.[28] This was for us to get the views of the party out of power, a practice Caio had quite wisely followed given the delicate and sometimes Byzantine politics of the region. Our host, also a member of the Likud, was moderate in his political views and seemed supportive of the peace process. But the other members of the party were adamantly opposed. They told us that they welcomed the bank's humanitarian initiatives, but did not see any possibility of a Palestinian state being formed in their lifetime. Not what we had wanted to hear, but at least we were getting it straight. In the middle of the dinner, our host left to take a phone call and returned to announce with some excitement that "Jimmy" had been appointed by President Clinton as the next president of the World Bank. There was much cheer all around the table. I was only to learn later that "Jimmy" was none other than James Wolfensohn, a very successful investment banker from New York.

The Washington press was full of stories about Wolfensohn. He had left a successful investment banking career at Schroeder's in London when passed over for the position of its chairman to start his boutique investment bank in New York where he had made millions. He had been involved in various philanthropic activities. He had served on the board of the Kennedy Center and the Population Council. He had taught himself to play cello at a late age and had given a performance at the Carnegie Hall in New York. One story dubbed him the "renaissance man." It all sounded very good and all of us in the bank were genuinely excited.

Then stories began to trickle about his other side. Even before he formally assumed his position, he summoned each of the vice presidents to New York to see him, and every one of them came back with disturbing stories. He disparaged them. One vice president was berated on not having briefed him about his visit to Tokyo. Wolfensohn was adamant that he should have known that he (Wolfensohn) was also due to visit Tokyo at the same time. Others reported the use of profanity, something that was unheard off in the bank's multicultural environment. There was a wide gap between the press stories and what senior colleagues were reporting. As we were to all learn later, there were indeed two Jim Wolfensohns: the public persona that was charming and went to some length to cultivate a positive image of himself, and the private persona that was ruthless, crude, insecure, and distrustful of his staff. Perhaps not an entirely atypical profile of investment bankers.

I was to personally experience Wolfensohn's management style within a couple of days of his assuming office on June 1, 1995. Wolfensohn had received a letter from (late) Shimon Peres, who was Israel's foreign minister at that time. It was largely a letter of congratulations, but Peres took the opportunity to suggest that the World Bank help the Palestinians by financing the construction of hundred thousand new apartments in Gaza. Those who know Peres are quite used to him putting one new proposal or another all the time. He was widely known as somewhat of a visionary, or perhaps even a dreamer in many people's eyes. I happened to be the acting vice president for the region at the time, and the letter was forwarded to me for action. As had been my training all along right from my days as a young professional working on evaluating the Gabon railway in 1972, I wrote Wolfensohn a note saying why Peres's proposal did not make much sense for a number of reasons. First, there was a surplus of housing in Gaza since it is not uncommon for Diasporas to send funds to relatives back home who often use them to build housing. Adding to the housing stock would have only added to the glut. Second, our worldwide experience had shown public sector-built housing to be a disaster—Singapore and Hong Kong were the only exceptions to this—and there was no reason to believe that a fledgling Palestinian authority would do any better. I suggested that we should decline Peres's proposal politely but propose that we will study the situation to see what maybe the constraints to having market solutions such as housing finance. I attached a draft letter of response to my memorandum.

The next day, I was summoned to Wolfensohn's office. By then my vice president had also returned from his trip and was present in the meeting. We settled into Wolfensohn's private conference room adjoining his office. Wolfensohn entered the room and sat at the head of the table and began to leaf through the folder that contained Peres's letter and my proposed response. I could immediately tell from his body language that he was not happy. He began by complaining that my memorandum was nothing but a "classical bank bureaucratic" response. He did not understand why a simple matter like this needed study and why we could not just send some people immediately who could get on with the contracting. He thought housing was such an obvious thing to do in Gaza. "I built projects like this in Australia in six months," he said, showing disdain for our understanding of development. I tried to explain to him once again what I had already said in the memorandum but he was in no mood to listen. He concluded by saying, "It is up to you how you want to proceed. But it does not make sense to me."

At which point my vice president immediately jumped in to say, "Jim, you have a good point. We will come back to you with a proposal." He was among those managers who had decided that agreeing with Wolfensohn was safer than expressing any different views.

I was appalled by what I had witnessed. What a contrast the meeting had been from the dozens of other similar meetings at various levels that I had participated in the very same office where the discussion was always on the merit of the proposal and nothing else, no matter who the proponent was. What I did not know at the time was that Peres because of his strong support for settling the Israeli-Palestinian conflict was literally worshipped by the liberal Jewish community that Wolfensohn belonged to. My guess was that he was offended that I had not shown due respect in my memorandum since I called the proposal as "not making much sense." In addition, I had not known at the time the importance Wolfensohn placed on being on the right side of the U.S. State Department, who had itself been promoting such proposals in order to create their dream of "warm peace" between the Israelis and the Palestinians. With what I was to learn subsequently in the short period I had the responsibility for managing our work in the

Palestinian territories, it is almost certain that the proposal had been discussed with the State Department as well prior to our meeting with Wolfensohn.

As we were to learn over the following few years, Wolfensohn had an enormous ego but at the same time suffered from great insecurity. He resented competence in others and trusted none of the existing managers; the most competent ones left either in disgust or were pushed out by him. But he was very meticulous about cultivating his own image externally. Over time, as documented so well in the book by Sebastian Mallaby,[29] he was a deeply flawed man who did considerable damage to the bank from which it has not yet recovered.

I do not intend to dwell on Wolfensohn's deeply flawed personality and poor management style here. Mallaby's book provides a rich account that an interested reader can refer to. I discuss here one aspect of his leadership that had a particularly adverse and lasting impact on the bank.

All the previous bank presidents in its fifty-year history had been accomplished Americans who considered the job as their way of giving something back to society. Wolfensohn was the first president to have actively lobbied for the job. He was initially recommended for the job by Robert McNamara to succeed him in 1980, only to discover that he was not a U.S. citizen and thus ineligible for the appointment. He had since been preparing for it by becoming a U.S. citizen, sharpening his resume by being active in various philanthropic activities, and cultivating important U.S. politicians, mostly Democratic, by generous campaign contributions. It was all a very carefully orchestrated campaign. However, his first real opportunity came only after a Democrat (Bill Clinton) was elected U.S. president after a hiatus of nearly two decades. He was determined to make the best of the opportunity, and his goal from day one after assuming office was to solidify his reappointment for a second term. He had a two-pronged strategy. First, to demonstrate to the opponents of the bank—NGOs who claimed that the bank was insensitive to poverty and suffering and destroying the environment—that he agreed with them and would work to "reform" the bank, and second, to be responsive to the important political constituencies, particularly the U.S. administration and Congress.

He started his reforms of the bank immediately on arrival. He had come with a prior notion that the place is run by a group of stodgy and arrogant technocrats who were insulated from the many valid criticisms of NGOs and resistant to any reforms. They were not to be trusted. He questioned everything that had been done before his coming and was dismissive of any dissenting views to his numerous initiatives that he launched. He had managed to convince the board that they should allocate some $250 million in additional budget for three years for a "Strategic Compact" that would not only improve the bank's effectiveness, but also subsequently yield efficiency savings to more than offset the cost. He hired management consultant, KPMG, without competition to carry out a study on the basis of a skimpy three-page terms of reference. I was designated by the managing directors as one of the group of bank managers to guide KPMG. But we found the KPMG team clueless about the bank or its work. The poor terms of reference also did not help. In the end, the only usable finding of the KPMG team was that there would be savings if we were to cut down the size of staff offices. The study was an utter disaster and a butt of jokes around the bank. The Strategic Compact in the end was an utter failure as documented at length by another ex-colleague, David A. Phillips.[30] The onetime additional budget for the Compact that was to be recouped after three years through improved efficiency turned out to be a pipedream as many had predicted. The fact that the bank's board of directors approved his proposal without any skepticism, and glossed over the negative findings of the critical ex-post evaluation three years later, says much about the problem of governance of the World Bank that I will discuss later.[31]

With funding from the Strategic Compact, Wolfensohn began to launch numerous initiatives, notwithstanding the KPMG fiasco. He decided that NGOs had been right in accusing the bank staff of not really understanding poverty. Every World Bank manager was asked to spend two months at the Harvard Business School to learn development management, followed by a period of time living in a village in a poor country. No one questioned why and how Harvard was the right place for this, although many eager beavers did not mind their stints in Cambridge.

One of Wolfensohn's legacies was the expansion of the bank into peripheral areas that it knew little about or that were not its business. While Preston had emphasized focus as one of the key principles for the bank, Wolfensohn was exactly the opposite. There was hardly anything someone influential suggested or that came to his mind that he did not turn into an initiative. During a visit to Egypt, when President Mubarak mentioned the difficulty Egypt was facing in relocating the beautiful Cairo museum from the city center to the outskirts, Wolfensohn immediately promised help and instructed me to line up a team, never mind that we had no expertise in this area. After meeting the archbishop of Canterbury, he launched an interfaith initiative. Fascinated by the subject of distance learning, he launched a Global

Development Learning Network with the idea that the bank would promote learning about development through creation of networks.

One year, Wolfensohn returned from his Christmas holiday at Jackson Hole to announce a new initiative based on a new revelation he had had. He wanted the bank to develop a "new development framework" that articulates a country's development priorities, identifying linkages between different sectors, and plans all donor assistance around this plan. As an example, he asked how we could build a school in a village if there is not a road that connects the school to the village or there is no drinking water supply available for the school. He saw his new development framework, subsequently renamed "comprehensive development framework" or CDF, as a new way of thinking about development comprehensively, although most of us thought of this nothing more than central planning of the 1960s. But no one in the bank dared suggest that what he was proposing was no different than central planning that had been tried and failed just about everywhere. Even Nobel laureate Joe Stiglitz, who at the time was the bank's chief economist, went on to extol the idea.

Outsiders were not so charitable. Columbia University's renowned development economist Jagdish Bhagwati puzzled in the pages of *Financial Times* what could explain "mistaken assumptions" and "outright fallacies" on which Wolfensohn and Stiglitz had based their framework. He charitably concluded that it was probably a result of "plain ignorance." On the same pages, T. N. Srinivasan, another prestigious development economist at Yale, expressed his disdain for CDF, dismissing it as "cliché ridden and banal."[32]

Of course, none of this prevented Wolfensohn from going forward with still another new initiative. A secretariat was set up to help a group of twenty or so selected "pilot" countries where this concept would be tested. Some directors eager to please Wolfensohn embraced the program enthusiastically and began to talk in the "CDF language." But others found ways to drag their feet or beg off from the program completely. The Jordanian minister of planning, an eminent economist, and one of my clients and close friends, decided to put a slow man on the job, predicting (correctly) that the initiative would soon be forgotten. India refused to participate, saying that its five-year plan was its CDF. In the end, as often happened with such initiatives, the countries that remained on the pilot were generally the smaller and weaker countries on which the bank could impose its new ideas.

Responding to criticism about the bank not having a "social conscience," Wolfensohn decreed that every project must be subjected to a social impact assessment. He viewed this an essential part of understanding how different members of a society maybe impacted by different projects and policies so ameliorative actions could be taken when a particular group was impacted adversely or conversely, when it was good social policy to have specific groups benefit from an intervention. This all sounded good, but no one, even to this day, has a clear idea about the appropriate scope of social assessments or the methodology for carrying it out. It has brought hordes of anthropologists and social scientists in the bank, to the delight of NGOs who think anything "social" must be good but never questioning its value. For the clients, it has become yet another requirement of the bank that they must comply with.

There are, of course, valid social issues that one can come to grips with—e.g., are measures being taken to encourage girls to come to school, whether women are not discriminated against as beneficiaries, how the community participation is to be organized, etc. But these do not require fancy social analysis by eager social scientists. Wolfensohn's ambition was that we should figure out "societal impacts" of interventions, something easier to think in theory than doing it in practice. A whole industry has sprung up in the consulting world and within the bank staff around this requirement that many clients think as yet another cost of working with the bank. I know of no client that has adopted such assessments for their own development plans and projects.

These are just few of the examples of diffusion in the bank into peripheral issues during Wolfensohn's era. Many of these have since been discontinued or, more likely, they continue to exist but have been forgotten. These detract from the bank's core mission and actually reduce its effectiveness. The more effective bank will need to take a much more disciplined approach to development if it is to continue to be relevant.

Having sought and won his appointment, Wolfensohn was soon working to solidify support from the major shareholders, cultivating relations with the United States for his foremost priority. As indicated earlier, getting the bank unreservedly behind the United States-led Middle East peace process was important to him. He wanted the bank to get behind any proposal coming from the U.S. State Department, irrespective of whether it made any sense from a development perspective. I have mentioned earlier the episode involving Shimon Peres. He reversed an earlier decision by Preston for the bank to not become the disbursement agent for Palestinian government salaries as demanded by the United States because it clearly was neither in the bank's development mandate nor within the bank's competence. There were many more similar episodes. As I will discuss in the next chapter, my insistence on focusing on the merits of the proposals ultimately led him to take the responsibility for the Palestinian territories away from me, apparently responding to the complaint from the State Department about I not being cooperative.

While previous presidents knew well the importance of having good relations with the United States, they had managed to strike a balance and by and large maintained their independence despite themselves being Americans. They limited their dealings with the highest levels of the U.S. government on big policy issues, and even on these, did not hesitate to go against the U.S. views. Wolfensohn, however, was different. He would go to any extent to keep the United States happy. He would agree to meet with third and fourth tiers of political appointees from the State Department, officials who should at best have been dealt with at my level.

Besides the United States, Wolfensohn also cultivated other shareholders who he thought could be helpful to him or who could be helpful in boosting his image. The most common tool he used for this was to make appointments to many senior positions based entirely on political considerations, similar to what the UN organizations are known for. This too was something very new to the bank that had, with a few small exceptions, largely avoided following this path to politicization. The fact that many of these appointees replaced some very competent and experienced managers who left in disgust further added to the problem.

Sometimes he would miscalculate and appoint people who had other baggage or did not earn him as much favor with the constituency as he had expected. He had decided on winning over African leaders as a way to burnish his credentials. Many of them blamed the bank for their ills. This was not an uncommon phenomenon I observed in my career: the worse performing a country, the more critical it was of the bank. Wolfensohn wanted to show that he was sympathetic to them. Saying no to leaders, as I had learnt to do starting with my first task in Gabon, was now out of fashion. The bank managers had to be accommodating. He also appointed several Africans to high positions, again irrespective of qualifications to pander to the African leaders. He loved their applauding him in international fora. However, one somewhat humorous but sad episode demonstrates how his overtures sometimes backfired.

Wolfensohn had become very popular with most African leaders but found it difficult to penetrate Mbeki, South Africa's president. Mbeki is a proud nationalist who, I suspect, did not like being patronized. As he often did with other important political players, Wolfensohn invited Mbeki to his summer hangout in Jackson Hole. In one of the rounds of many social events, Wolfensohn told, "Thabo"—he liked to be on first name basis with the world leaders—that he had decided to appoint Mphela Ramphele, a South African woman, as a managing director, the highest position after the president. Ramphele had neither experience in development nor had she managed anything in her life. She was an academic, and her claim to fame was that she was Steven Biko's widow. Mbeki is reported to have responded, "Mr. Wolfensohn. I am glad you wish to appoint a South African to a senior position. We have many qualified people in my country and will be happy to suggest names." Wolfensohn had not realized that Ramphele was not from the Mbeki camp. She left the bank a couple of years later when her lack of preparedness for the job became all too evident and even Wolfensohn could not support her anymore. She was just one of many Wolfensohn appointees who suffered such fate.

Ever since I joined the bank, a common question in cocktail conversations when I would tell someone that I worked for the bank, would be, "So it is a U.S. organization? Or surely, you must be answerable to the United States." Even now, news stories commonly talk about the United States having a veto power, which is not true (the United States share was around 22 percent in the 1970s and has since gone down to about 15 percent).

It was not easy to explain to them how the bank functioned in practice. Although the United States as the biggest shareholder and a major contributor to IDA is clearly important, previous presidents had managed to maintain the bank's independence, although they were sometimes forced to make concessions, for example when the U.S. Congress would threaten to withhold U.S. contributions to IDA. Still, overall they managed to keep the bank apolitical and free from undue influence from the United States and others.

Wolfensohn was the first bank president to overtly politicize the bank. For the first time, we began to see appointments to senior ranks that were always based largely on merit being made on political grounds. The bank traversed even further on the slippery slope of politicization in 2005 when President Bush appointed Paul Wolfowitz as Wolfensohn's successor. Wolfowitz was an overtly partisan political appointee from within the U.S. government.[33] He appointed several senior managers of questionable qualifications from the countries that formed the "coalition of the willing" for the Iraq war. Eventually Wolfowitz was forced to resign in disgrace in 2007 under the cloud of corruption, but the Bush administration continued to defend him to the bitter end.[34] Wolfowitz was followed by yet another political appointee, Robert Zoellick, who had been the U.S. trade negotiator and had been on the team that defended George Bush's reelection in Bush v Gore in 2000. And the latest is Jim Kim, who again was a political appointee by

President Obama, after pretentions by the bank's board of having followed a worldwide competitive selection process.

Whether and how the bank can recover from its politicization over the last fifteen years and regain its old reputation as not taking political considerations into account in any of its decisions is unclear. Many have argued the need for a non-American as the next president. In my view, this will be nothing more than a hollow gesture. Many Americans have served the bank with distinction, and there is nothing to be gained by making the issue of nationality as a battle cry. It detracts from the real issue facing the bank which is its poor governance whereby the board of directors is unable to exercise any real oversight, including in ensuring that a transparent selection process is followed that attracts a reputed leader and manager as the bank's president.

The politicization of the bank started by Wolfensohn, and continued by his successors, has led the bank far from its original charter of not taking political considerations into account in its development activities. The weak oversight by the bank's board has allowed this situation to develop. There is a need to reverse the decline by having an apolitical process for the selection for the future bank presidents and by strengthening the oversight by the board of the activities of the president.

13. The Middle East: An Impossible Dream[35]

The Middle East, I found, on taking over my position in March 1995, could not have been more different from East Asia where I had cut my teeth in development. My department handled the bank work in six eligible developing countries—Egypt, Jordan, Lebanon, Syria, and the Yemen, and West Bank and Gaza. In addition, it was responsible for providing technical assistance to six oil-exporting Gulf Cooperation Council (GCC) countries that was paid for by them. The developing countries varied from very low-income (Yemen) to middle-income (Lebanon) and in between. I liked the variety of countries that I was to manage.

Most countries were facing economic crises of one form or another—stagnant economies that had not experienced much growth in per capita incomes for over a decade, significant consumption subsidies that were increasingly unaffordable, and large and pervasive public sectors and inefficient civil service. Most countries had maintained fixed exchange rates over many years, with some even maintaining dual or multiple administered exchange rates. Most had yet to adjust to the secular decline in oil prices that affected them negatively through reduced oil revenue or worker remittances or both. In addition, Lebanon and the Yemen had experienced major civil wars from which they had yet to recover. On the positive side, most countries in the region (except the Republic of Yemen) had invested in education and health, which—along with food subsidies and civil service employment—had kept most of the population above the absolute poverty line. But those programs were not affordable in the new realities of constraints on public expenditures. In addition, the social expenditures faced major problems of efficiency and effectiveness. There was a clear need for economic policy reforms. Yet commitment to reform was at best halfhearted or—more usually—nonexistent.

The bank was blamed by the public in most countries for causing economic hardship and misery. This attitude was surprising given the fact that no country had really undertaken much serious structural reform. In large part, the public did not distinguish between the bank and IMF, the latter having supported stabilization programs in the Egypt and Jordan, in both of which riots greeted government attempts to eliminate the bread subsidy. This problem of the bank image, unfortunately, continues even today and is one of the factors that has led me to think about a totally different approach to the bank lending: away from structural adjustment lending with ex-ante conditionality to budget support based on ex-post performance—but more on this later.

The demand for project lending was modest for different reasons in different countries—reluctance to borrow expensive World Bank funds (Egypt), more interest in balance of payments support (Jordan), recent civil war (Yemen), loan arrears to the World Bank (Syria), and political pressures (Iran). Lebanon was on the bank's watch list because of concerns about its economic stability due to excessive public spending under its businessman turned prime minister, Rafic Hariri, who was more concerned about quick rebuilding of the war-torn country rather than massive budget deficits. When Iran was added to my department two years later, we were stymied by strong opposition from the United States and its allies to any bank engagement. West Bank and Gaza (WBG) was the only country[36] with an active lending program. The department staff was thus underutilized and often busy selling their services to the Gulf countries for a mixed bag of assignments from important to make work. This context illustrates why the Middle East had the reputation as the bank's backwater.

I was determined to change the status quo. I had a strong belief that it serves neither the country nor the bank if there is not a healthy degree of mutual trust and shared vision of the development agenda. I was not satisfied with the low level of equilibrium at which our relationships appeared to have settled. I told my staff that I would rather have no program in a country than be constantly pushing at the end of a string, trying to gin up work that the country did not want or appreciate. A lack of client receptivity frustrated the bank staff, and the more capable ones would soon find assignments elsewhere, leaving only the weaker staff to work on the country. One of my bosses used to talk about the vicious cycle: poorly performing country—bad bank staff—bad projects—bad outcomes—poorly performing country.

West Bank and Gaza (WBG) was very much in the limelight at the time. The Oslo Peace Accord had been signed two years earlier and created a great sense of hope about the emergence of an independent Palestinian state living peacefully side by side with Israel. The bank (along with the IMF) had been entrusted the job of helping with economic development. There were lots of U.S. groups that wanted to talk to me soon after my appointment. They were by and large promoters of peace between the Palestinians and Israel. They worked under titles such as "Builders of Peace," "Bridge Builders," etc. Many had prominent backers from the American Jewish community who had long-standing friendships or business relations with Wolfensohn. Many had implicit or explicit backing of the U.S. State Department. They all had suggestions for projects we should finance. Some groups had good ideas but many had grandiose plans to "transform the region." One such idea was for an elevated highway passing through Israel to connect Gaza with the West Bank. Others were a bit self-promoting in that they involved engaging the proponents somehow in the process.

I decided to make WBG as the first place to visit. It was a depressing visit. The Palestinians already were much more pessimistic than the international community. The constant humiliations they suffered daily at Israeli checkpoints had left them bitter. Even more importantly, they were beginning to lose hope in achieving their goal of independence. I met with Yasser Arafat in his office in Gaza. It was an indescribable feeling for me to be meeting this man who I had often seen on television ever since I was a boy. It was unreal to meet him in person with his trademark beard; his big, round, twinkling eyes; his army fatigue jacket and the classic kaffiyeh as his headdress. He greeted me warmly and seemed to develop a liking for me. I quickly learnt that it was because of his affection for India. He said he will never forget India's steadfast support for an independent Palestine. He was relieved to find out that I had come from Israel through the Rafah border without any problems. He had been distressed when, a few days earlier, the Israelis had insisted that the visiting Indian foreign minister walk across the border.

I had come to talk about how the bank could help. He would listen politely but immediately turn the conversation to his frustration with the lack of political progress. He complained about various Israeli actions in the name of security and lamented the lack of impartiality of the Americans. "You know when the Americans say 'be reasonable,' what they really mean is, accept the Israeli position," he remarked with a slight chuckle. He put his finger on freedom of movement without harassment and the ability to import and export freely as the key issues that were impeding Palestinian development. I suspect he saw development aid as more of a game by Israel and the United States to delay having to act on the real issues, which were political.

It was difficult for me to see how the projects we were pushing were the answer. Palestinians are smart and industrious people, and I had no doubt they would flourish once there was a clear political settlement. Building grandiose projects was not the answer. It was also disconcerting to know that any investment the bank makes may well be destroyed the next day in Israeli attacks. The Americans were pushing for a "warm peace" between the Israelis and the Palestinians by promoting various joint projects that would involve both parties as partners. One such proposal was to build large industrial estates on the Israeli border, which would attract Israeli investors and managers and workers from Gaza. They would come in from their respective side during the day and go back at night. This, in their view, would avoid the necessity of crossing the border and meet the Israeli concerns about security. It was an absolutely crazy proposal with no precedent for such enclaves being successful. But it was difficult to convince the Americans. I wanted our team to focus instead on some of the smaller and easier investments that could be done in the very tough political environment.

This did not endear me to the U.S. State Department. Moreover, they were not used to in the Wolfensohn era to have a mere World Bank director deal with them as an equal. To them, my job was to carry out their directions, never mind that none of them had a clue about development.

I had an American who was my resident country manager in WBG. He was an opportunist who was all too ready to do anything the Americans wanted. He enjoyed the limelight as the focus of many Western governments had been on the bank as the lead institution for development. He resented my intervention and used the opportunity of my rift with the Americans to push for a more prominent role for himself. He got the assistant secretary in the State Department to call Wolfensohn to complain that I was not giving sufficient authority to my resident representative in the field, who knew the situation best.

The call was received by Rachel Lomax, the director of Wolfensohn's office (he had expanded his office from a mere five people before he came to over fifty people). Rachel had been a very senior and highly regarded British civil servant before she joined the bank. Wolfensohn had picked her with big fanfare to mange his office and given her the rank of a vice president. As someone who knew how an organization should function, she had rebuffed the Americans by telling them that they should talk directly to my boss and not come to the president. But as mentioned earlier, the State Department officials had a direct line to Wolfensohn and ultimately got through to him over Rachel's head. I knew that Wolfensohn would want to do what the Americans wanted and could not in good conscience accept this. I asked my boss to take the responsibility for WBG from my department and give it to the country manager reporting directly to him, something he had been clamoring for. I was sorry to lose the Palestinian file but in the end was happy to not have the professionally unsatisfying task of working on a short American leash.

I have continued to follow developments in WBG over the years and have not been surprised that it has not only not progressed very much but has largely regressed since the Oslo accords. The political situation between Israelis and the Palestinians seems even more distant. I was never a believer in the totally contrived concept of warm peace and am not surprised that it has not only not panned out but probably has created even a greater hostility between the Palestinians and the Israelis.

Yemen was the poorest country in my department, and I decided early on that it deserved greater attention. In 1995, it was not on anybody's map. It had not yet been linked to terror. Osama bin Laden was an obscure figure, with only tenuous links to the country. Outsiders only knew Yemen as a peculiar country with rather fascinating tribal traditions. The bank had had an active lending program in the previous People's Democratic Republic of Yemen (South Yemen) and Arab Republic of Yemen (North Yemen), but the bank projects had suffered badly in the early 1990s, first from the consequences of unifying two diametrically opposed economic systems and later from the ensuing civil war. When I arrived in 1995, there was a lot of pessimism about Yemen in the bank. The combined economy was highly distorted. It looked as if it had joined the poor economic policies of the communist People's Democratic Republic of Yemen with the poor governance of the Arab Republic of Yemen. Most development projects supported by the bank and other donors had come to a standstill. The new bank lending had naturally come to a halt.

My staff responsible for the country had little faith in the government of Yemen—in its capacity and in its commitment to development. They told me that there was no will to carry out any reforms since the key policy makers benefited from the distortions in the economy and had shown no willingness to change. The bank had recently completed a study of the economy that had recommended certain reforms, most notable being the need to liberalize the exchange rate and remove trade distortions.

I decided to use the study as the basis of discussions during my first visit. I was received courteously by most of the key policy makers from the president on down. Contrary to what I had been told, they were all anxious to carry out the reforms. Perhaps the timing was right since the worst aftereffects of the civil war were now behind. What concerned them, however, was whether the bank would be ready to support them with funding that would be needed to back up the reforms. They had never been told by anyone what they could expect from the bank. On the portfolio, the fixed exchange rate pegged at an artificially low level (12 rials/dollar vs. 150 rials/dollar in the black market) had destroyed the contracting industry. No one could afford to bid under such conditions. The Yemenis also had numerous complaints about the bank staff not clearing things in a timely manner—this had been a growing problem the bank wide in the last few years partly as a result of the many diffused tasks its staff were chasing—and the little time the bank staff spent in Yemen, solving issues jointly with them.

I decided to use the technique I had learned from my East Asia days and employed with every client. I told them that there would virtually be no limit to our assistance if they were to do the right things, but that they must take the lead and back the reforms forcefully. As a poor country, Yemen was eligible to receive IDA funds that are rationed among various recipients. I knew that for a small country, I could easily increase the allocation if they performed well by simply taking away a small amount of funds from the bigger recipients. I seem to recall that I may have mentioned $200 or $300 million per annum as a possibility, as compared with less than $20 million they had received recently. However, I repeated to them that the ball was in their court, repeating my favorite phrase with the clients, "You will not find the bank lacking if you show determination." I was going off on a limb since I did not yet know if my staff in the Middle East department would be up to this challenge.

On the existing projects, I decided to recruit a number of national staff whose job it was to help solve implementation bottlenecks in the field and not wait for instructions from Washington. My experience had been that even in the countries with the so-called weak institutions and weak capacity, one could find capable and motivated people who would perform well under the right working conditions. I recall finding some excellent Yemenis to work for us at something like $1,000 per month compared with several hundred thousands we would be spending on sending an expatriate.

I tried to explore the allegations of corruption at the highest levels that I had been told about. Such allegations were common in almost every country that I have worked in. Often these were topics of conversation in gatherings of foreigners, particularly in countries where the locals do not mix much with foreigners. I had learned to keep these in perspective. As elsewhere, I found that there was no hard basis for these allegations. They invariably represented hearsay and secondhand rumors that were then circulated among foreigners as "facts." This is not to say that the allegations were wrong. There was surely corruption going on. But I could not find any basis for the serious charges of "insider manipulation" by the finance minister and the central bank governor that my staff had been talking about. The situation to me looked no different than many other poor countries I knew. I told my staff to stop gossiping about the issue but be very vigilant in monitoring our projects and bring to my attention situations that looked serious. I had one such instance brought to me in five years—for an airport runway contract in Aden—and we promptly decided to cancel it. I also told the Yemenis about our approach and put them on notice that we could not tolerate any malfeasance in our projects. They agreed with me.

In the last few years, the bank presidents have made fighting corruption as a centerpiece of the bank. This is a good gesture to win public applause, but in my judgment, it has seriously detracted from the bank's development mission. There is no evidence that corruption is any less than before in any of the poor countries because of the donors' anticorruption initiatives, or that any of these have worked better than the classical approach of vigilance in contracting.

We had a very productive relationship with Yemen in my five years in the Middle East. We made progress in several areas, although much more still needs to be done. The Yemenis were very grateful to us for all we did. In 2000, a neighboring country, Djibouti, asked to be moved from the Africa region to my department because they had been watching the bank's work in Yemen and wanted the same kind of relationship that they felt they were not getting from the Africa managers.

Toward the end of 2000, the bank had begun to enforce more seriously the governance indicators in determining the IDA allocation for a country. Yemen was tagged as a "poor governance" country, and there was pressure to reduce its IDA allocation. I did not see any sense in this since Yemen had actually made great progress in five years and managed to maintain Yemen's allocation. I did not believe in such a mechanical application of governance as a metric for allocation. I subscribe to the concept of "good enough" governance that Yemen certainly had, for otherwise it would not be poor. The formula enforcers won the day after I left in 2001, and Yemen's allocation was reduced significantly, only to be upped again later because of Yemen being a country of interest in the war on terrorism.

It makes me sad to read reports of civil war having erupted once again in the country, again with external interference. It is once again on the list of fragile states with no realistic solutions in sight. It demonstrates the limits of aid donors to influence matters. Rebuilding failed states, as I discuss n a later chapter, is far from a science that many donors have come to believe.

My biggest challenge was presented by the three largest economies in the region: Egypt, Syria, and Iran. Due to their size and political importance, developments in these countries, economic and political, have a major significance for what happens to the region as a whole. But economic progress in all three was stalled for different reasons. I tried tackling all three, but with varying degree of success. We did engage all three but did not succeed in achieving a lasting impact. Effective leadership was the missing ingredient in all three cases.

Egypt is the acknowledged leader in the Arab world. It is the largest country (in terms of population) and the largest developing economy in the region (excluding the GCC countries). Its importance also derives from its history and politics. It has been a close ally of the United States since it made peace with Israel in 1979, ties that give it considerable clout in the region and with the donors. So a natural thing for me to do when taking over as director was to visit Egypt. This plan, however, turned out to be not so simple and revealed some important issues between Egypt and the bank. The first response from Egypt to my expressed desire for a visit resulted in the usual polite response that I was most welcome to visit but that the "timing was not convenient for the government."

I did not think much of that response and went on to visit other countries first. But when, in the next four months, we still had not found a mutually convenient time, I became concerned. Fortunately, Khalid Ikram, an old Egypt hand who was highly regarded by the Egyptians and who later became country director for Egypt when the bank reorganized the Middle East department, had taken over at about the same time as the bank's resident representative in Cairo. In due course, Ikram was to discover that the Egyptians' reluctance to receive me was based on the apprehension that, as had apparently been done by some others before me, yet another bank manager would lecture them yet again about their reform program. Thanks to Ikram's personal relations at the highest levels of the government, I conveyed to the Egyptian officials my message: I wanted to come simply to see what was working and what was not, and I had no agenda to pursue. I also assured them that I did not plan any press statements that would embarrass them. I never believed in outsiders pushing reforms on a reluctant country.

The visit was thus arranged for late summer of 1995. I was received most warmly. The Egyptians are gracious hosts. They have a long history and an ancient culture (of course, an understatement!). The government officials had taken me at my word and used the visit as an opportunity to educate me from their perspective on their development priorities and relations with the bank. On my part, I was determined to be true to my word and be a listener.

The Egyptians had two gripes. First, they detested the bank's pushing them on economic reforms, believing that what they had done was quite adequate. Second, they expressed unease with the bank's pushing lending on them when they had ready access to significant bilateral grants. They acknowledged the bank's intellectual contributions and hoped that we could find ways to help them technically.

The complaint about the bank being too pushy on economic reforms is an interesting story that offers some pertinent lessons. By virtue of having signed the peace treaty with Israel and its subsequent pro-United States stance during the first Gulf War, Egypt had won very significant support from the United States and other group of seven (G-7) industrialized countries. That support included a virtual write-off of its large debt to the G-7. However, as a condition of this debt write-off, the G-7 had imposed the customary requirement: having an agreed IMF program in place, with successive tranches of debt relief being linked to continued compliance. The main elements of the program were the customary IMF fiscal and monetary targets. The principal conditionality on structural reforms was defined targets for privatization of SOEs. Unlike programs in most other countries, the IMF program was not accompanied by the bank's structural adjustment program because the Egyptians presumably did not need more money. Rather, the bank had agreed to be the monitor for the privatization program.

The program included nothing (or not much, as I recall) on regulatory reforms or exchange rate policies—the former, I suppose, because of the difficulty of defining a meaningful program absent a willing client in an inherently difficult area, and the latter because IMF was perhaps unable to carry the day with the Egyptians and had obfuscated the issue through the usual phrases such as "improving competitiveness through productivity improvements."

My briefings had advised me that the Egyptians were not committed to economic policy reforms, and my discussions in Cairo certainly confirmed that view. It was clear that they saw the IMF agreement purely as a way to get their debt write-off through and as nothing more. IMF was in an untenable position. Even though in theory it had the ability to obstruct or delay the debt write-off, in practice IMF understood that some members of the G-7 were not beyond pressuring it to take an understanding view of Egypt. But IMF had to go through at least the semblance of some monitoring to satisfy its board of directors. It was truly caught between a rock and a hard place.

The monitoring role that the bank had taken on puzzled me. Our staff members had been clear that the Egyptians were unlikely to implement agreements on privatization, for which the United States had provided an enormous amount of technical assistance that had resulted in nothing more than massive studies by highly paid foreign consultants that lined the shelves of the privatization ministry. Moreover, the bank had virtually no leverage (although I have little faith in the bank leverage as a way to influence government behavior), given that Egypt did not want or need the bank lending. Under those circumstances, the only value added by the bank was the nuisance value of making pronouncements from time to time about the "slow pace of privatization" and of throwing sand in the well-oiled Egyptian machine that was nicely and surely headed toward debt write-off.

I was also very skeptical of the argument that is commonly made in the bank that somehow by staying involved howsoever low the government commitment, we could add value to a country's thinking. The Egyptian officials individually were as qualified and competent as any of us. They surely did not need the bank staff to teach them about the concept of economic reforms. What was clearly inhibiting a serious reform effort was political considerations—some well founded and perhaps others simply a fear of the unknown. We had little to offer the Egyptians on this score. My experience in numerous countries had taught me that our advice is good when the client knows what it wants and uses the excellent bank staff for cross-country experiences that can refine the approach and ensure smooth implementation. Absent the political will, we could never turn a country into a reformer by sheer force of our technical advice.

Soon after my return, I convinced my bosses that we were spinning our wheels in Egypt on economic policy reforms. We decided (to the chagrin of IMF) to withdraw from monitoring privatization. It was not that I did not believe in privatization. Quite to the contrary, I was, and continue to be, a strong proponent. But I also had a strong belief that unless the policy makers at the highest levels believed in the private sector, any external pressure to force the issue was virtually assured of failure. In Egypt, as it turned out, IMF eventually declared the country in compliance. The debt write-off was completed, and the privatization program continued to flounder. On the positive side, I earned some good and lasting personal friendships with the Egyptians.

The Egyptian economy was (and to some extent continues to be today, although to a lesser extent with the reforms that it finally did undertake a few years back) mired in serious structural problems—

118

regulatory impediments, a state-owned financial sector with administered interest rates, an overvalued exchange rate, and a poor quality of civil service. What it needed was not just a push on privatization (which had become the focus of dialogue on policy reforms between the bank and Egypt), but also a comprehensive package of reforms that over time could transform the economy into a more efficient private sector and export-led economy that created sufficient jobs to absorb the still-growing, young labor force. However, such a reform could succeed only if the Egyptians themselves came to the conclusion—as the Indians did in the early 1990s—that continued slow growth is untenable. With the good fortune of having abundant grant flows from bilateral donors, Egypt was in a good position to defer reforms for political reasons. It was surprising that donors did not see the contradiction of pushing reforms with one hand while with the other hand pouring in large sums of aid that allowed the Egyptians to delay reforms. The Egyptian case is an illustration of how aid can sometimes not only not do good, but also causes harm.

The second complaint about the bank's pushing lending had an equally bizarre story. Egypt's per capita income meant that it was still eligible for International Development Association (IDA) funds. However, some in the bank questioned this status, given that Egypt was receiving large amounts in grants from bilateral donors and because of its creditworthiness for borrowing IBRD funds. Egypt, on its part, had no interest in IBRD borrowing because of its access to large amounts of soft bilateral funds. It found IBRD loans too expensive, anyway. So it preferred to borrow only IDA funds (although many in Egypt found even the IDA terms too onerous). The compromise reached permitted the bank to continue to give Egypt some IDA funds (about US$150 million per year), provided that there was a 50:50 blend between IDA and World Bank funds in Egypt's overall program. Egypt had accepted this compromise, but in practice it found reasons either not to go forward with the World Bank projects at all or, for blend projects, to cancel the bank-loan portion during project implementation. In some cases, the bank staff members had worked hard to develop a project for World Bank lending only to be told by the Egyptian officials, at a very late stage, that the Egyptians had changed their minds about the project or that a bilateral donor had decided to fund the project as a grant. That situation caused a lot of consternation in the bank and inevitably caused friction with the Egyptian authorities.

I could not find any merit in the bank's position. Forcing a more costly World Bank loan on Egypt just so we could justify IDA lending to the bank's board of executive directors made no sense. Egypt's access to other, more favorable external sources made borrowing from the bank unnecessary. I was again able to convince my bosses that we should go with a small IDA-only program, focusing on a few sectors where we had positive experience (such as agriculture) and on the social sectors (The Egyptian Social Fund, which we funded, has become one of the most successful social funds in the world). Again, the Egyptians were grateful for the decision. But it did not satisfy the internal needs of the bank—bank staff members were unhappy with having less work, and the bank management was unhappy about the modest program for a country as large and important as Egypt. It illustrated how pressure to show a large lending volume can sometimes become a perverse motive in the bank (and, I am sure, among other donors as well).

After Egypt, Syria is the next biggest developing economy (excluding GCC countries) in the Middle East. Its economy is highly distorted, resembling in many respects the socialist economies. It had not been in any crisis, having kept a lid on public expenditures and borrowing. But like most other countries in the region, Syria suffered from a crisis of slow growth and inadequate job creation. The population had been restless, but it had been kept under control in the tight grip of the Ba'ath Party.

The bank could have helped Syria with both advice on reforms and with investments in some of the key sectors. However, we were constrained from helping Syria because of some US$550 million in arrears to the bank it had accumulated since 1988. It had the ability but not the will to clear the arrears. As a part of our attempt to bring Syria around, we made a deal on arrears whereby the bank management agreed (and the board of executive directors approved) the proposal to let Syria clear its principal arrears first and clear the interest arrears over three years. This plan kept the Syrian arrears from growing (since, contrary to the normal financial practice, the bank did not charge interest on interest arrears). The deal was a bit unconventional and was opposed vehemently by the bank's finance staff since it implied a theoretical loss of about $50 million to the bank. But Jim Wolfensohn personally endorsed the plan because he saw the benefit of a normal relationship between the bank and Syria as greater than the theoretical chance of recovering the small additional amount of interest on interest. This was one instance of Wolfensohn exercising real leadership and not allowing the normal bureaucratic practice of important decisions being held up for a prolonged period.

Despite having resolved this obstacle, the Syrians continued to be reluctant to seek the bank assistance. We did manage to provide some technical assistance and developed some project ideas. But none of these found any traction during my tenure. I suspect a decision to get assistance from the World Bank would have required a decision by President Hafez Assad himself who, as with most things external, probably was suspicious of our real intentions and whether the World Bank was an agent of the United States if not Israel. Wolfensohn, with his keen interest in the Middle East peace, himself visited Syria to try to engage Assad. He was received most cordially and spent several hours with President Assad, but nothing came out of this overture. Syria has continued to be a highly distorted economy, despite a few steps it has taken from time to time to open up.

The challenge for Iran was still different. Iran is one of the founding members of the World Bank. It was in good standing in terms of having always serviced its debts to the bank. It had also made good progress—much better than any other country in the region—on the social indicators, including some of the key gender indicators. However, because of the strong opposition from the United States, variously joined by some of the Europeans, the bank had not funded any projects for many years. The only projects that were funded were after the 1990 earthquake on humanitarian grounds. Iran, as an oil exporter and a middle-income country, did not exactly need World Bank loans. Rather, the government was more interested in the principle. It asserted its right to borrow from the bank, being a member in good standing. The bank management used to skirt the issue when raised by the Iranians, citing its poor economic management as the reason for a lack of bank support. This was not entirely untrue, since the Iranians had mismanaged the economy since the revolution. So it provided a useful shield to having to acknowledge the political pressures and continue to maintain the bank's apolitical mandate.

I and most of my colleagues felt that the Iranians were justified in their unhappiness. They had a much better record of implementing projects than most other countries in the region. They had also done very well in dealing with poverty through effective interventions in health and education. In this regard, they should have met with the donors' approval. Also the main point of contention with the United States at that time was not the nuclear issue. Rather it was the U.S. complaint about embassy hostages in 1979. Howsoever unpleasant and irritating that episode, many people did not understand why the United States insisted on continuing to isolate Iran. All of the developing countries on our board and several developed countries favored engagement, particularly after Khatami's election. But we were stymied by insistent U.S. opposition. Few industrialized countries were willing to go against the United States, irrespective of their own views. I guess they did not consider it worthwhile to support Iran at the expense of their relations with the United States. So when people assume that the

United States has a veto power in the bank, they are partly right. It is the ability of the United States to arm-twist other countries that allows it at times to mobilize majority opposition.

During the 1997 annual meeting in Hong Kong, the Iranians asked for and were granted a meeting with Jim Wolfensohn. The Iranians once again complained about the bank letting political pressure from the United States determine its policy that they pointed out, correctly, was a violation of its charter. Wolfensohn, who was meeting the Iranians for the first time, decided to respond candidly. He told the Iranians that indeed there were pressures, but that these were not from the United States alone. He told them that a number of other industrialized countries had also been opposed, and it was against the long-standing World Bank tradition to have a polarized vote, even if the majority were in favor. The Iranians genuinely seemed to appreciate his candor and went on to point out that the European attitudes had changed since President Khatami assumed office and had been telling them that they would be supportive of a resumption of the bank lending. It was obvious that the Europeans were doing some double-talk. Wolfensohn told the Iranian delegation that they needed to get clarity on this from the Europeans and suggest to them that they needed to tell us the same thing they seemed to be telling the Iranians. He went on to say that he would be willing to resume lending if there were "significant" support among shareholders, leaving the implication that United States opposition alone will not stop us from proceeding.

I thought Wolfensohn was brilliant. The Iranians found his candor refreshing and told me so. They were also impressed with his commitment of going against U.S. opposition if most others were supportive. I was personally surprised by his statement, knowing his strong connections with the various Jewish groups who adamantly opposed Iran, and his subservience to the U.S. State Department. Perhaps he himself had underestimated the opposition, as the events that followed would show.

Subsequent to the meeting, the Iranians did start a major political offensive with Europe and Japan. Khatami's conciliatory overtures toward the west ("the dialogue of civilizations") had already softened much of the political opposition in Europe. It also helped that some countries—Germany, Italy, and Japan—had significant commercial interests. It is not uncommon in the foreign aid business for principles to be subservient to commercial interests. In my meetings with the ambassadors in Tehran, I also started getting positive signals, which I reported back to Washington. Based on my reports, Wolfensohn gave the go-ahead to start preparing a few projects. For tactical reasons, we decided to have the initial projects in some of the "good" areas, such as health and environment. I was always amazed at how the opposition was suddenly less in controversial cases when one talked about such sectors, as if the concept of fungibility of money was unknown. This was a tactic we had often used successfully in difficult situations such as lending to China post-Tiananmen and to India post-nuclear tests.

The Iranians on their part worked diligently to prepare the projects. The civil servants are generally of a high caliber and had little difficulty in doing the technical work. With our help, they also made sure that the projects were prepared well and met all our requirements. We did not want to give anyone an excuse to oppose them on technical grounds.

Soon word was out about the bank preparing projects for financing. The bank rules required that it disclose summaries of projects under preparation. Most of these summaries go unnoticed. But Iran was different with lots of people watching it. We began to get a barrage of letters in opposition. As is often the case, many were standard letters orchestrated by organized groups, but some letters were very specific. Most would have some sorts of threat about getting the U.S. Congress to withhold funds. The most vicious ones were from U.S. Congress members.

The supporters of Israel also mobilized in opposing any World Bank support to Iran. Israel has always been suspicious of Iran, although this was even before Ahmadinejad appearing on the scene with his vitriol about Israel and the Holocaust and the logjam on the nuclear issue. I was called to attend a meeting in Wolfensohn's office with the representatives of AIPAC, the premier pro-Israel lobby in the United States. The meeting was very cordial but the AIPAC representatives were quite firm in their opposition.

Wolfensohn at first talked like he agreed with them. Then, all of a sudden, as if he was hit by a realization that there were others from the bank present who knew that every step had been taken with his approval, he looked at the group and said, carefully choosing his words, "You are all my friends, and I respect your views. But you have to realize that not only as the president of an international organization but as a Jew, I have to be careful. I need to be mindful of the broader board." It was a correct answer, but I was sure that the answer was as much for the consumption of us from his staff as for AIPAC. Wolfensohn was badly conflicted.

We continued to prepare the projects and finally sent them for approval to our board in April 2000. Now the opposition intensified, this time officially led by the United States. Secretary Albright sent letters to the foreign ministers of all G-7 members asking, or rather telling, them to oppose the loans. She also made several phone calls to her counterparts. The Iranians on their part made our life difficult by convicting some Iranian Jews of espionage on behalf of Israel. Their sentences were to be handed down any day.

Wolfensohn convened a meeting of his senior managers to discuss the matter. He asked each of us our individual opinions. "My presidency is at stake. If they hang the Jews, I will have to resign." All of us directly involved with Iran told him that he had the responsibility to uphold the bank's mandate and that we should proceed with presenting the projects to the board. He asked that I call the finance minister of Iran and ask him that they should act "responsibly" in handling the sentencing in the espionage case. I told him that this would be very counterproductive and in any event it would be highly presumptuous on our part to be interfering in the Iranian judicial system howsoever worthy the cause. He listened and glared at me.

What we did not know is that some of his confidants had been telling him that the board support for Iran had evaporated. Wolfensohn decided to convene an informal board meeting first to discuss the matter. This is a technique often used by the bank presidents when faced with a tough situation to avoid the embarrassment or discomfort of open discord in the board. Recall a similar technique that we had used during the controversy on Thailand's Pak Mun dam project.

The meeting was an eye-opener for Wolfensohn. Every one of the twenty-four executive directors spoke. The developing country representatives were particularly vocal in voicing their support for the bank having a normal relationship with Iran. Some of them blasted the bank management for being influenced by political pressures. Many industrialized country representatives spoke of the desirability of engaging Iran. Only the United States and Canada spoke in opposition. The U.S. representative couched his opposition on economic grounds: he did not think that Iran had managed its economy well and thus should not be supported. But everyone knew that this was just an excuse to cover the real reason for US opposition, which all knew was political. The meeting lasted all morning well into the lunch break. The board views could not have been clearer. As a concession to the United States, the board agreed that the two projects should be accompanied by a country strategy, a document that lays out the bank's three to five-year plans for the country. It normally takes several months' work to prepare such a strategy. We had one week.

As we walked back to Wolfensohn's office, he was clearly unhappy. He had expected to find consensus against moving forward that he could then cite to the Iranians. What he found instead was even stronger support. Even the British, who normally tow American line on most issues, were strongly supportive.

I had a very capable economist from Tunisia, Habib Fetini, leading our work in Iran. Habib was not only an excellent economist but he also enjoyed excellent relations with the Iranians. He worked with me day and night to produce a strategy document as required by the board. Wolfensohn reviewed the document personally every step of the way, a highly unusual step for the president, before it was finalized. He thought we were too positive in describing Iran's social progress and tried to get us to downplay them. It was clear that he was torn between his obligation as the president of the bank, and having to please the United States to secure a second term or another suitable job in the U.S. administration (rumor had it that he wanted to be the secretary of state). He wished he did not have to face this situation, and I am sure he blamed some of us for having forced him into it.

I left the bank a year later, but our work had opened up once again a full-fledged World Bank relationship with Iran. The two projects were followed by several other loans in the following five years. However, lending to Iran was stopped again in 2005 by Wolfensohn's successor, Paul Wolfowitz, who was a well-known neocon, and even more beholden to the U.S. administration. The Iranians made it easier for him to do so when they elected a highly controversial man as their president to succeed Khatami. Iran once again is a pariah country internationally. It has also now lost the support among the Europeans that Khatami had worked hard to gain. Indeed, I myself would not be arguing for Iran today, were I to be in my old job. However, I am convinced that opening up Iran was the right thing to do during the Khatami era. Indeed, I wonder whether Ahmadinejad would have come to power had the United States been more willing to support Khatami, at least by not opposing so vehemently even small costless overtures like Iran's engagement with the bank. Recall the main point of contention between the United States and Iran at the time was the U.S. complaint about the embassy hostages and the Iranian complaint about CIA interference in installing the Shah in 1953, and not nuclear weapons.

By the time I left my position in 2001, we had reestablished a coherent dialogue with the three most important economies. There was a more stable and predictable program in Egypt. Relations with Iran had been resumed. And we had removed the obstacle to resuming work in Syria. However, none of the three economies can be said to have turned around. All three remained in need of major structural reforms. None had any prospect of becoming a dynamic economy capable of not only achieving a significant improvement in the lives of its people, much less to become a catalyst for broader growth in the region. This also applied more generally to the region as a whole. We had good active engagement with most of the countries and financed projects that in a narrow sense were successful. But looking at the forest, the Middle East remained mired in the slow growth trap and, in that sense, I cannot say that we had succeeded. This is an important point to keep in mind before we get into the question later in the book of whether aid works.

One aside before concluding the discussion of my Middle East days. Jordan was the only country in the region that was committed to reforms. It has a very capable economic team led by Dr. Rima Khalaf Hunaidi. Rima was a brilliant economist and a dedicated public servant. She spearheaded Jordan's reform agenda successfully in a difficult environment. Jordan is basically a conservative society and not naturally inclined toward greater openness. The fact that a woman took the lead is all the more remarkable. Of course, Rima enjoyed strong support from King Hussein that helped insulate her from the charge routinely leveled against her by some of the traditionalists in the assembly of being an agent of the World Bank. We supported Jordan's reform through a series of adjustment loans where for the first time we broke new ground by linking our support to reforms Jordan had already done on its own rather than on ex-ante conditionality. King Abdullah has continued the reforms, and even tried to accelerate them.

The results of the reforms, however, have been mixed with unemployment particularly among the youth continuing to be an intractable problem. Unfortunately, Jordan cannot insulate itself entirely from the region and thus continues to be hampered by the overall negative regional environment. Jordan is a success story of the bank support, but only to a limited extent since it has not really succeeded in becoming a truly dynamic economy.

In early 2001, I began to contemplate my next assignment. I had thoroughly enjoyed my six years working in the region. Although it was nowhere near as rewarding as working in Asia, I felt that I had been able to turn a moribund region into a more interesting place to work. But I also left reinforced in my view that the bank or any other donor cannot push reforms until the country's leadership itself is prepared to take the lead.

On a personal level, I enjoyed the people many of whom have been friends ever since. But I was increasingly disillusioned with Wolfensohn's management style and the direction he had taken the bank. I resigned in May 2001 and joined the faculty of George Washington University to pursue teaching, research, and consultancy

14. Postscript: Rebuilding Failed States

It was the fall of 2003. I had happily "retired" from the World Bank and started my new career as a part-time professor of international development at the George Washington and Duke universities, and doing occasional consulting. I received a call from a colleague at the World Bank telling me that Dr. Ashraf Ghani, at the time Afghanistan's minister of finance would be visiting Washington the following week and had asked to meet me. He did not know why, but thought it may be a follow-up to the discussions Ghani recently had with Jim Wolfensohn, the president of the bank.

I met Ghani at the faculty club of George Washington University. He was accompanied by Claire Lockhart, his loyal and able chief of staff, who had been seconded to him by the British Government. Ghani was a busy man and got to the point of the meeting quickly after exchanging a few pleasantries. He asked me to help him in the implementation of massive amount of foreign aid that had been promised to Afghanistan. He went on to explain that only a fraction of the aid that had been committed by numerous donors had actually been translated into anything concrete on the ground. There was a big mismatch between good intentions and the reality on the ground. Ghani was worried that the Afghani people were beginning to lose patience, and there is a danger that they will become totally disillusioned if they do not see tangible improvement in their lives. He said that having observed me in action in the Middle East, he was convinced that I was the right person to help him. He pleaded, "I can really use your help."

Ashraf Ghani had been a colleague at the bank. He was a respected social scientist working in the social development unit. We had never worked together directly, but had a few interactions in the context of occasional support he would provide to my teams working on projects in the Middle East. He had always impressed me as one of the few social scientists in his unit who could think practically. I knew that he had left the bank a few months before me to join the faculty of Johns Hopkins University, from where he had been drafted to become the finance minister when the Karzai government was installed after the Bonn accords in 2002. I had occasionally read his op-ed pieces and watched him appear on television talking about Afghanistan, but other than that had not been in contact with him. So I cannot say that I knew him well. It seemed that he knew me much better.

I was honored by Ghani's heartfelt request and the confidence he seemed to place in me. I had somewhat anticipated his request based on whatever little I had heard from the bank colleague who set up the meeting. But I had not expected him to ask for it in such strong and personal terms. I was also impressed with what he was trying to do for his country at great personal sacrifice. The prospect of once again taking on a difficult challenge also intrigued me. After some further discussion, we agreed that I would assemble and lead a team of two to three senior specialists with specific sectoral expertise to work with the Afghan ministries to help them debottleneck implementation of the stalled aid projects and to prepare a pipeline of future investments that could be funded by future donor commitments. I tapped two other World Bank retirees, a specialist in energy and another in roads, water, and urban development for this purpose.

Since 2002, when the first donor meeting for Afghanistan was convened in Bonn after the overthrow of the Taliban, the donors had pledged over $5 billion for reconstruction over three years. The United States alone had committed over a billion dollars per year. There were also promises made to deliver the aid quickly so the Afghan people could see an immediate improvement in their lives. This had raised great expectations among the Afghani people about finally seeing a better life after years of misery under the Taliban rule.

However, by the time of my first visit to Kabul in December 2003, there was already discontent emerging among the people. None of the infrastructure services were functional. There were many signs everywhere of the destruction and deprivation after years of civil war. Most city streets were nothing more than dirt paths and the few paved roads that did exist were full of potholes. The public water supply was nonfunctional. Most of the city had no electric supply and the parts that did had intermittent supply for only a few hours a day. This made for considerable suffering during the bitter Kabul winter that had already set in. The poverty and desperation was all too evident. Numerous beggars on the streets with amputated limbs were a constant reminder of the horrors of war.

The situation was similar in other cities and even worse in the countryside. An average Afghani had seen little of the improvement that had been promised by the donors with great fanfare. The only Afghanis who seemed to derive any benefit were those who could siphon off the

128

aid funds or the lucky few who found employment working for one of the donor agencies, consultants, or any number of NGOs that had cropped up to deliver donor programs at princely salaries by Afghani standards. There was a growing resentment against the very visible presence of foreign aid workers in the city driving around in their white land rovers equipped with large radio communication antennas.

As we assessed the situation, it was clear that the methods of delivering aid utilized by most of the donors were inappropriate and did not offer the possibility of delivering results. There was a need for a complete rethinking of the approach.

The most urgent need in Afghanistan was to have a functioning government that could inspire the trust and confidence of the population. It was important for people to see their government effectively providing them personal security and delivering essential services. This meant developing the capacity of most government institutions, particularly the civil service that had been decimated by years of war and turmoil. But capacity building is a slow process that requires a great deal of patience and perseverance. Instead, the donors were not only not doing much capacity building but were draining away whatever limited capacity that did exist by diverting the few capable civil servants toward donor projects. The large and visible donor presence everywhere was also delegitimizing the government since the Afghanis viewed donors instead of their leaders running the show.

The preoccupation of donors and much of the Karzai government on the volume of aid rather than its quality was at the root of the problem. Since the volume of aid promised was far in excess of what the fledgling government could absorb, most donors engaged "implementation agents" of various types—UN agencies, contractors, NGOs, etc.—to implement their projects. These implementation agents often themselves did not have the necessary capacity, so they turned around and hired away from the government itself the few qualified people it did have attracted by very high salaries. A large number of civil servants were left to rot in the ministries as mere bystanders to things they should have been doing. In addition, the implementation agents had to hire large numbers of foreigners to run the show in part to manage the Afghanis who were not familiar with the donor contraptions, and also to satisfy the donors' anticorruption requirements. This further increased the foreign donor footprint, adding to the resentment referred to earlier, and to very high overheads. All donors utilized such mechanisms to a varying degree, but the case of the USAID was a particularly egregious. It employed expensive American contractors—or "Beltway Bandits" as they are known in Washington DC—to act as intermediaries for their assistance. These intermediaries serve the purpose of insulating USAID bureaucrats against the charge of having "corrupt Afghani officials" handling aid funds. So U.S. aid was being delivered through multiple layers of contractors outside the control of the government. In a study we did for the health minister, we found that overheads accounted for 70 percent of the funds spent by U.S. aid. As a government minister once remarked to me, "They are not here to help us. Rather, they are here to fund themselves."

What made the situation even worse was that despite the rhetoric about donor coordination, every donor was pursuing its own agenda further taxing the limited capacity of the government. Some of it was because of domestic constituencies back home such as pushing for laws to modernize overnight a tribal society. At one point, there were some 120 laws drafted by individual donors and their advisors that were pending before the Afghan Parliament. No matter how worthwhile the individual proposals, it was difficult to see how the members of parliament could ever even read the drafts much less digest and debate them. Some initiatives were pet donor projects. Still others were proposals pushed by the dozens of Beltway Bandits to get more business. Let me illustrate with two incidents that I personally witnessed.

My energy specialist colleague and I were in the ministry of energy, discussing ways to expedite procurement of a very critical transmission line that was the bottleneck for improving the electricity situation in Kabul. The ministry did not know even the basics of international procurement, and we were going step by step to help them. In the middle of the meeting, we received a message that the minister would like us to join him in a meeting with the Americans who had been advising the ministry on its institutional strengthening. There were two gentlemen representing the U.S. government who were actually private contractors funded by USAID. They were making a presentation to the minister on how the ministry of electricity should build a regulatory framework for the electricity sector so as to be able to attract private investment. I was appalled. Here was an entity that is still learning the basics such as procurement and contracting, did not know the extent of its system and the shape it was in, how many customers it had, and did not even have rudimentary accounting methods to be able to keep proper books. And the visiting experts were recommending work that even the more advanced developing countries were struggling to do. It was obvious that they were suggesting the work so as to increase their business and not because this is what the country needed. All they had to do is to get the ministry of electricity to say yes, and they would go back to USAID and sign another multi-million dollar contract for advisory services that were not needed. It would be one thing if all it meant was that the U.S. taxpayer's money would have been wasted, unacceptable as that should be. What was more disturbing was that it would have diverted scarce Afghan human resources to a useless exercise.

One time, Ashraf Ghani asked me to go and meet with the education minister, Mohammad Yunus Qanuni, who he (Ghani) believed could use some help in his ministry. Every donor had been wanting to help in the education sector but had somehow not been able to get Qanuni's cooperation. Ashraf tasked me to talk to Qanuni to see if I could somehow break whatever logjam existed between the donors and Qanuni.

I was slightly apprehensive about this assignment. I knew that Qanuni was a very important politician. From the Panjshir region of the country, Qanuni had been a prominent member of the Northern Alliance that overthrew the Taliban in 2002, and a close confidant of the late Ahmad Shah Masood. He was reputed to have been a warlord. He had previously been the interior minister in the first interim Karzai government and was appointed the education minister in the second government in 2003. I decided to wait for a couple of days before calling to set up an appointment. But the next day my cell phone[37] rang, and it was Qanuni's assistant calling to set up a time for me for that afternoon. I was relieved since it avoided my having to take the initiative.

I did not know what to expect. I had assumed that the donors must be complaining because as an ex-warlord, he was not serious about education, particularly of girls. I had been told by my World Bank colleagues that he did not speak English, so I expected difficult communication. I pictured meeting a bearded, turbaned person in traditional Afghan clothes. As I was ushered into his large office to see him, I saw a clean-cut, handsome man, dressed in a well-tailored, Western suit walk up to me and shake my hand warmly. We settled in two facing couches. An Afghani man sat nearby with his notebook. I knew he was the translator.

After a few small welcoming words in Dari that were translated to me, he looked at me and asked in fairly fluent English if I thought his English was good enough. It clearly was, and when I said so, he seemed delighted and dismissed the translator.

"My friend Ashraf Ghani told us in the last cabinet meeting about you and how you are so knowledgeable about development, and that you are available to help the sector ministers. I am very interested in your help in my ministry," he started the conversation.

I had met many leaders who, despite knowing English well, refused to speak in English with foreigners either as a matter of pride or because they did not think they could express themselves fluently when talking about a difficult subject. Qanuni's talking to me in English immediately told me that he was comfortable with me. Ashraf had obviously been very generous in his praise of me in the cabinet. But I suspect that my nationality was also helpful. India had supported the Northern Alliance in the overthrow of the Taliban and many Afghani leaders had lived or studied in India. I never thought of myself as ever representing India in the World Bank. One of the greatest joys of working in the World Bank had been that most of us in the bank almost never considered our nationality as anything of consequence. In my official travels to more than fifty countries, never once did I think of paying a visit to the Indian ambassador. But in this instance, I did not mind if my nationality happened to be a useful icebreaker with an important person.

I demurred in response to Qanuni's compliment and said something to the effect that I was by no means an expert, but would be happy to share whatever knowledge and expertise I did have.

"I am having a very difficult time getting help from the donors," Qanuni started the conversation, "and this is where I would like your help first." He said that he had been trying his best to have the donors support him but each time he ended up finding a huge gap between what he asked and what the donors offered.

He mentioned how much he had enjoyed his meeting with Elaine Wolfensohn (the wife of Jim Wolfensohn) in New York where they discussed the challenges in basic education and how she had encouraged him to seek donor help. He said that he had followed up on Elaine Wolfensohn's suggestion and tried to get help from donors, only to find a complete disconnect between his requests and what the donors offered. "I seem to speak a different language," he said, looking at me showing some puzzlement.

"But you speak perfect English," I said using friendly humor to put him at ease and to probe further his concern. I knew how anxious the donors were to be involved in education. After all, most of them were judged by their bosses by how much of their aid had gone for the social sectors. I asked Qanuni to give me some examples.

Qanuni went on to describe two recent instances. He said that as we all knew, Afghan summers can be extremely hot, and there were many schools all over the country that did not even have a roof under which children could sit. He had asked the donors to help him with a crash program to provide a simple roof over four pillars—not even walls. The donors had sent a team of experts who did not want to give him the roofed areas he had asked for, but recommended equipping the schools with electronic blackboards.

Citing another example, he explained that most of the teachers had become out of date during the prolonged civil war and the Taliban rule. At Elaine Wolfensohn's suggestion, he wanted the donors to finance a two-week long refresher training in Kabul or another suitable place for every teacher. The expert team sent by USAID had instead proposed that they use distance learning on radio. "Can you imagine that we do not even have electricity in most places, and the chances of replacing batteries that the experts recommended for the radios would be a close to an impossible task? Moreover, in Afghanistan we just do not have the tradition of such learning." The expression on his face was now showing a great sense of bewilderment.

We spent two hours together. I promised to take up the matter with the donors whom I was to meet as a group later in the week. Qanuni jumped at my suggestion that we should organize a one—or two-day retreat with everyone present to thrash out the issues openly. I even offered to act as a facilitator for the meeting, and Qanuni accepted my offer enthusiastically. "Let us meet in Panjshir. You will find it beautiful," Qanuni said as he shook my hand to say good-bye on my way out. In the event, Qanuni resigned his position shortly thereafter to run for president against Karzai, and the retreat I had proposed never materialized.

I was not surprised at what I had heard. I had seen this type of lack of communication in far too many poor countries. Donors give a lot of lip service to "country ownership" and "home-grown solutions" but their own incentive systems push them to pursue their own different agendas. I consider this to be one of the most serious shortcomings of project aid.

I have continued to follow Afghanistan, although from a distance since Ashraf Ghani left his post in 2006, and later to become its second elected president in 2009. The developments have not been encouraging. Despite billions of dollars in foreign aid, numerous surveys have shown that the average Afghani does not consider his life any better. Some of this is frustration about not seeing "quick results" that donors foolishly promise in post-conflict reconstruction. If foreign aid cannot achieve quick results in normal countries, what chance is there to do this in a war-torn country? The noble attempts to accelerate progress through armies of advisors and NGOs cannot accelerate progress, and their highly visible presence in the country only serves to delegitimize the government. Indeed, the civilian surge that President Obama had promised, but that fortunately never materialized, would have been yet another blunder. What Afghanistan needs is to learn by doing, and walking before running. It needs funds—even on a much smaller scale than what the donors currently provide—to be channeled to its national budget that the Afghani leaders plan and implement themselves. The Afghans must set their own priorities and phase in reforms consistent with their unique history, culture, and circumstances. The imposition of "good governance" requirements that is talked about so casually in the United States is a fool's errand. Afghanistan was destroyed by the Afghans, and it is only they who can rebuild it. Foreign aid at best will be a catalyst.[38]

****

In the last 15 years, particularly since 9/11, the issue of how to help failed or failing states has been a much-discussed and researched subject. The World Bank set up a special unit to provide leadership on the subject, and most major donors followed suit. There is much discussion on what constitutes a failed or failing state, and what tools are available to help them. There have been dozens of international conferences on the subject, but we are none too close to discovering the holy-grail.

The Afghanistan experience had vetted my professional appetite to do some more thinking on this knotty problem. I articulated my views on the futility of various quick-fix donor approaches in a paper[39] I was invited to present at a Wilton Park conference in 2013 that was attended by high-ranking donor and Afghan Government representatives. My findings resonated with the participants, but as happens with such meetings, nothing came out and everyone reverted to business as usual.

Since working in Afghanistan, I have worked in numerous post-conflict and fragile states – Tajikistan, Timor-Leste, Papua New Guinea, Sierra Leone – to help assess effectiveness of World Bank programs. In each case, while the situation is different, donor approaches seem to be the same: pour lots of money to fix problems, and provide myriad of "technical assistance" by experts with the expectation of seeing a functioning state in 3-5 years. The situation in each country has been different but the challenge has been the same: how to get leaders in these countries to develop and implement home-grown solutions that are perhaps second or even third bests, but are fully-owned by them. This is an imperative in all development efforts, but more so in fragile and failed states.

PART II.

Does Foreign Aid Work?

Introduction

Before getting into the future directions for the World Bank, it is necessary to take stock and try to answer the age old question that has been with us since the inception of foreign aid: does it work?

There are two subsidiary questions that need to be addressed to answer this broader question. The first is how have the aid-financed projects performed? This question helps the provider of aid funds—the public in the donor countries—appreciate whether the money they have provided has been well used. The second part is the broader question of how well a recipient country of foreign aid has done in reducing poverty, which is after all the ultimate goal of the providers of foreign aid.

In the previous chapters, I have described specific experiences my over forty years of work in development from which I can draw my own conclusions. During this period, I saw countries that grew and reduced poverty within a generation, and also others that are still struggling to make a dent. The difference, based on my experience, is not foreign aid. Rather, it is first and foremost the country's own development efforts that make a difference. Development theory provides only a broad guidance to the appropriate policies for development that each country must adapt to its own unique circumstances. Donor-led efforts have invariably failed in moving the countries to a sustained path toward growth and prosperity. Domestic leadership is the key.

My experience at the World Bank also indicates that it can be an important partner in development provided it plays a supportive rather than a directive role. It has managed to acquire worldwide knowledge of what works and what does not. It has many highly trained experts whose advice is valued, particularly by countries that are self-assured about their own policies and programs and strategies. However, the World Bank's effectiveness has been eroded over the years because of a diffusion of its agenda, growing politicization of its leadership that has allowed Western interest groups to dictate its approach to development, and insufficient attention to learning from the successful developing countries. A weak governance structure has allowed the situation to persist.

Extrapolating from my experience at the World Bank, I conclude that aid in its present form *has* worked, but in a limited set of circumstances. There are wide differences in performance of aid in different countries, determined largely by the quality of leadership and commitment in the country. Lacking such leadership, there is little prospect of development being driven by donors. So while there are no doubt many success stories, there are far too many failures as well. In many cases, aid has failed to make a difference, and in some cases, may even have caused harm. On the most important issue of the day—how to help failed and fragile states—the aid agencies still are a long way from figuring out the effective approaches to channeling foreign aid.

Yet these conclusions are subjective being based solely on my experiences. It would be useful to examine these in light of the available analytical evidence on aid effectiveness. Unfortunately, despite by now over five decades of experience with foreign aid, there is paucity of data on outcomes of aid-funded projects, and whatever is available is often not shared in a systematic manner that lends to outside scrutiny. The broader question of aid effectiveness—whether aid contributes to poverty reduction—there have been well over hundred scholarly papers, many published in reputable journals, but which present widely divergent conclusions without any consensus view. I examine further in the chapters that follow whatever limited evidence that is available.

15. Outcomes of Aid-Funded Projects: A Mixed Record

Project aid is the most common, and by far the largest, form of aid to developing countries. It is the form that most observers would recognize. Aid funds are provided to finance specific investments that are agreed between the donor and the recipient country. Donor projects cover virtually every sector of development—roads, power, water, telecommunications, irrigation, agricultural research, forestry, industry, education, health, social protection, environmental improvement, and many more. There is virtually nothing in most developing countries that has not received funding from some donor at one time or another.

The projects are prepared meticulously to the requirements of each donor. The donor wishes to be satisfied that the project it finances is indeed of high priority for the country, is prepared well to an acceptable technical standard, meets environmental and social safeguards the donor considers necessary, and follows certain procurement procedures to ensure that there is no malfeasance. The projects have over time become increasingly complex both as we have better understood the complex, multifaceted development agenda, but also because of increasing donor requirements in response to pressures from their domestic constituencies. In return for providing the funds, the donor may ask for specific commitments from the government that it will undertake certain reforms such as levying adequate user charges, eliminate wasteful subsidies, conduct studies, etc. Such commitments constitute what is commonly known as "conditionality."[40] The conditionality can be to ensure compliance with donor requirements or to accomplish what the donor considers is good for the country.

The donors follow the project closely during its implementation to make sure that it is proceeding along the lines agreed, helping resolve problems that may have arisen in implementation, and monitoring compliance with the agreements. Donor representatives visit the project periodically for this purpose. The World Bank terms these as "supervision missions" and considers them critical to not only project monitoring but as an ongoing source of advice to the project entity and the country. A typical World Bank-financed project is planned for implementation over five to seven years, but in practice it can take up to ten years because few projects get implemented without any hitch.

All in all, a project involves intensive interaction between the donor and the project entity and the country over a prolonged period of time. While in the early years, it was considered to be a welcome process by most developing countries as providing valuable learning opportunities from the donor experts, it is now seen more and more as a highly intrusive, time-consuming, and increasingly less useful process as both the number of donors and projects have grown exponentially.

Donors do not keep a ready inventory of all the projects they have financed over the years. The count probably runs into several hundreds of thousands, of which thousands are still active in the sense that they are in various stages of implementation. The World Bank alone finances some 250-300 projects per year, the number having risen steadily over the years.

How these projects have actually performed and how they have contributed to development is not an easy matter to come to grips with. The World Bank, however, systematically evaluates each project at completion to determine its outcome, which is subjected to further audit by its Independent Evaluation Group (IEG).[41] The results are maintained in a database that goes back to projects completed since 1964. This database includes outcomes ratings from highly satisfactory to highly unsatisfactory for all completed World Bank-financed projects and thus provides a useful starting point for answering the question: do aid-funded projects succeed? Until a few years back, the World Bank did not make this database available publicly but only reported it in bits and pieces in its Annual Reports on Development Effectiveness (ARDE) prepared by IEG. This inhibited an independent review of projects or an analysis of trends. However, faced with public pressure, it decided to disclose the full database on the IEG website that allows us to develop a complete picture of project performance over a long period of time.

The aggregated data provides a reasonably positive assessment of success of World bank-financed projects. In the forty five-year period, 1971-2015, evaluation of over 9,000 completed projects representing over $700 billion in funding from the World Bank, some 72 percent were assessed to have satisfactory outcomes. Although some would argue that 72 percent success rate is too low, I consider it to be a reasonable outcome considering the inherently difficult task of development in poor countries.

However, this somewhat positive assessment outcome is subject to two caveats: first, the outcome numbers are generally based on self-assessment by World Bank staff responsible for the particular project. IEG audits a sample of these and generally finds that the self-assessed project ratings by the bank staff are high by about 10 percent. However, contrary to what good statistical techniques would suggest, IEG does not use the gap in ratings from its sample to adjust the ratings for the entire portfolio. Instead, it only adjusts the rating of the project that was in the sample. Applying the adjustment factor to the portfolio would lower the satisfactory outcomes to about

Second, satisfactory outcome as defined by IEG simply means that the project has been completed and could yield expected benefits. What it does not say is whether the project would continue to work satisfactorily and yield the expected developmental benefits once put in operation, e.g., whether the facility is likely to be maintained and not fall in disrepair, or whether we can expect health clinics built under the project to also have medicines and nursing staff, or whether a village water supply would not fall into disuse because of a lack of community ownership, etc. Using this broader measure of sustainability, the number drops to 47.5 percent for projects that completed between 1971 and 2000.[42] In other words, only one in two projects would continue to perform what they were intended to do.

Based on these caveats, it would probably be reasonable to conclude that perhaps somewhere between 50 and 70 percent of bank-funded projects have satisfactory outcomes.

There is, however, a significant variation in outcomes among countries. Assessed outcomes are worse in some of the poorest countries/regions that ostensibly are in most need of foreign aid. Africa has the worst outcomes, with only 62 percent of projects assessed as satisfactory, but one in three projects assessed as likely sustainable (table 15.1). South Asia, home to most poor people, also fares badly with only 45 percent of projects assessed as sustainable. Country-level data is equally enlightening. Some forty countries had 0 to 35 percent of projects assessed as being sustainable in the 1971-2000 period (Appendix 1).

Table 15.1. World Bank Project Outcomes 1971-2015
By Regions

		Project Outcomes	
Region	No. Projects	% Satisfactory	% Sustainable
Africa	2,832	62.1	33.1
East Asia & Pacific	1,534	79.9	65.2
Europe & Central Asia	1,317	78.7	64.7
Latin America & Caribbean	1,943	74.5	52.6
Middle East & N Africa	852	72.1	51.1
South Asia	1,108	75.2	44.4
All regions	9,588	72.3	47.5

Notes: Sustainability numbers only to 2000. IEG stopped systematically reporting sustainability after 2000.
Source: IEG Project Evaluation Database

Looking at the data over time indicates a much higher proportion of projects completed in the earlier period (1971-1980) were assessed to be satisfactory than in the latter periods, a deteriorating trend between 1980 and 1995, and a small but steady improvement since then (table 15.2). The Independent Evaluation Group (IEG) in its annual reports on project outcomes also reported a steady improvement in project performance in its Annual Review of Development Effectiveness (ARDE) that it issues every year. Its report in 2009, when aggregate project performance appears to have peaked, reported that 81 percent of projects that exited in 2008 were satisfactory, "continuing the upward trend that started in 1993:" (Figure 15.1)

Table 15.2 World Bank Project Outcomes 1971-2015
By Decades

| | | Project Outcomes | |
| | No. | % | % |
Period	Projects	Satisfactory	Sustainable
1971-80	958	84.5	48
1981-1990	2,134	67.7	43.3
1991-1995	1,178	66.1	45.6
1996-2000	1,320	70.8	55.5
1971-2000	5,590	70.8	47.5

Source: IEG Project Evaluation Database

Fig. 15.1. Trend in World Bank Project Outcomes Reported by IEG

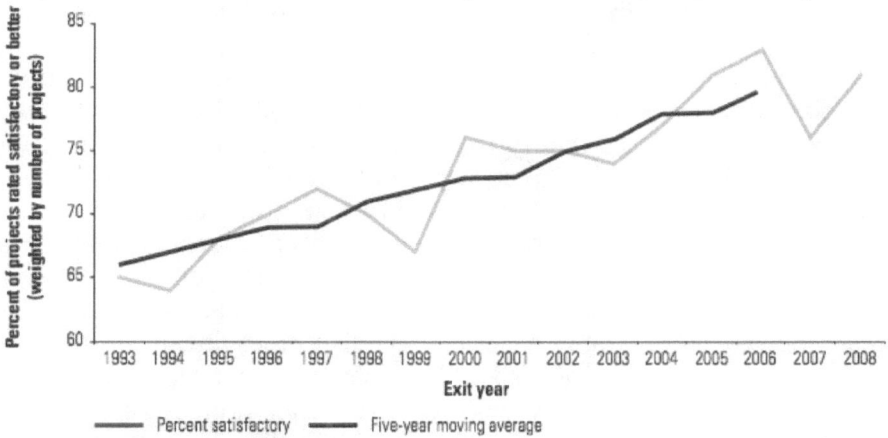

Source: IEG: Annual Review of Development Effectiveness, 2009

Encouraging as these trends may appear, however, these need to be viewed with suitable caution. It is a well-known axiom in bureaucracies that any number that management focuses on improves. The reported improvement since mid-1990s coincides with a period when there had been widespread concern among Bank's shareholders about the deteriorating bank project portfolio leading the bank to appoint a task force under the leadership of a well-respected Vice President, Willi Wapenhans. Jim Wolfensohn who became president in 1995 made improving project outcomes as one of the goals of his "Strategic Compact"[43] that lasted over three fiscal years, 1998-2000. And sure enough, the target of 75 percent satisfactory was duly met in 2000. This would seem surprising since projects that are reported as "exiting" in 2000 would have been approved prior to 1993 based on the normal seven—to ten-year implementation period for the most bank projects. It is remarkable that the benefits of the strategic compact were felt retroactively!

In general, the IEG findings also do not quite pass the smell test of experienced hands at the bank. I have interviewed many people over the years and most are surprised to hear that project performance is showing an improving trend. It contradicts their perceptions of the reality from the ground. Most believe that the quality has declined since the 1990s as the bank projects have been overburdened with more and more requirements.

It is possible that there indeed had been improvements in the outcomes, at least after 2000 when many developing countries' economies, led notably by China and India, were showing renewed vigor. Latin America was also emerging from years of decline. As I will discuss in a later chapter, countries that do well economically generally tend to have better project performance also. But as long as IEG remains a less than fully independent entity and closely connected with the bank management, and always pushed by the board to be "balanced" in its reviews, its reports will always be suspect. The coincidence of improving trends of project performance with the Strategic Compact stretches IEG's credibility.

Overall, my assessment is that the outcomes of bank-financed projects continue on the historical record of some 50-70 percent satisfactory. Whether this is an acceptable record given the complexities of the development business is open to debate. In the 1980s, when the project performance data first began to emerge for sufficiently large numbers of projects, some of the aid proponents began to offer a new rationalization. In his widely heralded book, *Does Aid Work* (Oxford: Oxford University Press, 1986), Robert Cassen of the London School of Economics, and at the time with the Overseas Development Council, concluded that aid fails at about the same rate as "complex human endeavors." He went on to suggest that even when projects fail, they have net positive externalities such as "demonstration effects" and "policy changes." So according to Cassen, there is bright light even in failures.

I, however, take a different view. I believe that the record can and must be improved if the bank were to implement serious reforms and address the reasons for failure of projects. But even more importantly, the relevant question is not just whether a donor-funded project succeeds. Rather, the question is whether the country is making progress in development as measured by growth and poverty reduction as a result. This is an issue I discuss in the following chapters.

16. The Missing Aid Growth Linkage

Measuring project outcomes is useful in providing assurance on whether the particular aid funds were spent prudently and not wasted. This is an important measure to reassure the providers of aid funds. However, it does not tell us anything about whether the aid funds actually helped reduce poverty, which is the ultimate objective of foreign aid. Reliable data on poverty levels over time is not available for many of the developing countries. For countries for which it is available, it is spotty in its coverage. It is therefore difficult to assess long-term trends in all but a handful of the more advanced, developing countries. We can, however, use economic growth as a proxy since there is ample evidence that economic growth is positively correlated with poverty reduction.[44]

However, finding a relationship between aid and economic growth has not proven to be easy. Scholars have grappled with this issue for a long time, producing at last count over hundred scholarly papers based on elaborate econometric studies. Up until mid-1990s, the main focus of these studies was on finding a correlation between foreign aid and savings, investment, and economic growth. The conclusions varied widely, in part depending on the ideology (conservatives and libertarians not surprisingly found aid as retarding growth and aid agency-affiliated researchers found a positive relationship). There was no consensus on the subject among development economists, which was also hindered by the limited availability of data, and the lack of clarity about the mechanisms by which aid would affect growth in different types of countries.

Then in late-1990s, a study by World Bank researchers Craig Burnside and David Dollar and published in 2000 in the prestigious journal *American Economic Review*[45] reignited the debate. Using regression analysis on a new dataset on foreign aid that the World Bank had released, they found a positive correlation between aid and growth but only in countries with good fiscal, monetary, and trade policies. Based on their analysis, they went on to suggest that a 1 percent of gross domestic product in aid given to a poor but well-managed country can increase its growth rate by a sustained 0.5 percentage points.

The Burnside and Dollar paper received considerable attention and acclaim among the aid community. Their conclusion was intuitively appealing and many aid agencies, including the World Bank, used it to neutralize the mounting criticism of aid effectiveness by arguing that aid *can* work if channeled to countries with "good" policies, and this indeed would be the future direction that aid agencies would follow. In the earlier World Bank publication on which their *American Economic Review* paper was based, Burnside and Dollar extended their conclusions to also suggest that aid itself can promote good policies and institutions. These conclusions were not included in the paper because I suspect they were not supportable by hard evidence. These conclusions, however, did provide justification for continued World Bank's lending to countries that did not have "bad" policies.

The Burnside and Dollar conclusions unleashed a host of other studies, some of which supported their conclusions while many more questioned the validity of their analysis. Danish researchers Henrik Hansen and Finn Tarp were among the notable supporters, albeit they dispute the Burnside and Dollar notion of aid promoting growth only in good policy environment.[46] Bill Easterly of New York University was the most vocal critic of their methodology. By running the same regressions as by Burnside and Dollar, but using what he considers more accurate measures of aid and alternative definitions of "policies" and taking growth over longer periods of time, Easterly concludes that the relationship between aid and growth is tenuous.[47] A recent study that uses meta-analysis[48] to try to draw conclusions from the various conflicting studies on aid effectiveness concluded that "the preponderance of the evidence indicates that aid has not been effective."[49] But I doubt that this will be the last word on the subject.

So here we are, back to where we started. Such is the state of academic research despite decades of experience with aid.

I am not a great fan of regression analysis. It can at times be useful but it is a much overused technique by economists. I find it preferable to fall back on my own experiences working in countries that I think did well (e.g., the East Asian tigers and a few others) and not so well (most of the rest of the developing world).

Over the thirty-year period, 1971-2000, developing countries received some two to three trillion dollars in foreign aid from various sources. The World Bank alone provided about eight hundred billion of this in soft loans. Still, only fifteen of more than 150 developing countries receiving foreign aid had a GDP per capita growth above the modest benchmark of 2.5 percent per annum over 1971-2000. Seven of these countries were in Asia, including the Asian tigers. Despite the fact that foreign aid was provided much more generously in Africa than in any other region of the world, only three relatively small African countries make the list: Botswana, Lesotho, and Swaziland.

The 2.5 percent growth benchmark is rather modest for developing countries. It is the rate of growth experienced by the rich industrialized countries in this period; the poorer countries should be expected to grow much faster in accordance with the economic theory of convergence. It is also barely enough to double incomes in a generation, almost a minimum requirement to make a dent in poverty. And of course it is far below the growth rates experienced by the dynamic East Asian economies that have been most successful in reducing poverty.

There also does not seem to be a correlation between the amount of foreign aid provided to a country and its growth performance. .1 below shows for a group of selected countries in Asia and Africa the aid per capita, and the growth record over 1971-2000. The selected countries include those that have had satisfactory growth performance (over 2.5 percent per annum) and a few others like Bangladesh, Uganda, Kenya, Liberia that have been favored by foreign aid donors at various times. With the exception of three countries —Botswana, Lesotho, and Sri Lanka— there does not appear to be any link between the amount of aid and growth performance. Indeed, the converse seems to be true for several countries. Bangladesh, the darling of foreign aid donors in Asia, and most countries in Africa, are notable examples of a negative correlation between foreign aid amount and growth performance.

Table 16.1. Aid and Growth in Selected Countries: 1971-2000

	Total Aid ($billion)	Aid/Capita $/Year	Avg. GDP/Capita Growth (% p.a.)
Asia			
Bangladesh	35.3	11.0	0.7
China	38.0	1.5	7.1
Indonesia	33.0	6.5	4.2
India	48.5	2.1	2.5
Korea	2.1	2.2	6.0
Lao PDR	3.8	29.0	NA (<2%)
Malaysia	3.5	7.6	4.3
Nepal	7.7	13.4	1.5
Philippines	18.2	10.0	1.0
Sri Lanka	12.1	24.0	3.2
Thailand	14.1	8.5	4.6
Vietnam	15.0	8.0	NA (>2.5%)
Africa			
Botswana	2.7	75.0	7.3
Ethiopia	15.7	10.8	NA (<0%)
Ghana	10.7	24.6	-0.4
Kenya	14.4	22.0	1.1
Lesotho	2.4	53.0	2.8
Liberia	2.4	38.4	-4.6
Nigeria	3.8	1.4	0.2
Senegal	12.0	55.4	-0.5
Swaziland	1.0	44.0	2.9
Tanzania	20.6	28.2	NA (<0%)
Uganda	10.3	18.2	NA (<1%)

Notes: NA not available; author estimate in parenthesis
Source : World Development Indicators, The World Bank

Africa, the region of most concern to the aid community, as a whole has performed very poorly despite having received massive foreign aid. Easterly illustrates this point vividly in the fig. 16.1 below:

Fig. 16.1. Aid and Growth in Africa

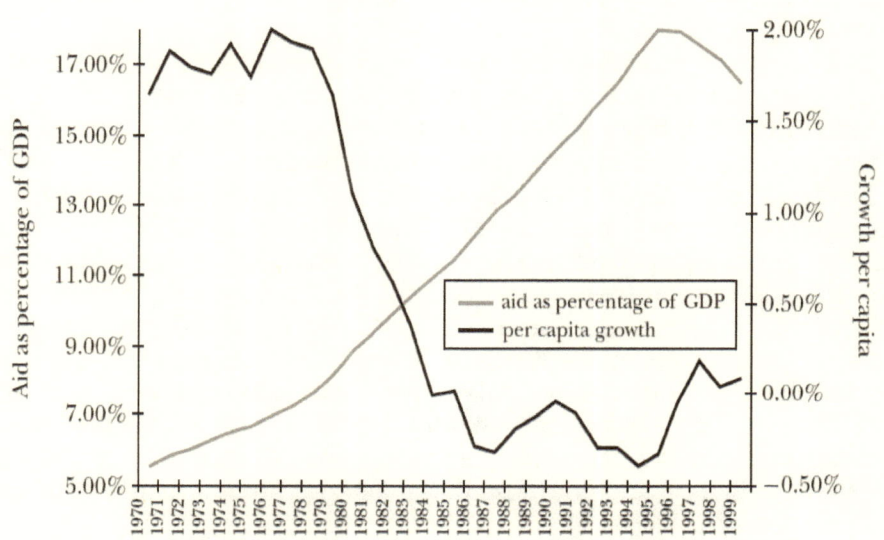

Source: William Easterly, "Can Foreign Aid Buy Growth in Africa?" *Journal of Economic Perspectives*, (2003) 17.3, pp. 35.

The data presented above does not necessarily contradict the Burnside and Dollar conclusions to the extent that the fifteen countries that experienced sustained growth beyond 2.5 percent are among the "good policy" countries and they also received some foreign aid. However, in my experience working in these countries, it is strong and committed leadership over a long period of time that matters the most. In the successful countries, such leaders no doubt introduced good policies, although perhaps not always the full range of policies that underlie the Burnside and Dollar analysis. Episodic good policies are not enough, as we have seen in the numerous failures of the World Bank-supported structural adjustment programs. So my slight variation form the Burnside and Dollar conclusions is that aid can help in countries that have demonstrated their own efforts through a record of performance over several years.

Aid advocates like to argue that they have internalized the Burnside and Dollar argument and now channel their aid much more toward countries following good economic policies. In a speech in advance of the Monterey Conference on aid flows to developing countries, president of the World Bank, James Wolfensohn, argued, "We have learned that corruption, bad policies, and weak governance will make aid ineffective." He went on to argue that corruption, bad policies, and weak governance had improved in poor countries that donors had become more discriminating in directing aid to "good" countries and that therefore there should be "roughly a doubling of current aid flows."[50]

The actual record of aid flows since then unfortunately does not bear out this assertion. No doubt the most egregious cases like Zimbabwe and Burma were weaned out during the worst of their periods of governance, but most other countries continue to receive significant new commitments irrespective of performance. World Bank lending continues apace in all countries in Africa despite many countries suffering from poor policies, weak governance, and a high level of corruption (see Appendix 2 for World Bank loan commitments to Africa in the last ten years). The Dollar and Burnside study it seems provided the convenient rationale by also suggesting, without much evidence, that aid can actually "midwife" good policies and good institutions.[51] Past experience should tell us that aid is best provided to countries that have established a track record of sustained growth and poverty reduction and not those that make promises of better policies to get foreign aid.

In the last few years, many African countries have been showing signs of growth following four decades of stagnation or even decline. It will be premature to conclude that the growth is caused by foreign aid as some would no doubt suggest. It is more likely that growth is ignited by the general global growth driven by the major developing economies of China, India, Brazil, and Russia. At long last, Africa may well be benefiting from strong global growth. But there will indeed be a strong case for foreign aid to these countries if the growth is sustained over a number of years.

17. Why World Bank Projects Fail?

So why do World Bank-funded projects sometimes fail? This seems particularly curious since the long and thorough process it employs in the preparation of the projects is well-known. The bank also stays with the project over its seven to ten year implementation, monitoring progress, resolving bottlenecks, and cajoling action from the government on critical issues. So why a 30-50 percent failure rate? In order to understand the reasons and answer this question, one has to look deeper into how in practice the projects are prepared and implemented. What seems on the surface to be a thorough process in practice results in projects that are disconnected from the broader development effort of the country. They are far from "country-owned" as all donors like to suggest. Instead, they are isolated islands of attempted perfection that fail when subjected to the ground realities. Indeed, I would suggest that discreet donor projects not only do not contribute to development, but they may actually detract from it. Let us see how.

Funding of discrete projects is a long-standing tradition of the World Bank going back to its origins that envisaged building or rebuilding infrastructure as its main task. The objective was straightforward: to finance a high priority investment that a country may not otherwise be able to finance from its own resources. As an institution that had to initially gain, and subsequently sustain, the trust of the financial markets, it set fairly stringent requirements for projects it would finance. Up until ealy-1970s, the focus was on technical, economic and financial soundness. The key question addressed was: is this the least cost investment that yields the most benefits for the people, and that can be afforded by the government and the beneficiaries? The environmental aspects were considered as a part of the technical review. These were the questions Raj asked when we appraised the Jamaica water supply project in 1972 or when we turned down the request for the railway line in Gabon.

The bank's charter requires that the funds it provides are used only for the "intended purposes" and with due consideration of "efficiency."

In these coded words, the message is that there should be no corruption in the bank-financed projects. This message was drilled into all the bank staff as far back as I can remember, not only because the charter required it, but because we knew that no donor to the bank would ever tolerate misuse of their taxpayer-provided contributions. The objective of preventing corruption was achieved through stringent guidelines for procurement that emphasized competition among bidders, and openness and transparency of the process. These procedures were highly regarded by the bidders and borrowers alike, although there were at times complaints from the borrowing country when the guidelines prevented it from awarding a contract to its favored or preferred contractor. There were also sometimes complaints from one or more of the losing bidders who faulted their failure to bag the contract on some flaw in the bidding and complained through the executive director representing their home country on the World Bank Board.

Following the disastrous episodes of the Polonoroeste project in Brazil and the Sardar Sarovar dam in India, the environmental and resettlement requirements were made more stringent and explicit in mid-1980s.

In totality, the bank requirements were stringent but were generally accepted by most borrowers, albeit many of them grudgingly as the price of getting the bank loans. Most required services of foreign consultants to prepare and implement projects to the bank's standards. A few countries like Korea and China, even adopted the bank's standards for the major projects they financed from their own resources.

In the 1970s, there were two developments that fundamentally changed the nature of projects. First, the bank began to see projects not just as discreet investments in itself, but in the broader context of economic and sector policies. The bank realized, correctly, that there is no such thing as a "good" project in a "bad" policy environment. If a municipal water system is built, one has also to try to get the government to levy appropriate user charges that not only recover the cost of the project, but also generate a surplus that could be used for further expansion. If a power plant is built to add to production capacity, one could not overlook the structure of the sector that was inefficient and wasteful. A school building project could not succeed if the teachers did not teach and the quality of instruction was poor. Building of public health clinics could only be appropriate if the government at the same time did not spend less on costly curative care. And so on.

In some cases, the bank knew what should be done and made it a condition of the loan. More often, either the bank did not know exactly how to tackle the issue or could not convince the country to follow the bank's advice, and in such cases the conditionality often took on the form of studies to be done by consultants on the basis of which the government would then make appropriate policy changes. Some borrowers agreed to the studies as a way of postponing hard decisions.

There was a premium placed on policy reform, the logic being that funding from the bank is really secondary, and only a means to the much more important task of policy and institutional reforms. In fact, an additional requirement was instituted that asked project proponents to give the "rationale for the bank involvement"[52] in the particular project and demonstrate the bank's value added beyond merely providing funding. A typical review meeting of project proposals would have managers grilling the team if the reforms proposed are sufficiently meaningful. Embellishing what a project could achieve by adding more components or policy studies became the *modus operandus* of the bank staff to win approval for their projects. The executive directors encouraged this further by routinely applauding projects for their "innovative" approach.[53]

So what emerged in much of 1970s and 1980s were projects that were increasingly complex and well beyond the capacity of the government agencies to manage. The problem was exacerbated by an increasing volume of loans that the bank staff was pressed to process. There was pressure to increase the size of the projects beyond the capacity of the agencies and at the same time load projects with multiple components and conditions that sounded good to the bosses in Washington. The results were predictable: a continuing deterioration in project quality that was picked up in the project assessments at completion by OED discussed in the last chapter. The Wapenhans Task Force that was constituted in 1992 to examine the reasons for deterioration in project quality placed the blame squarely on these pressures.[54] A senior official from a borrowing country interviewed by the task force described the problem as such: '[T]here is so much pressure put on the responsible ministry by the bank that, you know, you just have to have it done . . . The bank adopts a take it or leave it stance. The borrower agrees to conditions that it has no way of honoring, and they end up with a contract that cannot be implemented.[55]

OED in its 1992 annual report of evaluation results, produced before the era of public disclosure, put the issue bluntly: "The central challenge faced by the bank is to reconcile the expanding scope and ambition of its development agenda with a need to improve project performance."[56]

Reflecting the imperviousness of the bank to learning from experience, the Wapenhans Report lamented: "The problems we are encountering in today's projects are the same problems encountered in projects many years ago. We keep making the same mistakes because we did not learn from earlier experience . . . Most project officers think that their project is unique and will succeed where others have failed."[57]

Lew Preston, who was the president then, took the recommendations of the Wapenhans Task Force seriously. He stressed the need for selectivity in the bank's work, emphasizing his long-held view that an organization should limit itself to what it does best. A group headed by Armeane Choski, vice president of Human Development, was tasked to devise an implementation strategy.

Lew Preston died prematurely in 1994 before this and many other of his sensible ideas could be implemented. His successor, Jim Wolfensohn, could not have been more different in his approach. Instead of emphasizing selectivity, Wolfensohn immediately set out to expand the bank's agenda. There was no initiative he did not like. Arguing that culture was central to development, he wanted the bank to support projects to preserve cultural heritage, and sure enough, the eager bank staff responded by producing such projects despite the fact that this was precisely an area of UNESCO's competence and there was little expertise in this area in the bank. Believing that the bank had ignored the valuable contributions NGOs could make, he decreed regular consultations with them for every project, and again, the eager bank staff complied uncritically. The initiative that left everyone puzzled was his "faith-based development" where he decided that religious organizations should play a role as a partner of the bank, and a director-level person was designated to coordinate this work. And I have previously mentioned his "comprehensive development framework" that required the bank to take a "holistic" view of development and, you guessed it, a department was created for this purpose.

Wolfensohn not only expanded the scope of the bank's work, he also mandated new requirements that made project preparation and implementation more, not less, complex. Viewing development nothing short of a complete social change of the society, he mandated social assessments for every project, and before long, a few hundred social scientists were on the bank's payroll. Matters like poverty impact, gender, participation, etc., that were dealt with as deemed necessary for a particular project were now mandated as yet another set of "fiduciary safeguards" issued under various "operational directives." Later, with Wolfensohn's crusade against corruption, the procurement rules designed to promote good procurement processes were made even more rigid, and the primary goal moved from efficiency to controlling corruption. In addition, new requirements were introduced for complicated financial management processes for individual projects bypassing the budgetary and reporting processes of the governments, creating yet another layer of complications. Governance became the new buzz word of development notwithstanding the fact that the donor community still has little understanding of how good governance is built and whether it can be done at all by external pressures.

The underlying rationale for each of these requirements is understandable. After all, no one is in favor of corruption or for excluding women or ignoring valuable inputs that civil society could offer. Such issues arose even previously in the bank projects and dealt with as appropriate. However, previously such requirements were deliberately not coded as "rules" but rather as "guidelines." There was room left for the bank experts to exercise reasonable judgment as to when and to what extent these requirements would apply. The bank understood that development is a complex business with widely varying conditions in different countries and circumstances that can be different at any given time. Indeed, staff was encouraged to apply the project preparation and implementation requirements flexibly to deal with specific problems. As I mentioned earlier, these were the marching orders I received from my boss when I first became a manager in East Asia. What was new now is the cumulative effect of all these new mandatory requirements that made complex projects now impossibly complex. The bank under Wolfensohn forgot OED's démarche in the 1992 report of the need to "reconcile the expanding scope and ambition of its development agenda with a need to improve project performance."

Most of these Wolfensohn initiatives withered away with his departure in 2005 as one normally expects at the demise of authoritarian leaders. But the additional "fiduciary requirements" continue, with some like anticorruption pursued with even greater vigor by his successors. Overall, the focus of the bank requirements for projects has in the last fifteen years shifted from what would contribute most to development and people's welfare to a checklist of numerous safeguard requirements covering social, environment, and anticorruption (procurement and financial management) aspects. Since these requirements were a result of onerous negotiations with western (mostly United States based) advocacy groups who have a culture of seeing themselves as the guardians of the people against bad behavior of their governments and litigation as their tool of enforcement, these requirements have now become rigid rules that the bank staff must follow at the risk of being hauled before the Inspection Panel, another requirement that was imposed on the bank by western donors in 1993 as a condition for their continued contributions to IDA.[58] The bank experts have increasingly been put in the role of compliance officers rather than sources of high-quality advice they previously thought of themselves and that the clients appreciated. The concepts of "reasonable application" and making "sensible judgments" in specific situations have been lost.

The net result of all these requirements has been that the bank-funded projects have their own world in which they exist, with little relationship to the realities on the ground. The various requirements are put into projects not because they are considered practical, within the capacity of the country, or consistent with how the country develops its own projects, but because these are required to pass scrutiny of those who view development as a pursuit of a perfect world. One harried senior official in a developing country that I have been advising mused whether the bank's requirements could be fulfilled by Denmark!

Few developing countries have the capacity, and indeed interest, to prepare projects with all the trappings required by the World Bank. The ones that do—mostly the better-off countries that borrow on harder World Bank terms—refuse to spend their own resources or borrowed funds to meet the requirements they consider unnecessary. Faced with this, the World Bank tries to mobilize grant funds from a bilateral donor or from its own resources to hire consultants who can translate the World Bank's onerous requirements into project proposals. The cost of these consulting services can be substantial, running into several million dollars. The poorer and generally low-capacity countries go along with the requirements since the IDA funds that they are given are grants or near grants and thus are willing to use these for such consulting services. The entire project preparation process is time-consuming and resource-intensive, where the country is often a bystander in a bank-driven process. The weaker the country's capacity - as is the case in many low-income countries in Africa - the greater the dominance of the bank in the entire process. It does not exactly promote "country ownership" of projects.

Implementation of the projects is equally cumbersome. A typical World Bank project is designed to take seven years to implement and in practice takes about ten years because of delays. Most projects get marred with difficulties at the outset for a variety of reasons, including a lack of familiarity of the implementing agency with the World Bank processes, a mismatch between the capacity of the country to implement and the complex requirements of the project mentioned above, and other procedural delays. Many of the policy reforms embedded in the project get sidetracked to the more pressing need to get things going. Much time and effort are expended by World Bank staff in resolving the nuts and bolts of procurement than on dialogue with the client on the substantive aspects of sector policies and programs that is the ultimate goal of World Bank's project assistance.

It should, therefore, not come as a surprise that a not insignificant number of projects fail to deliver the development outcomes they were designed for. The entire project preparation and implementation process is highly taxing on the limited capacity of poor countries. Instead of building country capacity, a key objective in almost every project funded by every donor, donor projects often siphon away whatever limited capacity that does exist. The more capable staff in the country is lured to work in donor-funded project management units, where they can draw higher salaries and enjoy additional perks such as cars, overseas study tours, and opportunities for making money by working in a cash-rich environment. This can leave the core functions of running the organization depleted. Hence, donor-funded projects can sometimes not only not contribute to development, but actually deter it. The more limited the country's capacity, the more the damage done by this drain of talent toward donor-funded projects. The World Bank's vice president for Africa in the 1990s put it bluntly when discussing various donors' efforts to build capacity in Africa: "Donors and African governments together have in effect undermined capacity in Africa; they are undermining it faster than they are building it."[59]

Establishing a better sense of priorities among all the different goals and objectives that the bank has accumulated over the years and making explicit decisions about what are the minimum set of essential goals that would contribute to the success of the project are the critical needs if the bank-funded projects are to show better outcomes. Unfortunately, this will not be an easy task with the current governance structure of the bank that is incapable of doing this. Moisés Naim, one-time minister of finance of Venezuela and an executive director of the World Bank and later the editor of *Foreign Policy,* put the issue bluntly in his excellent background paper prepared for the high-powered Bretton Woods Commission:[60]

> One of the reasons for the Bank's accumulation of goals is that its governance system is not very good at sorting out priorities, at least formally. Once an objective is incorporated as part of the Bank's agenda, it becomes almost impossible to delete it from the list. Political factors, organizational inertia and the way strategic decision-making is formally organized make it very difficult to explicitly exclude an item from the Bank's priorities. One of the more insidious effects of this goal-over-load is that it impacts more negatively the weaker countries. Countries with little bargaining power have to accept the conditions and objectives that, in a given period,

acquire great visibility and priority within the Bank. Instead, stronger countries can—and often do—manage to persuade the Bank to be more lax on conditions that are not central to the loan being negotiated.[61]

18. Obsession with Volume of Loans Adds to Project Failure

You can be very proud of contributing to accomplishments that have marked new highs in the history of the Bank Group. In FY 2010, we have committed $72.2 billion to support our clients:

- IBRD lending increased to 44.2 billion.
- IDA commitments rose to $14.5 billion—with more than 49 percent of commitments going to sub-Saharan Africa.
- IFC provided more than $12 billion in financing for private sector development, and almost 40 percent of the projects financed were in IDA countries.
- MIGA issued $1.5 billion in guarantees.

—Excerpt from end-year message from
Robert Zoellick to all World Bank staff, July 2, 2010

I do not recall a single year at the World Bank when a similar end-year message was not delivered by the bank president to all staff. While the messages also listed other accomplishments—more allocation for AIDS, the bank's quick response to a crisis, internal reforms, etc., the volume of lending was always the central part and the one most focused on by the bank management and staff. Every World Bank staff member knows that it is the volume of lending that ultimately matters for career advancement. The executive directors see this as the main metric of judging the bank's performance as an institution. And of course, the volume of IDA commitments is used by the bank to justify going back to the donors with requests for increased contributions for the next three-year replenishment cycle.

Unfortunately, this emphasis on volume of loans has long been one of the reasons for poor performance of the bank-financed projects. Pressure to make ever-growing commitments over previous years often means staff pushing additional and larger projects on country institutions that are not capable of handling the projects. This creates a mismatch between the bank's ambition and the reality on the ground, exacerbated by the increased burden of project requirements discussed in the last chapter. The result is an inevitable deterioration in project quality, which ultimately contributes toward unsatisfactory outcomes. And ironically, in the last ten years as the concessional IDA resources have become abundant, the pressure from the western donors to increase commitments is felt more and more in Africa and countries in conflict, or precisely in countries that have the weakest institutions and the poorest record of performance. This does not bode well for the future outcomes being any better than the record of the past.

Pressure to lend is not something new in the bank. It goes back to the McNamara era and continued since then by almost all presidents. Soon upon arrival in the bank in 1968, McNamara declared his goal of doubling the volume of lending in the next five years and then doubling it again in the following five years. Under him, every year will start with each unit establishing lending targets, which he monitored personally, and he accepted few excuses for slippages. By the time he left in 1980, World Bank loans had grown from about $1 billion in 1970 to $7.5 billion (fig. 18.1). Soft loans from IDA also grew, thanks to McNamara's vigorous efforts to persuade increasingly reluctant donors, particularly the United States, to increase their contributions.

Following McNamara's departure, World Bank loans continued to grow as the middle-income and larger poor countries (notably India and later also China) were willing to borrow significant amounts on World Bank terms to meet their needs. The volume of World Bank lending reached an annual level of $12-15 billion, a range that it has since found difficult to breach except during periods of crisis such as the East Asian crisis in 1997-2000 and the current world financial crisis, when many middle-income countries have borrowed to build a cushion against shocks. Most of the bank staff working in these countries expect World Bank lending to be back in the historical $12-15-billion range, barring a major change in the way the World Bank does business. The World Bank borrowers have become increasingly vocal about the growing "cost of doing business" with the bank that has reduced their appetite for bank loans.

Fig. 18.1. World Bank and IDA loans
(1971-2015)

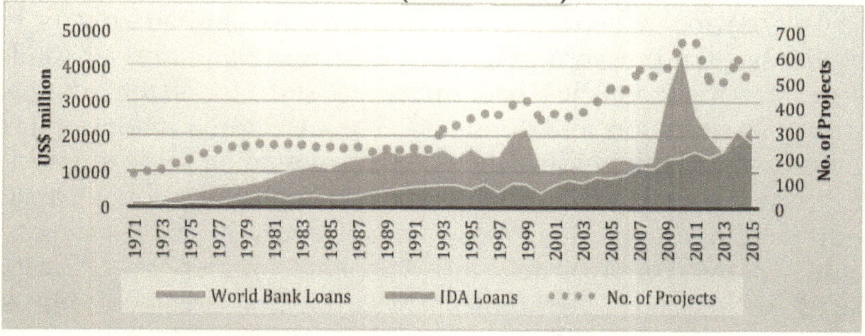

Source: The World Bank.

IDA, on the other hand, is a different story. After McNamara's departure in 1980, getting donor contributions to IDA became an increasingly difficult task. With Republicans controlling the White House and the Congress, it became even harder to obtain contributions from the United States. The conservatives had always been opposed to foreign aid and had even less of a liking for the World Bank, which they considered to be a bloated and ineffective bureaucracy. Nevertheless, the bank presidents were able to maintain some growth in IDA funds by getting the some western European countries and Japan to increase their shares and by transferring significant amounts from the World Bank's net income to IDA. In the fifteen-year period, 1980-1995, IDA commitments grew from $3 billion to $5.6 billion, while World Bank loan commitments grew from $7.5 billion to about $17 billion, a slower rate of growth in IDA but growth, nevertheless.

The IDA funding situation improved dramatically after the attacks of 9/11, when the Bush administration began to view foreign aid as an essential part of its security strategy. Increased U.S. pledges for IDA also meant a significant increase in pledges by the other donors, most of whom in any case had been more supportive of IDA. Thus, IDA commitments increased from $4.4 billion in 2000 to about $20 billion in 2015.

All this would be good news if there were evidence that the increased resources would result in better development outcomes. Unfortunately, this is not likely to be the case. As long back as the mid-1970s, as the volume of the bank and IDA lending began to grow rapidly, there was also a growing concern both within and outside of the bank about the quality of World Bank projects.[62] As previously mentioned, projects that were deemed satisfactory were below 75 percent overall, and under 50 percent in Africa. When looked through the lens of sustainability —will the benefits last?— the results were even lower.

The 1992 Wapenhans Report had confirmed what had already been known widely: the pressure to commit increasing amounts of funds to poorly performing countries had often led staff to disregard quality standards of preparation and appraisal. The task force made a number of recommendations, including the need to give much more attention to lessons from previous interventions and to the institutional capacity. Jim Wolfensohn often cited Wapenhans Report in his first year to justify his plans for restructuring the bank under his "Strategic Compact." To his credit, Wolfensohn was the first president who sent the message that he did not care about the volume of lending. Indeed, lending in Wolfensohn's first years in office did not increase, although it should be noted that these years coincided with a period of slow growth in the availability of IDA funds, and when many middle-income countries were reducing their borrowing from the bank because of their complaints about "high cost of doing business" with the bank mentioned earlier.

The restrain, however, did not last long, and soon the bank was back to asking donors for more contributions and once again began to make large commitments to countries despite poor record of performance. It had to show to donors that it had committed the available funds in order to ask for larger contributions. The bank was back in the business of using growing lending volumes as the metric of its success. Two examples illustrate this point.

Bangladesh and Nigeria are currently among the top three recipients of concessional loans from IDA. Between 1971 and 2000, the World Bank committed $6.0 and $5.4 billion respectively of soft loans to each (table 18.1). Both have large populations and a significant number of people in absolute poverty. As such, both can be considered to be in need of foreign aid. However, the performance of World Bank projects in both countries has been dismal, with only 38 percent of projects in Bangladesh and 20 percent in Nigeria between 1971 and 2000 rated as sustainable by IEG. Both countries have had a poor thirty-year growth record in the past. Nigeria is well known for its high level of corruption, and Bangladesh for its highly inefficient public sector, factors that explain their poor past performance.

Table 18.1 Bangladesh and Nigeria – Key performance indicators
1971-2000

	Bangladesh	Nigeria
No. Projects	89	89
Commitments ($ billion)	6.0	5.4
Projects Satisfactory	72%	52%
Projects Sustainable	38%	18%
Avg. Annual GDP/capita Growth	0.70%	0.20%

Sources : IEG Database; World Development Indicators

Yet the World Bank continued to increase commitment of IDA funds to both countries—some $3.8 billion to Bangladesh in the years 2001-2008 growing to $10.3 billion in the period 2009-2015; and $3.1 billion and $8.1 billion during the same periods to Nigeria (1999-2007). The buildup of the Nigeria program was a response to the democratically elected government of President Olusegun Obasanjo coming to power after many years of military rule. President Obasanjo immediately went about courting the World Bank and other donors by instituting a number of reforms, including the establishment of a widely heralded anticorruption commission. As most Nigerians know, the reality of Obsanjo's reforms fell far short of his public relations efforts, and the country still teeters on collapse. Nigeria ranks number 14, just ahead of Yemen, in *Foreign Policy* magazine's 2010 index of failed sates.

An evaluation of the 1998-2007 program of the World Bank in Nigeria carried out by IEG in which I participated[63] rated the program performance as "moderately unsatisfactory," a fine gradation by IEG that, along with an equally ambiguous label of "moderately satisfactory," allows it to avoid the staff before it finalizes the country's evaluations. However, in the classical clutching at the straws, the IEG report goes on to state that "[i]n the Nigerian context this reflects an improving trend relative to a previous IEG assessment of the 2000 to 2004 period, which rated the outcome of the bank assistance as unsatisfactory."[64] Six months after the IEG's evaluation, the bank approved a new country partnership strategy (CPS) for Nigeria for the period 2010-2013 that proposed committing $4.5 billion of IDA funds to Nigeria over four years. The ambition to increase IDA commitments as usual trumped the record of development performance over many years, which cannot be described as anything but dismal as any Nigerian would testify. The "chairman's summary" of the discussion at the board of the bank's proposed country program contains the usual platitudes about directors "commending the authorities . . . " "welcoming the emphasis on governance . . . ," "broadly supported the CPS . . . ," etc. (Appendix 3). The discussion shows no concern that the past record has been poor or that 80 percent of over two billion dollars of IDA funds committed in the last five years was unutilized.[65]

The Bangladesh story is not much different. Successive IEG evaluations have rated the bank's assistance program as "moderately satisfactory." Even without discounting the upward pressures on IEG ratings, this is not a record of great accomplishment. But it was enough for the World Bank to increase the IDA allocation from $461 million in 2006 to about a billion dollars a year in 2009 and 2010, and an intention to double it over the next three years.[66] This intended increase was all the more remarkable when at the time the lending allocation was made, 85 percent of IDA funds committed in the previous five years was still lying undisbursed.[67] Bangladesh has no doubt benefited in recent years from the spillover effects of the economic boom in Asia. But ask any donor to Bangladesh and he will tell you the enormous challenge of getting the bureaucracy to implement anything in the country.[68]

The cases of Nigeria and Bangladesh are not unique. The story is the same for most of the countries that receive IDA funding. IEG evaluations of the eighty-seven country programs since 1998 that have been disclosed rate only twenty-five as satisfactory or highly satisfactory, most of which are for middle—or upper-income countries (Appendix 4). Thirty-four country programs, most of which are for low-income countries that receive IDA funds, are rated "unsatisfactory" or "moderately unsatisfactory," with the remaining twenty-eight as "moderately satisfactory." Like Nigeria and Bangladesh, a large portion of the funds committed in the last five years to projects in most of the low-income countries remains unutilized. But we can be sure that all of them would continue to receive ever-growing IDA funds to meet lending targets despite the poor performance to date. It is not difficult to forecast that a large number of projects are headed toward failure.

19. Why Successful Projects Do Not Result in Successful Development?

Although the overall record of project success has been mixed, there are countries where at least a significant number of projects are assessed as having satisfactory development outcomes. Recall that for the thirty-year period, 1971-2000, the World Bank considers 71 percent of its projects to have had satisfactory implementation and 50 percent judged as sustainable. With this record, it would be reasonable to ask why the successful projects have not resulted in economic growth and poverty reduction in more than a handful of developing countries.

The World Bank has long recognized that appropriate development policies and institutions in the country are the most important ingredients for development. It considers projects to be simply instruments to achieve policy reform and institutional development.

Most projects include conditionality for policy reform that the bank considers necessary for the development of the sector. This could be, for example, assurance by the country that it will provide adequate funds for maintenance, change its policy of teacher transfers and postings, grant more autonomy in decision-making to the local governments, levy adequate charges for services, transform a power utility from a government department to a commercially oriented company, etc. Another form of conditionality is for things the World Bank considers as "best practice" based on the experiences of other countries, for example, commitment to set up a dedicated road fund funded from road users to finance the road program, or allowing private sector to participate in the provision of infrastructure services, ensuring greater voice for women, contracting out primary health care to NGOs, etc. In many cases, studies by consultants/experts are included in the project to thrash out a particular policy issue or sometimes simply as a way to postpone the decision because of client resistance.

Such policy reforms have been the recurring themes in all of the bank's work over the years, although the economic crisis of the late 1970s and 1980s shifted the bulk of the attention during this period on macroeconomic policies. The so-called Washington Consensus, with emphasis on fiscal and monetary policies, liberalization of trade and investment, and privatization at its core, became the main theme of policy reforms promoted by the bank. These reforms created much controversy, when it became clear that many countries had not been able to grow or reduce poverty despite having adopted the Washington Consensus policies. These criticisms led development economists to concede that the reform policies advocated under the rubric of the Washington Consensus were generally appropriate as "first generation" reforms, but these had to be followed by reforms of key institutions of development that are much more complex and difficult to implement. As Moisés Naim puts it, "Reforming countries were discovering that economic growth did not matter much to people if hospitals did not have medicines, and that a booming stock market could be highly dangerous if the domestic equivalent of the Securities and Exchange Commission was ineffectual. A competitive exchange rate could not do much to bolster exports if inefficiency and corruption paralyzed the ports, and fiscal reforms did not matter much if taxes could not be collected . . . [or] a reliable justice system, a well educated workforce and an efficient telecommunication infrastructure were some of the additional factors, among many others, that would give a country an edge in its effort to attract foreign investors. In short, it became apparent that stronger, and more effective institutions were urgently needed to complement macroeconomic policy reforms."[69]

Institution building has been at the center of virtually every project financed by the World Bank. Most developing countries, particularly the poorer ones, have weak institutions, and projects generally include two measures for institutional strengthening: "technical assistance," which is generally the services of foreign and local consultants to help develop one or more aspects of certain organizations relevant for the sector, and training to upgrade the capacity of civil servants to plan and implement development. These project components can account for as much as 30 percent of the total project cost in the poorer countries that also tend to have low institutional capacity. Estimates of total amount of funds provided cumulatively by the World Bank for institutional strengthening and capacity building run to more than $100 billion.[70]

Given the importance of good institutions for development, the significant emphasis on policy reforms and capacity building in the World Bank (and other donors') projects would seem reasonable. The problem is that it does not work. We have now known for some time that externally imposed conditionality invariably fails to bring about policy change, or when it does, it is not durable. The real policy change, as we saw in some of the more successful developing countries in Asia, is one that is home-grown, even when it may not the ideal that one would like to see. It should emerge from domestic consensus and be driven by strong leaders. Aid conditionality, howsoever well intentioned, simply does not promote such ownership. Most of the aid-dependent countries find it easier to simply accept donor conditionality even if they know full well that they stand little chance of implementing it. Unfortunately, aid donors, although aware of this reality, continue to push for reforms that they think are necessary, sometimes to satisfy their own interests and constituencies.

The same is true of technical assistance and training to build institutions. Numerous assessments by the World Bank itself confirm the dismal record of technical assistance for capacity building. Project performance data of IEG show that only 38 percent of the projects have a positive impact on institutional development, and less than 30 percent in Africa. The reason for the low success rate is simple: Capacity building and institutional change is a long and arduous process that requires perseverance, commitment, and leadership. Absent these factors, technical assistance would fail. A comprehensive assessment of the bank's capacity building efforts in Africa carried out by IEG points to the reasons, including, inter alia, poor designs, lack of expertise in capacity building, and inadequate quality control of the programs. It concludes that "the bank's traditional tools— technical assistance and training—have often proved ineffective in helping to build sustained public sector capacity."[71]

The truth of the matter is that despite more than fifty years of efforts trying to build capacity, we still do not, to this day, know the process by which institutions develop. As Naim puts it, "[I]nstitutional reform or institutional strengthening is a field with much action and little theory . . . (and) what passes for knowledge and institutional reforms is often nothing more than a series of partial findings with little capacity to provide universal prescriptions to guide efforts aimed at improving institutional performance in reforming countries. In fact, institutional weakness is not one specific illness but, like cancer, includes variety of maladies, each requiring different treatments." Unfortunately, the World Bank and other aid institutions have been throwing a lot of chemotherapy for institutional development with little success. The only thing I know for sure, based on the experience of successful countries, is that institutions develop slowly and over a long period of time. This is not different than what the developed countries also experienced. Home-grown solutions are critical. World Bank projects try in vain to compress these into the project time frame of five to seven years, something that is utterly unrealistic. The desire to see the project completed keeps all the energies focused narrowly on project-specific institutional issues, and the multiplicity of project goals means that the most difficult and the most important aspect of development is neglected. Not only this, but as noted in a previous chapter, the project efforts often drain whatever limited capacity that does exist. One World Bank report was frank enough to admit that "we do not understand fully how to help improve institutions and governance, especially in the poorest countries where the needs are greatest."[72]

I should also note here that technical assistance today is a major contributory factor to corruption in donor projects. In contrast with contracts for goods and services that can normally be assessed objectively, consulting service contract awards require significant subjective judgments. Project authorities often use this as a lever to extract funds or other favors from their preferred consultants. Lure of follow-on contracts also keeps the consultants on the hook. Developing countries will be much better served if the donors were to cut back significantly on the consulting services they provide. Unfortunately, the conjoining of the interest of the staff of project entities and that of consultants makes it very hard to break this link. World Bank staff too would resist this because they need foreign consultants to translate the complex bank requirements into concrete projects. In the end, despite statements to the contrary, the World Bank is judged by the volume of lending. A country-owned and country-prepared project would take too long and be too unreliable to allow it to meet its annual lending commitments that must show an upward trend.

To summarize, successful development requires putting in place good policies and institutions. Policies, however, can only be durable if they are owned and developed by the countries themselves and not imposed by donors. Similarly, developing durable institutions and capacity is a slow and long-term process that must be driven by the country adapted to their specific circumstances. Strong and sustained leadership is the key for both. Donors cannot accelerate these efforts by infusing large amounts of technical assistance. Indeed, donor projects can often detract from the effort that the country must make itself.

20. When Do Projects Succeed?

So far I have argued that the very nature of aid funded through projects is such that it is unlikely to succeed. It is impossible to reconcile the very intensive donor-driven project preparation and implementation process with the country-owned development that is essential for success. Aid projects are often disempowering rather than empowering. But it would be instructive to see why in some countries, few as they may be, projects succeed. The success rate, for example, in China has been in excess of 91 percent satisfactory and 85 percent sustainable, significantly better than the 74 percent satisfactory and a meager 47 percent sustainable in India, despite the fact that India has had much more experience with receiving foreign aid.

Table 20.1 provides for the same group of selected countries in Asia and Africa discussed earlier, thirty-year (1971-2000) economic growth and project performance. The well-performing countries, again defined as those that achieved at least an average of 2.5 percent per annum growth in GDP per capita in the period, are highlighted.

In general, countries that have performed well economically also tend to have better project outcomes, particularly so in the important dimension of sustainability. India is one outlier, probably explained by the fact that aid projects are generally implemented by the Indian states, which have a wide variation in the quality of governance and leadership, and the World Bank lending may have been tilted toward the less well-governed states that are also poorer. But otherwise, the conclusion seems to be clear: success breeds success. A country that is growing because of having its act together on development policies and programs is also likely to have successful outcomes of aid-funded projects.

Table 20.1: Growth and Project Performance in Selected Countries 1971-2000

	1971-2000 Avg. GDP Growth Rate (% p.a)	Project Outcomes	
		% Satisfactory	% Sustainable
Asia			
Bangladesh	0.7	67	31
China	7.1	91	85
Indonesia	4.2	81	54
India	2.5	74	47
Korea	6.0	90	81
Lao PDR	NA (<2%)	59	53
Malaysia	4.3	85	80
Nepal	1.5	64	38
Philippines	1.0	70	54
Sri Lanka	3.2	74	43
Thailand	4.6	84	64
Vietnam	NA(>2.5%)	100	67
Africa			
Botswana	7.3	83	83
Ethiopia	NA(<0%)	67	36
Ghana	-0.4	69	45
Kenya	1.1	38	23
Lesotho	2.8	70	65
Liberia	-4.6	50	0
Nigeria	0.2	42	18
Senegal	-0.5	70	37
Swaziland	2.9	88	100
Tanzania	NA (<0%)	53	37
Uganda	NA(<1%)	59	35
World Average		71	47

Source : World Development Indicators & IEG Database

There are two possible explanations for this. First, countries that are growing consistently generally have better leadership and steadily improving institutions. Thus they have better capability to implement projects. Second, these countries are generally not highly dependent on foreign aid. They thus have the ability to say no to donors when donor requirements conflict with their policies and priorities. Korea and China are two notable examples of successful donor management. Even in the 1970s, when Korea was just embarking on its long and successful development effort, it would only invite donor scrutiny of projects after its National Assembly had approved its annual borrowing program that listed very specific projects. This forced the donors to be much more disciplined as they were compelled to compress their long and tedious project approval cycle to one year. Korea also refused, always politely but firmly, to accept components of "institution building" and "policy reforms" that it considered unnecessary.

China followed the same process when it started borrowing in 1980. Every project that was put up for donor financing had to be approved by the State Planning Commission. China welcomed donor suggestions and ideas but ultimately decided what it considered best. For example, when the World Bank insisted that an intercity highway be four lane and not six lane that the Chinese considered necessary, it would award two separate contracts: a four-lane contract to be funded by the bank and adjacent to it a two-lane contract to the same contractor to be funded from its own budget. When it saw that the World Bank requirements for environment and resettlement would be a never-ending process for the proposed Three Gorges Dam, it decided to fund the project from its own resources even while continuing to draw on the World Bank's expertise and advice. Success allows the country to be in the driver seat and not be dictated to by donors. A few other countries have tried similar techniques for donor management, but unfortunately most lack the will or the capability to do so effectively.

The moral I drew from my experiences is that the World Bank is successful in countries that are successful and a failure in countries that are themselves failures. Our relationship was always excellent with the former and rocky with the latter. The lesson of this is that foreign aid should be targeted to those countries that indeed have a sustained track record of good policies and programs. Aid can be a catalyst, but it cannot pull countries that do not show the will or the ability to take charge of their own development. And that requires strong leadership within the country.

This conclusion, of course, poses a dilemma for the donors. The concern for aid effectiveness naturally leads us to conclude that aid should only be channeled to well-performing countries. But then how to reconcile this with the view that the "need" for foreign aid is the most in the poorest countries that have been left behind? The World Bank has tried to reconcile these two conflicting goals for allocating its soft IDA funds by adopting a performance-based aid allocation system whereby each country is scored on a composite index of twenty equally weighted criteria that attempt to measure the country's policies and institutions for economic management, structural policies, policies for social equity and inclusion, and quality of public sector and institutions. The composite index, referred to as the Country Performance and Institutional Assessment (CPIA) score is then factored along with the conventional income level cutoffs and past record of portfolio performance to arrive at the country's IDA resource allocation.

The performance-based allocation is a step in the right direction, but it does not go far enough. The CPIA scores embody the conventional World Bank approach of trying to predict the future based on a paper assessment of what it considers good policies and institutions, which suffers from its policy biases and preferences, rather than what a country considers to be appropriate. Each one of the twenty factors that comprise the CPIA is important for development, but no country that has been successful in development has dealt with all of these at once, as the composite CPIA score implies. The subjective nature of several of the components of CPIA also introduces the World Bank's biases about "good" policies and institutions, some of which tend to be based on the current fads and fashions of development. Some of the most successful developers in East Asia, who often followed their own unique policies and were led by dictators, would probably have scored low on CPIA. In the end, as I have suggested previously, it is good leadership that matters the most for promoting good policies and developing institutions. However, measuring good leadership is not so simple. In a paper I coauthored when the Millennium Challenge Corporation was created, I suggested that with the exception of countries dependent on extractive industries, the historical growth performance of a country sustained over a period of time is a more objective measure of policies, institutions, and leadership instead of the CPIA.[73] Ultimately, demonstrated performance in development is a much more defensible basis for allocating aid. This is a key feature of my recommendations for the future of the World Bank.

PART III.

Reinventing the World Bank

Introduction

Do we still need foreign aid? And, more specifically, do we still need the World Bank? These are the questions that have persisted from the earliest days of foreign aid. The debate continues to this day without any signs of a consensus emerging. Critics cite failing aid-funded projects and a lack of any correlation between foreign aid and growth to support their argument. Supporters cite the cases of several successful countries as evidence to support foreign aid.

Whichever side of the argument one takes, there is no denying the fact that there has been enormous progress by most developing countries in the last fifty years. The East Asian tiger economies virtually eliminated absolute poverty within a generation, and China now is well on its way to do the same. India finally changed course in 1991 in the face of a severe economic crisis from an inward to an outward-looking country and has been growing rapidly since then. The Malthusian predictions about India have now been replaced by glowing reports about it becoming an affluent society in one generation.[74] In much of Latin America, growth has finally resumed with the lingering negative effects of the debt crisis of the 1980s now behind it. Similarly, Eastern Europe and former Soviet Union countries have by and large completed their economic transformation to market economies, with many now integrated with Western Europe. Growth has resumed even in Sub-Saharan Africa, albeit unevenly, after having stagnated over much of the last century. Middle class is growing rapidly in many developing countries and fueling growth not just in their own countries but also in developed countries.

Overall, the developing world has gone from being predominantly poor and low income to predominantly middle-income. So whatever the argument about effectiveness, critics now can point to this dramatic change to argue that there is now no need for foreign aid or for aid institutions like the World Bank.

While recognizing the validity of the arguments, my view is that there is still a case for aid for a few selected circumstances (e.g. post-conflict reconstruction or emergency response to crises as is happening currently with the massive influx of refugees in Jordan and Lebanon) and the World Bank can be an effective coordinator of such assistance. But its most important role should be to facilitate flow of capital to developing countries. With its existing capital base of some $200 billion, the World Bank has the capacity to mobilize and channel significant resources for development. Developing countries, most of which at least now seem to be growing and joining the ranks of middle-income countries, need massive amounts of finance to meet their infrastructure needs. Even the successful developing countries that may not need financing for their normal development could need emergency financing to deal with spillover effects of financial crisis that have a tendency to spread across borders in a globalized world. The World Bank has a track record of being able to borrow significant funds from the world capital markets at very competitive rates, which it passes on to developing countries at very attractive terms.[75] The challenge is to make the transfer of resources more efficient and effective.

A second argument in favor of continued role for the World Bank is its enormous convening power and influence. Despite its weaknesses discussed earlier, it is arguably still the most competent of all the development institutions. It has assembled a number of well-qualified specialists—economists, agronomists, engineers, financial specialists, environmental specialists, etc.—in just about every aspect of development who can be a useful source of technical advice to developing countries, bringing to bear their global knowledge. Many developing countries, including the more advanced ones, welcome such knowledge transfer from global specialists. The challenge is to separate out such valuable expertise from the much larger numbers of "bean counters" that now populate the World Bank. This is a message one hears repeatedly from the World Bank's clients, particularly the more sophisticated and middle-income countries.

However, a case for continued aid from the World Bank needs to be accompanied by a radical change in the way it currently functions. The starting point should be the lessons we have learnt after fifty years of experience with development. Let us recapitulate these. First, aid cannot make development happen. Countries that have had a successful record of development so far are those that had strong and committed leadership that followed sound home-grown and owned economic and social development policies. It is precisely these successful developers that can make an effective use of foreign aid. The causality is not between successful foreign aid and development, but rather the other way around.

Second, the amount of foreign aid does not bear any relationship with the development of a country, but excessive foreign aid can actually retard development. Aid-dependent countries have generally not done well in achieving growth or poverty reduction. Aid can be a catalyst, but not a driver of development. The hard truth is that no amount of foreign aid can make development happen until and unless the country itself takes charge of its destiny.

Third, politicization of foreign aid and the emphasis both by the suppliers of aid funds and by many recipients on ever-increasing volumes of aid commitments as the indicator of success have contributed to reducing the effectiveness of the World Bank. There is ample evidence of aid being wasted in many countries in the absence of the right leadership that is committed to improving the welfare of its people. Need alone is not enough of a justification for providing aid.

Fourth, aid linked to projects has not been particularly successful. Besides having a poor record of success in the counties most in need of aid, isolated projects divorced from the countries' own development program drain away precious limited institutional capacity. And even when projects succeed at the micro level, there is no evidence that successful projects add up to good development outcome in terms of growth and poverty reduction.

Finally, there is little justification for "concessional" (meaning grants or subsidized) aid. Just like Muhammad Yunus postulated in the case of the poor, what developing countries need is *access* to finance not handouts. The World Bank should focus on providing access to finance from international capital markets rather than passing the hat around for unnecessary contributions from the rich countries that are themselves facing budget constraints.

These conclusions lead me to propose a different approach to aid from the World Bank that links funding to actual performance, jettisoning the current culture that implicitly rewards failure by providing more funding to the "more needy" countries. The bank would need a governance structure that is willing and able to make hard-headed decisions. It would also need a credible feedback loop that constantly assesses outcomes, identifies successes and failures, and indicates corrective measures that may be necessary for a country to receive continued aid.

The World Bank should also reconsider its project mode of financing and devise alternative ways that support country's own development plans and priorities, with the level of funding linked to past performance. I suggest providing support for the country's annual budget as the mechanism to do so.

Finally, the current size and scope of the World Bank would need to be reevaluated. The proposed approach of budget support would allow it to reduce its staffing significantly and focus it more sharply on the key development issues.

21. Strengthen Governance

The most critical element of reinventing the World Bank is to review and overhaul its governance structure and mechanisms. As presently constituted, it does not provide adequate oversight to its effectiveness as a development institution. Its governance structure is diffused over multiple objectives, many peripheral to its central mission, is often driven by narrow constituency interests rather than by the interest of the institution, and lacks coherence and consistency. It can be highly intrusive in areas that are best left to the management and very lax in other areas where it should be more diligent. The increasing political influences of recent years have further eroded the effectiveness of governance.

The governance structure of the World Bank comprises (1) a board of governors where each member country (currently 189 total) is represented by one of the economic ministers in the cabinet, normally the finance minister; and (2) an executive board of directors, currently consisting of twenty-five members, each nominated by a country or a group of countries, depending on their shareholding in the World Bank. Eight countries—the USA, UK, Japan, France, Germany, Russia, Saudi Arabia, and China—are represented on the executive board individually. The board of governors set the broad direction and limit themselves to only a few overarching issues. As such, they have a rather limited role in governance. The predominant oversight responsibility rests with the executive directors.

Each executive director represents a "constituency" of a single or group of countries and is nominated by them. Different countries view the appointment differently. Most tend to nominate a senior civil servant from one of the economic ministries, although a few, including the United States, nominate someone from the broader civil society. Nevertheless, since the executive directors report directly to one of the government ministries, they are for all practical purposes civil servants. Each executive director has an alternate executive director, also nominated by the countries represented. In constituencies of groups of countries, the executive directors or the alternates, or both, are rotated among the countries. The caliber of the appointees varies widely. Some countries treat it as an important position and nominate capable people, while others treat it as an end-service reward or a political favor. Most of the executive directors have a number of advisors and staff to help them perform their functions, and these positions too are used to balance representation among the group of countries in the constituency.

The executive directors are based full-time in the World Bank. They meet once or twice a week throughout the year, more frequently as the year progresses, with a few breaks for holidays. In between the formal board meetings, they meet in various committees and subcommittees of the board. They review and approve virtually every aspect of the World Bank's development activities, ranging from country strategies that are prepared every three to five years, strategy updates and progress reports, each individual project (although it has delegated some of it now to the bank management but while retaining its power to review), numerous economic and sector studies the bank carries out each year, policy papers on a variety of subjects, portfolio reports, internal evaluation reports, and so on. This is in addition to numerous other matters such as the World Bank's finances, personnel policies, research, external relations, etc. In addition, they routinely receive formal and informal briefings on matters big and small: status of discussions on IDA replenishment, administrative and process matters, agreements with other organizations, external relations, publication policy, arrangements for the forthcoming annual meeting, just to name a few.

In total, there are over two hundred staff members currently working with the executive directors supported by a budget allocation of about $300 million or roughly 10 percent of the entire administrative budget of the bank. This does not include the numerous other staff the bank employs to support the work of the executive directors.

All in all, the oversight is quite intrusive into the affairs of the World Bank. So why does it not work? The reasons are, first, the very manner in which the executive board is constituted and, second, the way it has chosen to function.

A board of directors is normally expected to make sure that the organization functions in such a way so as to maximize the shareholder interest while operating prudently. In the World Bank's case, everyone would agree that the interest of all shareholders—developed and developing countries alike—is growth and poverty alleviation in developing countries. In practice, however, this high-level objective is overtaken by individual country interests, which vary widely, from making sure that its contractors benefit from contracts funded by the World Bank, to having its nationals represented adequately among the World Bank staff and managers, to maximizing funding from the World Bank for its constituency, to ensuring that the views of legislators and other pressure groups from the country are reflected adequately, etc.

The directors from developing countries maintain solidarity of sorts with other developing countries and do not oppose any project or program that benefits a fellow developing country. The developed country representatives normally focus largely on issues such as "safeguards" that are pressed by their politicians or civil society members. The World Bank staff is quite attuned to such predilections of executive directors, or at least the ones representing an important country, and finds ways to dress up the documents appropriately on how every social and economic ill will be dealt with by the program being presented. A common saying among the bank staff was that if a project receives high praise in the board, we should mark it down as a potential problem project during implementation! Many of the mandates that have contributed to project failures discussed earlier have their origin in such attempts to please the executive directors, particularly from the developed countries.

The quality of deliberations is often shallow and full of platitudes. Most directors read prepared statements from their staff. Hard, penetrating questions are rare. There are hardly questions on why a country has been stagnating the last few years and what makes us think that it will do better in the future. Or why so many projects fail in the country and we are still planning to commit further large amounts? Or why so many projects are delayed and take more than ten years to complete? The goal is to make a statement and move on, generally voting in favor of all management proposals, be it the bank's strategy for a country or a lending project or a policy paper. The only rare occasions when the discussion becomes contentious is when there is a clear conflict with an important country's policy goal, as happened during the discussion about lending to Iran and, more recently, on lending for a large coal-fired project in South

Africa, or when faced with pressures from western pressure groups. But the general rule is to rubber-stamp everything that comes before it.

The second reason is the various processes the executive board has adopted over the years. By virtue of having assigned itself the responsibility of reviewing and approving everything, it receives an average of fifty to one-hundred documents a week. Some of these are substantive, often dealing with complex issues. Even with their large staff, it is virtually impossible for the executive directors to read, much less absorb, the documents they receive. It is not a surprise that they are unable to exercise much influence on anything. From time to time some executive directors complain about the excessive paperwork, as one (Per Kurowski, who represented a group of Latin American countries from 2002 to 2004) did in a memo he wrote in November 2003. He wrote, "[W]e are drowned in too many written and spoken words about too many topics so that our power, as a body, is completely diluted to such an extent that we could easily qualify as the most expensive rubber stamp in mankind history." Responding to the concern of the board at the time to increase the "voice" of underrepresented member countries, Kurowski went on to say, "It really doesn't matter if you are a Pavarotti if you have to sing in Madison Square Garden during a Knick's match . . . Because you will not be heard anyhow . . . Our Board's acoustics are so bad that . . . in reality, no one has a voice."[76]

The issue of paper overload at the board is exacerbated by the tendency of the bank staff and managers to themselves take the initiative and send papers to the board that have little relevance for broad bank policy. Having prepared a board paper is somehow considered to be a feather in the cap. The more sinister explanation is that it is a deliberate strategy long perfected by the bank management to make sure that the directors are kept overwhelmed. It raised quite an outrage among the board when one senior manager was reported to have said, "The board is like a mushroom farm. It is best to keep them in the dark and feed them garbage." But unfortunately it is not too far from the truth, although I suspect the practice has evolved and grown over the years without anyone stopping to question it, rather than by some evil design. The effect, nevertheless, is an inability of the board to exercise effective oversight.

One consequence of the weak governance is that the president of the bank is able to exercise substantial unchecked power in most matters that can have serious consequences. Much of the diffusion of the bank under Jim Wolfensohn was because of the executive directors' inability or unwillingness to question his numerous initiatives that I discussed previously. It was also surprising that the executive directors went along with Wolfensohn in overriding a long-standing practice of not allowing executive directors to be appointed as staff after completion of their service on the board. The sad episode of corruption by Paul Wolfowitz is largely because of the inability of the chair of the board's audit committee, Ad Melkert, to question Wolfowitz's outright fraudulent proposal to reward his girlfriend at the bank's expense. Melkert, instead, seemed busy trying to curry favor with him. What was even more surprising is the concessions Wolfowitz was able to demand before resigning despite the clear case of malfeasance. One wonders whether he would still have been at the bank had it not been for the open revolt by the bank staff.

Given the dismal state of affairs, it is tempting to recommend a far-reaching set of solutions such as having a nonresident board that meets periodically like normal corporate boards, not having all board members come from the government, or having elections for board members from among nominees, or even more dramatically, delinking the board members from their constituencies. Unfortunately, the realities of the world as it exists make it highly unlikely for such a drastic change. I suggest a few simple changes that, in my view, can improve the situation.

First, there should be a clearer demarcation of roles and responsibilities of executive directors. Their functions should only be twofold: set important policies and do retrospective reviews of its work. On the first aspect, it needs to be made clear that they need not entertain numerous papers that come to them in the guise of policy. Instead, they should clearly devote attention to important issues. A sharp curtailment in the volume of papers circulated to them would be a good indicator of whether this objective is being met. These should include a few annual reviews such as the current annual review of portfolio or an assessment of quality of lending, but it should also include some topical retrospective reviews done by the Independent Evaluation Group (IEG) that already reports to the executive directors. However, the independence of IEG from management should be further enhanced, as discussed later. The executive directors should not review any lending or non-lending operations, except as a part of the retrospective.

Second, the number of staff employed in the executive director offices should be curtailed sharply, probably to no more than one or two per constituency. It is a well-known axiom in bureaucracies that people create their own work that is not always necessary or useful. A smaller number of staff would also force discipline on not having thousands of papers circulated to them. In any event, the functions that the board takes on for itself should be determined by its own capacity rather than the other way around. A limit on numbers should discipline the board and curb its appetite for paper.

Third, all appointments of executive directors, alternate executive directors, advisors, and technical assistants should be for a fixed nonrenewable term with a ban on subsequent appointment to World Bank staff, closing the revolving door that has been gradually opened wider in the last several years.

Fourth, all proceedings of the board should be open to the public. This could be accomplished by accrediting a revolving list of five to ten representatives of the civil society as observers. In addition, minutes of all board meetings should be posted on the web shortly after each meeting. Shining light on the proceedings will bring a greater degree of seriousness in the discussion and create a more disciplined environment for the deliberations.

Taken together, these measures would go a long way to improve the functioning of the executive board and improve governance of the World Bank.

There have been periodic suggestions that one way to improve governance is to grant a larger voting power for developing countries, which is currently around 46 percent. Attractive as this proposition is on the surface, we must ask first how the developing countries choose to exercise the voting power they currently do have. The larger developing countries such as China, India, Brazil, and Mexico enjoy considerable leverage on the World Bank in relation to matters of direct concern to them by virtue of being large borrowers on whom the World Bank must depend to maintain its status as the premier development institution. What is needed is for these countries to exercise this leverage for the broader goal of making the World Bank a more effective development institution and resist the bank becoming an instrument of a few industrialized countries, notably the United States. Unfortunately, most of these larger countries seem content to pursue narrow parochial interests instead of trying to influence broader policies to any great extent.

The smaller and the poorer developing countries see themselves as largely in the business of getting as much funding from the bank as they can, notwithstanding its effectiveness. As such, they often opt to go along with whatever the bank proposes and consider it their duty to not question loans to other fellow developing countries. These countries will have much more "voice" in the bank if they were to insist on development effectiveness over the volume of loans both for themselves and for other developing countries. Opposing misguided donor-driven initiatives that are not appropriate for developing countries would empower them more than higher voting strength on paper.

So what is needed is not necessarily greater shareholding power for developing countries, although that would be welcome, but a willingness to use whatever power they do have.

The issue of greater voice for developing countries has been on the agenda of numerous meetings over the last ten or twenty years. The discussion was most intense in the 2002 meetings on aid held in Monterey, Mexico. The meeting concluded by asking the World Bank to develop specific proposals to achieve this objective. What emerged was nothing short of humorous. After some study, the World Bank concluded that the reason the developing countries, particularly the smaller countries in Africa, did not have an adequate voice was that they lacked the capacity to analyze and follow the World Bank processes. It proposed to address this issue through a "voice secondment program," whereby a group of twenty-five to thirty civil servants from various developing countries nominated by the respective executive director representing the country would be invited to spend a year in the World Bank learning its operations. A significant budget was allocated to meet the expenses of the program through contingency funds of the board. Some five years later, I and another retired senior colleague were asked to evaluate the program to see if and how it should be continued. Our findings were that the program had indeed been most welcomed by the participants and the executive directors, but that it had little impact in terms of the stated objective of giving more voice to developing countries. All it had done was to give a nice gift of training to one or at the most two persons in the country, who often transferred to better jobs in the government on returning home, or even when they stayed, could not possibly add much to the capacity because they were often relatively junior and/or were just one person among the group managing the country's relations with the bank.

We concluded that the program was based on a false premise that could possibly not accomplish its stated goals and recommended that it be discontinued. Our recommendations were opposed by the World Bank staff administering the program, who had found the job of interacting with people from world over as personally rewarding. When we presented our findings to the audit committee of the board on whose behest the review was done, we were given a polite hearing, but there was no desire to see any changes. The developing country executive directors were content to have the patronage power the program provided them, and the developed country directors were happy that the issue of voice has been diffused for a few years at a bargain price of a few million dollars!

22. Transparent Qualification-driven Process for Selection of President

As would be clear from the description of my various experiences, the president of the bank wields considerable power and, as a result, has significant ability to influence the direction of the bank. For the first twenty years, the bank was fortunate to have men (no women have served so far) who were appointed after having led major organizations in the private sector. Thus they brought proven managerial capabilities. In addition, they were mostly men who had taken the job as a call to public service after successful careers in the private sector. They were essentially apolitical and took the bank's mandate of not being influenced by political considerations seriously.[77]

However, all this began to change with the appointment of Jim Wolfensohn in 1995 and his three successors, Paul Wolfowitz (2005-2007), Robert Zoellick (2007-2012), and Jim Kim (20012-present). None of them had much prior executive experience. None had ever led a large organization. All three, but particularly Wolfowitz and Zoellick, were overtly political. All four have had mixed records as presidents.

The bank's president is appointed by the president of the United States but with the approval of the World Bank Board. Unfortunately, the board has not exercised its approval function credibly by effectively rubber-stamping whoever the United States nominates. This needs to change. The executive directors should establish clear qualification criteria and expect that the United States would make sure that the candidate they propose meets it. The most important criteria, besides a strong interest in development, on the basis of my years of experience, are (1) a successful track record of having led a large organization in public, private, or nonprofit sector; and (2) a lack of strong connections with the party of the president nominating the candidate, with a strong presumption that the person would not have served in the U.S. administration. Some would suggest expertise in development as an important criterion, but to me this is secondary. What the World Bank needs more than anything else is a proven leader. Once the criteria are established and publicized, the executive directors should make sure that their review process is transparent and forthright. They should be under no compulsion to accept a candidate who in their view does not meet the selection criteria.

One proposition that is commonly advanced these days is that the practice of always having an American as the president of the World Bank should be discontinued and the next appointment should be given to a non-American. I would argue that this is not the most critical issue in the selection of the president, nor is it the one that would necessarily result in an improvement. There is little to suggest that a non-American will be any less susceptible to American influence than an American—witness the experience of the UN secretary general and heads of several specialized UN agencies who are non-Americans. As previously discussed, many Americans have served in the position admirably and maintained significant independence, a tradition broken only since 1995. So the real priority is to fix a broken selection process.

Another point to keep in mind is that a mere change in nationality will not change the basic reality of the fact that the World Bank will always have to be responsive to some extent to the United States as its largest shareholder. Its location in Washington DC makes it particularly susceptible to the American politics. An American president has a cultural advantage of dealing with such pressures. What is more important is how the rest of the countries choose to exercise their rights in the process and not be a rubber stamp to whomever the United States proposes.

23. Increased Autonomy of Independent Evaluation Group

A major objective of strengthening the governance of the bank would be to shift the focus from mere volume of lending to development outcomes. This would require a constant feedback loop between what the bank tries to do and the results on the ground that then should provide the basis for corrective actions. As the East Asia experience has amply demonstrated, the theory of development is broadly accepted but also relatively limited. Each country's situation is unique, and development practitioners must adapt their approaches to specific circumstances of the country. There is much room for trial and error and learning by doing. Thus, in order for the World Bank to move toward an outcome-based approach to its lending, as I would argue, it needs a strong independent evaluation function as an integral part of its strengthened governance—a system that constantly asks the following hard questions: Are the interventions actually getting a country any closer to the goal of growth and poverty alleviation? What should we be doing different? How do we make sure that we do not get so much enamored by our own contraptions that we forget the real goal of development?

The World Bank is to be commended for having established an independent evaluation function more than forty years ago. Originally called the Operations Evaluation Department, or OED, the name was changed to the Independent Evaluation Group, or IEG, in 2006 to emphasize its independent role from the bank management. IEG oversees self-assessment by the World Bank staff of all completed projects, conducts in-depth evaluation of a sample of completed projects to calibrate the self-assessment, carries out assessments of the overall country programs over a number of years, conducts periodic review of major sectors of the World Bank activities, and carries out ad hoc assessments as requested by the board or management. It also prepares an annual review of development effectiveness (ARDE) each year, which was originally meant to report on the outcomes of the bank-funded loans and technical assistance but was broadened in the late 1990s to report on development progress more generally.

The head of IEG, the director general, is appointed by the board and reports to it, and has the rank of senior vice president, a two-step upgrading from the head of the old OED. The other IEG managers and staff are generally drawn from the World Bank for assignments of a few years before they either return to the World Bank or retire. In the last five years, IEG has hired many more staff from the outside, but there is a constant tension between inside knowledge and connection vs. evaluation experience.

IEG generally enjoys a good reputation among other development institutions, and many of them have modeled their evaluation groups on IEG. Its reviews tend to be generally well-researched and competent. Consistent with the general trend toward more openness, most of the IEG reports are now disclosed publicly, although after they have been vetted internally by the bank management and cleared by the executive directors for external dissemination, with the executive directors reserving the right to withhold disclosure.

Despite the official status of IEG as an independent group, in practice there are questions about the extent of its independence. It often produces valuable analysis of issues, but its findings are diluted as it goes through various internal reviews. Indeed, all IEG reports go through an extensive vetting process by the bank managers before they are even sent to the board. As can be expected, there are frequent disagreements that are resolved through negotiations of ratings or wordings of the critical findings. The Nigeria country assessment that I mentioned earlier went from being "unsatisfactory" at the draft stage to "moderately unsatisfactory" when the newly appointed vice president for Africa, who happened to have previously been a cabinet minister in Nigeria during the period under review, objected vehemently. The extensive negotiations also produced language that although rated "moderately unsatisfactory," had a gloss put over the stark finding by including the following caveat: "[i]n the Nigerian context this reflects an improving trend relative to a previous IEG assessment of the 2000 to 2004 period, which rated the outcome of Bank assistance as unsatisfactory." IEG's excellent report assessing the capacity building efforts in Africa that concluded what had already been widely known in the bank that these efforts were largely ineffective nevertheless goes on to add, "[but]recent country strategies for Africa do a better job of addressing the criticism."

In some instances, IEG has become a cheerleader for initiatives taken by the bank presidents. I earlier mentioned IEG reports immediately declaring progress toward meeting strategic compact goal of 75 percent satisfactory outcomes, full ten years before the fruits of the "new and better" processes under the strategic compact could possibly have been felt. IEG's review of the strategic compact was similarly soft-pedaled, when everyone knew that it had been a failure.

IEG also sometimes withholds or delays public disclosure of its reports in response to the bank management or board concerns about the disclosure, causing harm to the bank or to the bank's relations with a particular country. IEG does not disclose when a particular report is withheld or delayed from disclosure.

So in practice, IEG is not as independent in its work as one would be led to believe. Its independence is tempered by the close links it maintains with the bank. Although the head of IEG is appointed by the executive directors, she or he is in reality nominated by the president of the bank, both for the initial appointment and for subsequent renewal of term, with perfunctory approval by the executive directors. Thus, it is the president of the bank who exercises the real authority for appointment and renewal, and it should not be surprising that he is likely to nominate someone who will not be "too independent."

The staffing of IEG presents an even bigger issue. Almost all the managers and staff aspire to return to the bank on reassignment or promotion.[78] Even the outside appointees see themselves longer-term as working in the bank than in IEG, given the limited scope of advancement within the evaluation work. This acts as a restrain on their independence in the face of the inevitable opposition from the bank managers to any criticisms.

The bank management has steadfastly resisted the idea of giving more autonomy to IEG, continuing to believe that the present arrangements work well. The Meltzer Commission, set up by the U.S. Congress to examine the workings of the international financial institutions (IMF, the World Bank, and the regional development banks) in 1999, was the first one to question the objectivity of IEG (then OED) because of its lack of real independence.[79] However, there was little follow-up to the report because of partisan divisions within the commission members that resulted in a split vote on the recommendations. When Adam Lerrick, a member of the Meltzer Commission, persisted in a letter to the *Financial Times* on March 6, 2002, questioning the independence of OED and suggesting an independent audit of the bank's activities, Peter Stek, an executive director from the Netherlands and the chair of the Board Committee of Development Effectiveness (CODE) wrote a rebuttal that CODE was actively monitoring OED, only implicitly rebutting the charge of lack of OED's independence.[80] The issue has been largely dormant since then.

The record of IEG, in my view, does not support the confidence that Stek showed. From my own experiences, far from being active, CODE meetings are very passive with rarely much real debate and generally endorsing whatever joint position IEG and the bank management put forward.[81] This is in part because of the general weakness in the bank's governance, discussed earlier. In addition, many board members still view their job as protecting the bank from external criticisms, which no doubt at times has been vicious and unjustified. Nevertheless, I believe that IEG's work will be enhanced and more valuable if it were to be truly independent and seen by everyone as such. Indeed, the Gurria-Volker Commission, whose overall conclusions were much more supportive and friendly to the bank, also called for more independence for IEG.[82]

There are three steps that would enhance IEG's independence. First, the head of IEG should be appointed through an open competition that is managed entirely by an outside group that assists the board. The bank management should have no role in the process. Moreover, the term of the head should be fixed at five years with no opportunity for renewal. Second, all managers in IEG should become ineligible for reassignment back to the bank, or when they are appointed from the outside, they should serve no more than two fixed terms of five years each, without the possibility of reappointment in the bank. Third, IEG should issue its reports directly to the board without going through prior vetting by the bank management. They should also be disclosed publicly at the same time, without any exception. The discussion at the board (or in CODE) should be the opportunity for the bank management and the board members to offer their views, and whether they agree with the analysis and recommendations. The conclusions of the discussion should also be disclosed immediately after the meeting. Even when the executive directors or the bank management disagree with IEG findings, the public should know what the evaluators recommended and the reasons why the recommendations were not accepted or accepted with modifications.

Overall, the need to have a true evaluation function that has the standing and credibility externally by virtue of its caliber of management and staff and the true independence it enjoys.

There is one additional change that IEG should make. Most of its reports often have a long gestation, two years or more from the time an issue is identified to when the report is issued. Some of this time is necessary and justified in order to be sure that the analysis is sound. But a significant amount of time is spent in IEG's formalistic processes of task initiation and various internal reviews and clearances. IEG needs to find ways to shorten its assessment cycle so that its findings can be used to shed light on some of the issues in real time and thus have a better chance of being implemented.

The issue of IEG independence is ultimately linked with the broader question of the bank's governance discussed in the last chapter. The board of directors would need to understand that learning from experience is an important part of understanding what actually works in specific situations and not simply a mechanism for holding people accountable. It will need to shed its own aversion to any criticisms that many times force even the members of CODE to soft-pedal IEG's findings. The record of CODE discussions that is appended to the major IEG reports when they are disclosed to the public is invariably full of platitudes such as the subcommittee "welcomed the report" and its "clarity, comprehensiveness, and candor," "were pleased with the greater emphasis to XYZ," that "efforts should be redoubled," there was "some room for improvement," and "the issue will continue to require careful attention." It is no surprise that IEG reports are soon forgotten after they are issued, with rare instances of serious follow-up. I am aware of very few instances where IEG's work has led to a major change in the bank policy.

24. Performance-Based Budget Support Instead of Project Lending

The traditional mode of providing funding for discrete projects should be replaced by annual or bi-annual support of the country's budget, with the amount of funding determined by the country's absorptive capacity and its development performance. This would result in a sharper focus on the country's own development efforts and direct the bank's assistance on these rather than on projects isolated from the country's own development agenda.

The principal goal of aid should be to support the existing institutions responsible for the planning and implementation of the country's own development agenda. The annual budget is the key instrument to set expenditure priorities and to introduce policy changes. It tells you the direction the country's decision-makers are taking the country. It indicates the priority the country gives to issues such as education, health, social programs, etc., as reflected in the programs and projects the country's government and legislators choose to include in the budget. It indicates the government's revealed choices between different categories of expenditures, including recurrent and capital expenditures. I believe that funding from the World Bank (and other donors) would be much more effective if it were integrated with the annual budget cycle and planned and implemented as a part of the government's overall development program without imposing any requirements that do not also apply to the overall public expenditure. Loans from the World Bank should be made to supplement the budget. The entire energy and focus of the government and the World Bank would be on the budget as a whole instead of "donor projects."

Under such an approach, the quantum of financing for each country would be based on an annual or bi-annual review of the country's development efforts by the World Bank (jointly with other donors that may wish to work in concert with the bank), in addition to the normal considerations of the size of the economy, the country's creditworthiness, and the country's own resource mobilization efforts. The review would focus on assessing the three important pillars of development: growth, poverty reduction, and environmental management. The focus of the review would not be on plans and promises for the future as most World Bank lending is presently predicated on. Rather, the focus would be on the actual record of performance, with sustained economic growth being the key anchor of assurance of the country's prospects. These assessments would then be used to suggest the appropriate level of financing that the World Bank would provide to supplement the budget in the next one or two years. There would be no need for conditionality since the level of financing would be related to actual actions and achievements rather than on promises for the future. The timing of the reviews would be synchronized with the budget cycle of the country so that it can incorporate the finding in its budget planning. The funding would not be linked to any particular program or project, except to the extent these are financed implicitly by being included in the budget. The reviews would be done transparently with full disclosure to the public.

There would be no project lending in the country with the exception of a large transformational project as a rare exception. So the World Bank's economic and sector expertise would be fully harnessed to carrying out the above-mentioned development reviews and in providing technical assistance to countries in response to specific needs, instead of being spent largely on appraising and monitoring projects. The countries would have predictable levels of financing that would generally not vary dramatically from one year to the next. Issues such as procurement, environmental management, social development, and corruption would benefit from advice and technical assistance from qualified specialists, who are currently engaged to a large extent in project monitoring. Major issues in any of these areas would impact the quantum of financing, or even lead to withholding of financing if, for example, a government is assessed as being too corrupt, rather than being addressed for each individual project without. With a focus on overall development effort of the country as a part of the development reviews, their efforts would be much more effective than the current approach of focusing on numerous discrete project-specific issues. Overall, I believe the approach would have a much broader and durable development impact in countries that are pursuing a serious development agenda and have a track record of progress.

Budget support can also be at the state level in the larger countries with a federal structure, the metropolitan city level for the very large mega cities, or even at the entity level for the very large entities. However, the additional levels of government or entities should be chosen judiciously with an eye to avoiding proliferation and once again going back to, in essence, supporting discrete projects. The option should be reserved for only levels of government or entities that have large budgets, and mostly in the larger countries.

The approach would force greater discipline on the bank. The public disclosure of the reviews and the link they would have with the amount of lending would force the bank staff to be on solid grounds professionally. There would be less tolerance for the current hit-and-miss quality of a lot of the bank's analytical work. The need to synchronize with the budget cycle would also force a time discipline on the work that is currently missing in the large number of studies that the World Bank currently carries out as a part of its "non-lending services." There would be a standard approach to the assessments that would make cross-country comparisons more meaningful.

The proposed approach would free the truly experienced professionals in the bank—the educators, public health specialists, environmental engineers, ecologists, power engineers, transport planners—to concentrate on substantive issues of development rather than on the mundane aspects of project management that currently occupies most of their time. They will be serving as the true "knowledge bank" that the bank aspires to be.

The budget support loans would reduce the administrative burden on the bank and the clients alike. Instead of preparing numerous project loans for each country, there would be one loan each year (or every two years for the smaller countries). It would force the harmonization of donor requirements with those of the country, something that has been recognized as critical by every donor and has been the subject of numerous international meetings for decades but without concrete results. The World Bank, and other donors if they follow suit, would be forced to follow the excellent principle of the so-called Paris Declaration[83] to promote donor harmonization that has remained a hollow promise despite the good intentions. For its part, the World Bank would achieve significant savings in administrative cost by focusing on a much smaller number of budget support loans than the more than two to three thousand projects it is engaged in preparing and about five thousand in monitoring at any given time.

The idea of providing aid in the form of budget support is not new, and the World Bank has been increasingly using this instrument in recent years in many countries. The structural adjustment loans of years past, now rechristened as development policy loans (DPLs), in essence provide additional funding for the country's budget. In practice, their effectiveness has been limited for a number of reasons. First, the main focus of structural adjustment lending, and now DPLs, continues to be to achieving policy reform through conditionality. The failure of conditionality to achieve reforms is well known by now. Reforms are durable when they are fully owned by the country and led by its leaders, and the very concept of conditionality conflicts with this prerequisite howsoever window dressing the bank may do through "participatory consultations." In addition, as Harvard economist Dani Rodrik argues, there is a wide room around the standard prescriptions, including the sequencing of reforms that is unfortunately ignored in the neoclassic prescriptions that typically underlie structural adjustment conditionality. Finally, development requires a sustained effort in building institutions, something that is underappreciated in the prescriptive policy reform conditionality.

The budget support loans would not be based on any predetermined path of policy reforms. The focus would be on assessing the country's leadership, programs, and policies in relation to its actual development performance. The better-performing countries would be eligible for more funding, and the moderately performing countries less funding. There would be no funding provided to poor performers. This will represent a major paradigm shift in development thinking, which is currently based on the faulty assumption that donor funding can turn around poorly performing countries through money and conditionality. Budget support loans would require hardheaded analysis.

Second, DPLs are often employed by the bank as a quicker and easier way to transfer large amounts of aid funds to a country, which would be difficult to do with the traditional project lending. The bank economists can formulate a DPL for hundreds of millions of dollars in two or three months sitting in the offices of planning and finance ministries. Thus, budget support has been used generally as an instrument of convenience than a strategic tool of development.

Third, DPLs tend to be sporadic depending on when the bank and the country have an agreed reform agenda. Budget support loans, on the other hand, would be on fixed annual or bi-annual cycles linked with the budget process of the country. This would allow economic planners in the country to know the resource envelopes in which they are working, and that would not be expected to change abruptly from one year to the next. This predictability of funding would improve the effective utilization of aid funds.

Finally, the bank fundamentally remains a project lending institution, with budget support being only an adjunct. Project lending continues to drive its development thinking and that of its clients. Budget support requires very different skill set and approaches, which would develop only if budget support was its only mode of operation.

There have been a few studies on the effectiveness of budget support, the most important being a three-year study commissioned by a consortium of donors in 2003.[84] Although noting some weaknesses, the study generally found positive outcomes when aid is channeled in the form of budget support. Nevertheless, most donors and even many recipient countries remain resistant to this approach. The main argument from the donors tends to be that there is weak capacity in the country and thus providing aid funds not tied to specific goods and services for particular projects would lead to corruption. Ironically, it is the donor intention, often unfulfilled in reality, to move large amounts of aid funds quickly that is at the heart of the problem. As discussed earlier, the classical donor approach of resorting to numerous consulting services and specialized project implementation units for each project to make up for the weak government capacity has proven ineffective and expensive in project after project. More important, the intended project beneficiaries receive only a fraction of the aid funds that were ostensibly meant to reach them, as consulting services can often account for 20-30 percent of the project cost in many World Bank projects, and even higher in bilateral projects (70 percent as we saw for USAID-funded projects in the health sector in Afghanistan).

This is a classical chicken and egg story. As I have discussed earlier, capacity building is a slow process that is best done through learning by doing. It would be better to provide a smaller volume of aid funds consistent with the capacity and then increase the volume gradually as capacity builds up. This would be a better approach even in the most capacity-constrained countries, including those recovering from conflict.

There is also a psychological barrier donors face. Most of their staff like the visibility of a project that has the donor flag attached to it. Donor staff loves the ribbon-cutting opportunities. Supporting the budget would dilute or eliminate such opportunities. The population will not be able to distinguish donor funds from the government's own funds. But then this is what development should be about: having the government delivering and seen to be delivering for its people.

Some donors also argue that since many of the poorly performing countries are likely to be from among the poorest countries, a performance-based allocation along these lines would deprive these countries of aid funding. This argument, however, rests on the belief that aid can transform failing countries, which has proven to be a false premise in the fifty-year history of aid. Giving aid to such countries may feel good, but the hard reality is that it will not matter. Aid donors need to continue to hammer the message of the country being the driver of development and not aid.

Similarly, there are several reasons —some valid, but most self-serving—for resistance to budget support among the recipient countries. Like in donor countries, there are also strong constituencies and vested interests in the recipient countries that have been built up over the years who benefit from discrete donor projects. In some cases, it is for a good reason because they find the donor systems much simpler than their own national systems, but equally because donor projects allow a sector ministry to not have to compete with other budget priorities. Also as mentioned previously, there are people in the country who also benefit personally from projects either from the extra perks they enjoy or from the opportunities for corruption in procurement decisions, particularly for consulting services. During my tenure, I would often have project authorities prolonging the project unnecessarily and arguing for follow-on projects because they did not want to see an end to the project structures that allowed them much better salaries and perks than working in a government-funded program.

Whatever the reservations among the donors or the recipients, budget support is the direction aid has to move toward if it is truly to be in support of the country's development agenda.

Moreover, project aid as it has evolved offers little prospect for being effective. The World Bank should lead the way toward the much needed shift from project aid to budget support.

The only exception to budget support should be for the very large infrastructure projects. These are precisely the projects where the full range of project evaluation techniques, including the stringent safeguard policies, is relevant. There are several examples of such projects where the bank's role has been important: the Nam Theun Hydroelectric Project, which allows export of electricity from Laos to Thailand ($1.5 billion, approved 2006); the Jamuna Bridge Project in Bangladesh, which provides a vital connection across the Brahmaputra River ($750 million, approved 1994); the private sector-financed Bujagali Hydroelectric Project in Uganda ($582 million, approved 2001); more recently, the South Africa Coal Power Project ($10 billion, approved 2010); the (aborted) second bridge over Brahmaputra River in Bangladesh ($2.5 billion); and a major freight railways corridor project in India ($4.2 billion, approved 2011). Although in the early years of development thinking, most donors shied away from such projects because of the view that they had poor economics (because of large and lumpy costs up-front while benefits materialized over many years in the future), or poor public finances in most developing countries raising questions about their ability to afford large projects, or concerns about such projects displacing other vital investments in the social sectors, there is now a realization that such large projects if done properly can have a transformational impact on the country that is pursuing sound growth policies. The bank has a comparative advantage in such projects and is well positioned to help developing countries.

However, it would be important to keep a very tight grip on circumstances under which such projects are financed and resist pressures from the bank staff and clients to once again open up the project lending tap for the more routine project. A minimum project size in relation to the size of the economy will need to be established. I would expect that there would be no more than 50 such projects per year financed by the bank.

25. A Leaner Bank as the True Knowledge Bank

When I joined the World Bank in 1971, the total staff was around six hundred, which was housed in three small buildings. Today, its staff strength is more than fifteen thousand (including countless persons who work full-time as consultants), housed in buildings spread over several city blocks and in most countries around the world. Some of the growth is a direct result of the expansion of the World Bank lending, which grew from $2.5 billion for 129 projects in 1971 to about $50 billion for nearly 300 projects in 2015.[85] Another reason for the growth in staff is the increase in the number of its member countries (from 116 in 1971 to 189 today). But a significant part of the staff increase has been since the mid-1990s with the expansion of the bank's focus into newer areas. In particular, the greater focus on the additional "fiduciary aspects" related to social assessment and anticorruption required a large increase in staff for more rigorous monitoring of projects. Consequently, there has been an explosion of the administrative budget ($1.3 billion in 1997 to about $3 billion today).

This staff expansion has, unfortunately, not meant better quality of advice to developing countries. In fact, country clients havee been increasingly complaining about the deterioration in staff quality and consequently the quality of advice they get. In response to such complaints, particularly from the middle-income countries that themselves have by now developed much greater expertise and thus have even greater expectations from the bank staff, the bank has been looking at ways to address the problem. In a study I was commissioned to undertake in 2008 of staff quality in three of the bank's major sectors—energy, transport, and water—my conclusion was that less than a third of the staff have the skills and experience to be considered high-level specialists in their field. I also concluded that much of the dilution in staff quality can be attributed to the growing number of staff who are hired to meet the bank's growing internal requirements, including fiduciary monitoring and other bureaucratic requirements that are not valued by the clients. This contradicts the notion of a "knowledge bank" that the bank sees itself as.

It is difficult to envisage a bank of fifteen thousand staff as a center of excellence that the developing countries desire. It is simply not possible to attract and retain real experts in such large numbers. Also it is well known inside the bank that the large number of staff has resulted in an exponential growth in bureaucracy. Most specialists find themselves burdened by the internal processing requirements and complain about not having sufficient time to devote to substantive work of helping clients.

The move away from project lending provides an opportunity to get back to the original concept of the bank being primarily in the business of giving technical advice, lending being only a vehicle to deliver advice. The sharp reduction in the number of projects (from some 350 per year today to less than 50) would require a lot fewer staff. My rough guess is that the number will be no more than a third of the present strength.

Overall, I believe a smaller bank will not only save valuable budgetary resources, but will also be much more effective in meeting the real development needs of developing countries. It will result in a smaller footprint of the bank in the developing countries and allow room for "country-owned" development that is often talked about by donors but never practiced.

26. Implementing Reforms: Needed a 'Disrupter'

Confident though I am about my recommendations, I am not at all sanguine about whether any of these will ever be implemented. There have been numerous reviews over the years, including the most recent one by the Center for Global Development that brought together some 20 influential leaders and development thinkers. Their report,[86] like the reports of most other commissions, recommends largely a shuffling of the deck that, in my view, is mere tinkering around the edges. Witness their first major recommendation: change the formal name of the World Bank from "International Bank for Reconstruction and Development" to "International Bank for Sustainable Development"! Like their predecessor reports, this report will have a limited shelf-life among academics and the insiders in the aid community, but little will change.

Why do I think so? It is because there are by now so many vested interests and views that almost no one seems to be willing to start from the basic question: why do we need foreign aid in this vastly changed so-called developing world? Or, if aid is still needed for whatever purpose and in what form? The recommendations emerging from most reviews of foreign aid that are undertaken periodically by and large assume that the aid architecture as it exists will continue and changes can only be made at the margins. Perhaps the reviewers try to be realists. But most often, it is simply inertia. As the old adage goes, no bureaucracy ever dies, particularly one that has multitudes of widely differing interests.

The change in status quo would require a strong stakeholder that is clear-headed about the objectives and willing to think in the proverbial 'outside the box.' In the hay day of aid, the United States was the only major shareholder that had the will and ability to take an interest in the World Bank. It exercised strong leadership in shaping the bank in its early stages, and demanded strong financial prudence that would be recognized and respected by the financial markets. Later, it took a keen interest in moving its orientation towards poverty alleviation and in the 1980s on much-needed structural reforms. Unfortunately, now the main interest of the United States seems to be to make sure that the bank continues to be headed by an American who, in turn, makes sure that the bank continues to lend to countries like Pakistan, Palestine and Egypt that it considers to be of strategic interest, or to help re-build countries like Afghanistan and Iraq that it was responsible for destroying in the first place. So like most other shareholders, it has become a shareholder with a narrow parochial interest.

Unfortunately, there is no other country that has shown the will or the ability to be proactive in demanding reforms. The Europeans have always been subservient to the Americans and have shown little need or inclination to challenge the United States. China and India, two emerging powers from the South, have given up on their ability to reform the bank, preferring now to set up their own parallel development banks – the Asian Infrastructure Bank, and the BRICS Bank.

In my view, the United States is still the only country that has, despite its diminished shareholding in the bank, the capacity to lead the change. But some would ask why should it divert itself into what would seem like an issue of peripheral importance to it. I can cite at least two reasons to make the case. First, there are opportunities for budget savings. While I think there is a compelling case for the bank to continue to leverage its capital to mobilize resources for supporting development, there is no need now to have donors contribute to its soft window other than for very limited and specific purposes. And there is definitely potential for budget savings by reducing or even eliminating the vast array of bilateral aid programs.

Second, the growth in the middle class over the last thirty years is one of the primary reasons for fuelling growth not just in developing countries but also in industrialized countries. Indeed, a recent study by my old colleague Homi Kharas, previously Chief Economist for Asia in the World Bank and now at Brookings, shows that the bulk of the growth of middle class in recent years has been in developing countries, particularly in Asia, with only modest growth in industrialized countries. And he predicts this trend to hold for the foreseeable future. So to the extent World Bank can channel market funds to the successful developing countries to support their growth, it will be good for the United States and Europe as well.

Perhaps the current change in the United States administration, with a recognized 'disrupter' as its head, will bring some new thinking on foreign aid more generally.

Appendix 1: World Bank Project Outcomes: The Lowest 40 Performers

Country	No. Projects	Outcome % Satisfactory	Sustainability % Likely
Angola	6	50.0	0.0
Liberia	32	53.1	0.0
Belarus	3	66.7	0.0
Uzbekistan	2	0.0	0.0
Iran	19	73.7	0.0
Lebanon	4	50.0	0.0
Syria	18	45.3	0.0
Dem Rep Congo	61	28.5	5.1
Haiti	32	51.0	5.2
Guinea-Bissau	17	70.6	6.9
Sierra Leone	17	52.9	7.7
Comoros	11	45.5	9.1
Central African	23	39.1	10.1
Sudan	18	55.6	11.1
Somalia	38	48.7	11.4
Republic of Congo	18	33.3	12.3
Sao Tome	6	66.7	16.7
Nigeria	89	51.7	17.5
Zambia	58	56.9	19.4
Burundi	43	67.4	19.8
Moldova	5	60.0	20.0
Cameroon	60	58.3	20.8
Fiji	12	83.3	22.2
Kenya	110	49.1	23.2
Panama	30	56.7	23.3
Venezuela	19	48.4	24.6
Equatorial Guinea	9	22.2	25.0
Vanuatu	4	25.0	25.0
Yugoslavia	79	78.9	26.7
Niger	37	62.2	27.2
Samoa	8	75.0	28.6
Algeria	53	49.2	28.6
Malawi	63	64.7	28.8
Rwanda	38	50.0	29.4
Cote d'Ivoire	68	67.6	29.8
Bangladesh	89	71.8	31.0
Honduras	41	80.5	31.2
Togo	36	50.0	31.6
Guatemala	22	77.3	32.4
Gabon	9	55.6	33.3
Yemen	98	73.2	33.8

Source: IEG Project Evaluation Database

Appendix 2: World Bank Loans to Africa FY 1971-2015

Country	1971-2004		2005-2015	
	No. of Projects	Commitment Amount ($ million)	No. of Projects	Commitment Amount ($ million)
Angola	17	416	11	1,262
Benin	60	817	46	1,178
Botswana	0	0	32	912
Burkina Faso	61	1,661	67	2,518
Burundi	83	1,982	98	3,366
Cabo Verde	20	203	18	224
Cameroon	72	2,515	33	1,168
Central African Republic	26	440	32	356
Chad	49	1,029	17	261
Comoros	23	134	16	51
Congo, Democratic Republic of	76	3,038	55	3,204
Congo, Republic of	24	528	27	805
Cote d'Ivoire	92	4,944	35	1,701
Equatorial Guinea	12	46	1	-
Eritrea	17	447	4	104
Ethiopia	86	4,174	67	10,147
Gabon	14	173	8	134
Gambia, The	32	302	24	149
Ghana	121	5,977	80	4,470
Guinea	66	1,341	34	598
Guinea-Bissau	27	309	24	161
Kenya	129	4,595	68	5,251
Lesotho	33	512	21	277
Liberia	31	256	66	1,163
Madagascar	94	2,572	35	1,353
Malawi	93	2,313	41	1,625
Mali	74	1,801	46	1,668

Country	1971-2004		2005-2015	
	No. of Projects	Commitment Amount ($ million)	No. of Projects	Commitment Amount ($ million)
Mauritania	63	902	27	384
Mauritius	44	477	14	394
Mozambique	59	2,751	76	3,275
Namibia	13	8	8	24
Niger	56	1,206	44	1,390
Nigeria	112	8,118	90	11,312
Rwanda	58	1,200	52	1,784
Sao Tome and Principe	22	81	15	42
Senegal	110	2,400	56	1,870
Seychelles	8	13	11	50
Sierra Leone	37	1,007	55	634
Somalia	36	483	16	209
South Africa	20	102	9	4,017
South Sudan	0	0	35	535
Sudan	48	1,354	30	409
Swaziland	0	0	20	154
Tanzania	132	4,879	73	6,585
Togo	46	751	33	527
Uganda	100	4,119	70	4,495
Western Africa	4	59	39	3,508
Zambia	83	3,240	42	1,086
Zimbabwe	45	1,565	9	59
Overall Result	**2,528**	**77,240**	**1,830**	**86,849**

Source: World Bank

217

Appendix 3: Nigeria: Country Partnership Strategy Chairman's Concluding Remarks

Meeting of the Executive Directors
July 28, 2009

The executive directors discussed the country partnership strategy (CPS) prepared jointly with the United States Agency for International Development (USAID), United Kingdom's Department for International Development (DFID), and the African Development Bank (AfDB).

They welcomed this partnership in designing the strategy and underscored the importance of donor coordination, pointing to the benefit of a simplified organizational structure to monitor the implementation of the CPS. The need for enhanced coordination with nongovernmental organizations was also highlighted.

Directors commended the authorities for undertaking the ambitious and far-reaching reforms since 2003. They urged them to consolidate the gains, strengthen the momentum of reforms, and further enhance transparency and accountability in the use of public resources, particularly in the oil sector. Directors also noted the country's relative success in improving governance at the federal level and highlighted the need for further improvements at the state level. They pointed to the potential for development policy operations in states that have a relatively good track record on policy reforms and reasonably strong fiduciary systems. In this regard, some directors urged for more precision in the state selection criteria and underscored the importance for regional balance and distribution.

Directors broadly supported the CPS and its focus on improving governance, maintaining nonoil growth and promoting human development. They agreed with the lending envelope and the mix of instruments and analytical work. Some directors, however, would have liked to see a clearer link between the CPS and efforts to reduce poverty. Several other directors expressed concern about the low institutional capacity and weaknesses, especially at the state level. In this connection, the need for the bank to be more flexible to accommodate changing circumstances was emphasized. They noted, however, that the government needed to be vigilant in view of the uncertainty over how long and deep the global financial crisis will be and its full impact on the Nigerian economy and society.

Several directors expressed concern that Nigeria is behind in the millennium development goals (MDGs) and suggested that investments in the health and education systems would have a high impact on human development. The importance of paying greater attention to gender issues was also raised. With respect to the nonoil sector, directors suggested that the authorities focus efforts on the agriculture sector, key value chains with high growth and employment potential, and the country's infrastructure. They also encouraged greater attention to improvements in the investment climate to support private sector development. In this connection, directors welcomed IFC's role in promoting an improved business climate, which is critical in attracting private investment and spurring growth.

Finally, directors noted Nigeria's potential as a regional and continental hub and driver of economic growth. They welcomed the bank's support for and linkage to regional programs, including the potential for south-south cooperation.

Source: The World Bank.

Appendix 4: World Bank Country Assistance Evaluations

1998-2009

Country	Period of evaluation	Date of review (FY)	Rating	Country	Period of evaluation	Date of review (FY)	Rating
Highly Satisfactory Outcome							
Chile	(1985-2000)	2002	HS	Uruguay	(1987-1999)	2000	HS
El Salvador	(1989-2000)	2001	HS				
Satisfactory Outcome							
Ethiopia	(1990-1997)	1999	S	Vietnam	(1988-2001)	2002	S
Maldives	(1980-1998)	1999	S	West Bank and Gaza	(1993-2000)	2002	S
Yemen **	(1996-1998)	1999	S	Brazil	(1990-2002)	2003	S
Argentina	(1991-2000)	2000	S	Lithuania	(1991-2002)	2003	S
Ghana	(1995-1999)	2000	S	Peru **	(1990-1996)	2003	S
Uganda	(1987-1999)	2000	S	Armenia	(1993-2002)	2004	S
Mexico **	(1997-2000)	2001	S	Bosnia-Herzegovina	(1996-2003)	2004	S
Mexico **	(1989-1991)	2001	S	China	(1993-2002)	2004	S
Bulgaria **	(1998-2001)	2002	S	Croatia	(2002-2003)	2004	S
Guatemala **	(1990-2001)	2002	S	Tunisia	(1990-2003)	2004	S
Russian Federation **	(1999-2001)	2002	S	Romania **	(2000-2004)	2005	S
Moderately Satisfactory Outcome							
Bolivia	(1985-1996)	1998	MS	Jordan	(1990-2000)	2003	MS
Cambodia	(1992-1999)	1999	MS	Bhutan	(1993-2003)	2004	MS
Indonesia	(1990-1998)	1999	MS	Rwanda **	(1995-2001)	2004	MS
Sri Lanka	(1989-1998)	1999	MS	Albania	(1998-2004)	2005	MS
Burkina Faso	(1989-1999)	2000	MS	Senegal	(1994-2004)	2006	MS
Cameroon **	(1995-2000)	2000	MS	Turkey	(1993-2004)	2006	MS
Egypt	(1991-2000)	2000	MS	Indonesia	(1999-2006)	2007	MS
India	(1990-2000)	2001	MS	Mali	(1995-2005)	2007	MS
Kazakhstan	(1990-1999)	2001	MS	Ukraine	(1999-2006)	2007	MS
Kyrgyz Republic	(1993-2000)	2001	MS	Cambodia*	(1999-2006)	2008	MS

Country	Period of evaluation	Date of review (FY)	Rating	Country	Period of evaluation	Date of review (FY)	Rating
Mexico **	(1995-1996)	2001	MS	Egypt	(1999-2007)	2008	MS
Mongolia	(1991-2001)	2002	MS	Georgia	(1993-2007)	2008	MS
Dom. Republic	(1985-2002)	2003	MS	Bangladesh	(2001-2008)	2009	MS
Eritrea	(1992-2000)	2003	MS	Uganda	(2001-2007)	2009	MS
Moderately Unsatisfactory Outcome							
Yemen **	(1990-1995)	1999	MU	Honduras	(1995-2005)	2006	MU
Morocco	(1997-2000)	2001	MU	Madagascar	(1994-2006)	2006	MU
Mexico **	(1992-1994)	2001	MU	Yemen	(1999-2005)	2006	MU
Lesotho	(1990-1999)	2002	MU	Angola	(1991-2006)	2007	MU
Bolivia	(1998-2004)	2005	MU	Ethiopia	(1998-2006)	2008	MU
Pacific Islands	(1992-2002)	2005	MU	Nigeria	(1998-2007)	2008	MU
Pakistan	(1994-2003)	2005	MU	Nepal	(2003-2008)	2009	MU
Unsatisfactory Outcome							
Ecuador	(1994-1998)	1999	U	Guatemala **	(1985-1989)	2002	U
Jamaica	(1980-1998)	1999	U	Russian Federation **	(1992-1998)	2002	U
Nepal	(1990-1999)	1999	U	Peru **	(1997-2000)	2003	U
Ukraine	(1993-1998)	1999	U	Zambia	(1996-2001)	2003	U
Costa Rica	(1990-2000)	2000	U	Zimbabwe	(1990-2002)	2003	U
Papua New Guinea	(1990-1999)	2000	U	Moldova	(1993-2003)	2004	U
Cameroon **	(1982-1994)	2000	U	Rwanda **	(1990-1994)	2004	U
Paraguay	(1990-2000)	2001	U	Mauritania	(1992-2003)	2005	U
Haiti	(1986-2001)	2002	U	Romania **	(1991-1999)	2005	U
Bulgaria **	(1991-1997)	2002	U	Malawi	(1996-2005)	2006	U

Notes:
* The Cambodia CAE evaluated Bank performance and outcomes until calendar year 2006.
**A single CAE provided ratings for different evaluation periods.

Source: Independent Evaluation Group, The World Bank

Endnotes

Introduction

[1] Address on June 5, 1947, by George C. Marshall to the graduates on commencement day for Harvard College.

[2] Ludwig Erhard, "Veröffentlichung von Wilhelm Röpke," in *In Memoriam Wilhelm Röpke*, ed., Universität Marburg, Rechts-und-Staatswissenschaftlice Fakultät.

[3] The World Bank, formally known as the International Bank for Reconstruction and Development (IBRD), was created following a meeting of 44 Allied nations at Bretton Woods, New Hampshire, in July 1944 after the war ended. The primary purpose of the meeting, however, was to discuss the regulation of the postwar international monetary and financial system, leading to the creation of the International Monetary Fund (IMF). Together, the IMF and the World Bank are thus often referred to as the Bretton Woods institutions.

[4] Bilateral aid is aid provided on a country to country basis. When aid is provided from pooled resources of countries, as in the case of the World Bank, it is referred to as multilateral aid.

[5] History of USAID. *http://www.usaid.gov/about_usaid/usaidhist.html*

[6] Milton Friedman, *Economic Freedom, Human Freedom, Political Freedom.* Lecture delivered at the Smith Center for Private Enterprise Studies, California State University at East Bay, November 1, 1991.

[7] Peter Thomas Bauer, *Dissent on Development* (Cambridge: Harvard University Press, 1972).

[8] William Easterly, *The White Man's Burden: Why the West's Efforts to Aid the Rest Have Done So Much Ill and So Little Good* (New York: The Penguin Press, 2006).

[9] Monica Francois and Inder Sud, "Promoting Stability and Development in Failed and Fragile States," *Development Policy Review* (2006): 24(2).

[10] The World Bank, *Engaging with Fragile States: An IEG Review of World Bank Support to Low-Income Countries under Stress*, Independent Evaluation Group, 2006.

[11] As early as early 1980s, when the record of failure of aid projects in Africa was already evident, the proponents of foreign aid began to expound the rather novel view that even when a project fails, it still makes a contribution to broader development. See Robert Caseen & Associates, Does Aid Work? (Clarendon, Oxford, 1986).

[12] North Korea and Cuba are the notable exceptions.

Part I
Chapter 4

[13] The share has since been raised gradually to some 45 percent today in consideration of greater economic power of certain developing countries. The issue of greater voice for developing countries in the World Bank (and IMF) Board continues to be a contentious issue.

Chapter 5

[14] The term "underdeveloped countries" was used in much of the early years of development but was already out of vogue in the 1970s when it was replaced by the term "developing countries."

[15] International Labour Organization, Men Who Move Mountains (Geneva, 1963).

[16] The legacy of poor quality and standards of roads in India unfortunately has continued to this day. While the roads have improved significantly since the 1970s, they are still grossly inadequate to serve the traffic needs of today.

[17] This finding very much upset the Indian government representative on the World Bank Board when we presented our findings to them. He reportedly remarked to someone that he could understand the Western bias on the study in the work (my bosses were an American and a Canadian), but he was dismayed that "the Indian boy" was complicit in the findings!

Chapter 6

[18] *Learning by Doing* was the title of a retrospective of the urban work done by the World Bank in 1986.

Chapter 7

[19] Tarbela Dam was completed in 1968 at a cost of almost $700 million. It was one of the biggest projects in the developing world at the time.

Chapter 9

[20] Graduation means that the country is no longer eligible to borrow from the World Bank because its per capita income exceeds certain threshold (currently $6,725). Only a few previously classified developing countries have passed this threshold: Taiwan, Singapore, Korea, Chile, and more recently most of the countries in eastern Europe.

[21] The administrative cost to the bank of processing and subsequently supervising a small loan are often the same as for a larger loan. So the bank prefers to not process too many small projects

[22] Sebastian Mallaby, "NGOs: Fighting Poverty, Hurting the Poor," *Foreign Policy*, No. 144 (2004), pp. 50-58.

[23] Sebastian Mallaby, *The World's Banker: A Story of Failed States, Financial Crises, and the Wealth and Poverty of Nations* (New York: The Penguin Press, 2004).

Chapter 10

[24] IDA was created in 1960 when the World Bank realized that many of the newly independent developing countries were too poor to be able to borrow on World Bank's terms that, even though quite concessional, were still too onerous for them. IDA was created as a soft loan window to provide funds to the poorer countries. Unlike the World Bank, it derives its resources from contributions by industrialized countries that are replenished in a 3-year cycle. Loans from IDA are called "credits" to distinguish them from the World Bank loans. However, in order to simplify the discussion, I use the term "World Bank loans" to include both the World Bank loans and credits from IDA.

[25] The term was coined by economists to describe the very slow rate of economic growth in India in the 1970s and 1980s that barely exceeded the population growth in the country. Thus, India made little progress in reducing abject poverty in this period.

Chapter 11

[26] The Brady Plan, named after the architect of the plan, the then U.S. treasury secretary Jim Brady, has been credited with resolving the debt crisis in Latin America in the 1980s, although some critics consider it to have been a public bailout of the commercial banks.

[27] IFC, or International Finance Corporation, is the arm of the World Bank that supports private investment in developing countries without the guarantee from the government. MIGA, or Multilateral Investment Guarantee Corporation, provides insurance to private investors against political risks. They feared that guarantees from the World Bank, a much larger and more powerful institution, would displace loans or investments they could have made or supported. Most World Bank presidents have tried to get the three institutions to cooperate rather than compete, with varying degrees of success.

Chapter 12

[28] Since the dinner was completely off the record, I have decided to not name the attendees.

[29] Sebastian Mallaby, *The World's Banker: A Story of Failed States, Financial Crisis, and the Wealth and Poverty of Nations* (New York The Penguin Press, 2004).

[30] David A. Phillips, *Reforming the World Bank: Twenty Years of Trial—and Error* (Cambridge University Press, 2009).

[31] The minutes of the board meeting that discussed the evaluation starts: "[T]he Directors welcomed the clarity, comprehensiveness, and candor of the three reports and commended their authors. They also expressed satisfaction that solid progress had been made in improving the quality and effectiveness of Bank's operations. They commended the president, his management team, and the bank staff for their achievement, while emphasizing that there is no room for complacency . . . Several Directors expressed appreciation that management had made a concerted effort to prepare a draft program to address the areas of weakness . . ." ibid., 244.

[32] *Financial Times*, September 22, 23, and 27, 1999.

[33] Wolfowitz was the undersecretary of defense in the Bush administration and a prominent neocon.

[34] In a letter in the online edition of *Wall Street Journal*, Robert Holland, the acting U.S. executive director on the World Bank questioned the motives of World Bank staff and the board for seeking Wolfowitz's ouster, calling them "parochial, overpaid, self-interested, and ineffective." Robert B. Holland, "The Real World Bank Scandal-Why the Bureaucracy Wants to Oust Paul Wolfowitz," WSJ.com, April 20, 2007.

Chapter 13

[35] This chapter draws from my chapter "Reflections on Development," in At the Frontiers of Development: Reflections from the World Bank, Indermit S. Gill and Todd Pugatch, editors, The World Bank, Washington DC, 2004.

[36] WBG was (and still is) actually not a country. It was receiving funds from IDA under a special trust fund arrangement. For simplicity, I will refer to it as a country in this discussion.

Chapter 14

[37] One early and important contribution of the World Bank in Afghanistan was to finance a cellular network that helped greatly with communication by wireless phones and internet within the country.

[38] Foreign aid in its original design was always intended to be a catalyst rather than a driver of development, a fact that has unfortunately been forgotten over the years.

[39] Afghanistan: A Synthesis Paper of Lessons from Ten Years of Aid, January 24, 2013.
https://ieg.worldbankgroup.org/Data/reports/Afghanistan_Lessons_Ten_Years.pdf

Part III
Chapter 15

[40] To most people who follow foreign aid, normally equate the word "conditionality" with conditions imposed in structural adjustment loans. These conditions are normally associated with hardships for the people because they dealt with issues like cutting subsidies, balancing budgets, privatization, trade liberalization, etc. In reality, conditionality is also imposed in project aid, although because of its relatively more benign nature, it has not attracted much attention.

[41] The Independent Evaluation Group is ostensibly an independent arm of the board of executive directors of the World Bank. It evaluates upon completion all projects financed by the World Bank. Until 2004, IEG was called the Operations Evaluation Department, or OED. Further discussion on the extent of independence of IEG is in Chapter 23.

[42] Sustainability was a key aspect of IEG's evaluations until 2000 when it inexplicably began to de-emphasize it and stopped reported it completely around 2005.

[43] The Strategic Compact was an agreement Wolfensohn secured from the Board in April 1997 for a major reform initiative. By investing an extra $400 million over three years Wolfensohn aimed to deliver "a fundamentally transformed institution – quicker, less bureaucratic, more able to respond continuously to changing client demands and global development opportunities, and more effective and efficient in achieving its main mission-reducing poverty". It also promised to recoup the $400 million through efficiency savings after the three year implementation.

[44] Indur M. Goklany, The Improving State of the World (Cato Institute, 2007).

[45] Craig Burnside and David Dollar, "Aid, Policies, and Growth," American Economic Review (2000) 90.4, pp. 847-868.

[46] Henrik Hansen and Finn Tarp, "Aid Effectiveness Disputed," Journal of Development Studies (2000) 12.3, pp. 375-98.

[47] William Easterly, "Can Foreign Aid Buy Growth?" Journal of Economic Perspective (2003) 17.3, pp. 23-48.

[48] Meta-analysis is a statistical technique for amalgamating, summarizing, and reviewing previous quantitative research.

[49] Chris (Hristos) *Doucouliagos*, and *Martin Paldam*, "The Aid Effectiveness Literature: The Sad Results of 40 Years of Research*," Journal of Economic Surveys (2009) 23.3, pp. 433-461.*

[50] As quoted in A Case for Aid: Building a Consensus for Development Assistance (Washington DC: The World Bank, 2002).

[51] The Burnside and Dollar paper published in the American Economic Review does not include these assertions, presumably because these were unsupported by evidence. These were included in the original study published by the World Bank, Assessing Foreign Aid: What Works, What Doesn't, and Why (Oxford University Press, 1998).

Chapter 17

[52] The requirement continues to this day.

[53] A common saying in the bank, only partly in jest, is that when a project receives high praise in the board, one should immediately mark it as a potential "problem project" during implementation!

[54] The task force was comprised of the seasoned bank staff and managers and chaired by Willi Wapenhans, a respected vice president of the bank. The report of the task force carries his name: The Wapenhans Report, Effective Implementation Key to Development Impact (World Bank, 1992).

[55] Ibid., 5.

[56] 1992 Evaluation Results, Operations Evaluation Department, The World Bank, 1994, p. x.

[57] Wapenhans Report, "Effective Implementation: Key to Development Impact," op cit., Annex B, p. 3, box 1.

[58] The inspection panel was established as a check on the bank staff that they adhere to established bank policy on issues such as environment and resettlement. In practice, under its first chair, Jim MacNeal, it assumed a much more intrusive role and started investigating far-fetched issues that it decided should be adjudicated against "policy" as it saw it. This has created a great aversion to any risk taking by the bank staff. Sebastian Malaby, in his book, The World's Banker (New York: The Penguin Press, 2004), pp. 276-285, provides a detailed account of the overreach by the inspection panel in a project in China that led to considerable internal consternation in the bank when China threatened to stop any future relations with the bank. It led Wolfensohn to rethink his NGO engagement strategy.

[59] Quoted in The World Bank, World Bank Support for Capacity Building in Africa, 2005.

[60] The Bretton Woods Commission was convened by the World Bank in 1993 and headed by Paul Volker that examined reforms of the IMF and the World Bank.

[61] Moisés Naim, The World Bank: Its role, governance and organizational culture, in Bretton Woods: Looking to the Future, Report of the Bretton Woods Commission, July 1994.

Chapter 18

[62] Judith Tendler, Inside of Foreign Aid (Baltimore: Johns Hopkins University Press, 1976).

[63] The World Bank. Nigeria Country Assistance Evaluation: The World Bank in Nigeria, 1998-2007, June 30, 2008. Although all country assistance evaluations by IEG are supposed to be available publicly, the Nigeria evaluation was released only in July 2010, two years after its completion, leading to the possible

speculation that it was to avoid someone making a link between the poor evaluation and the increased allocation for Nigeria that was approved in 2009.
[64] Ibid., . x.
[65] The World Bank, Statement of Loans and Credits, June 27, 2010.
[66] The Daily Star, Bangladesh. World Bank to double assistance: $6b in 4 years, including $1.2b for Padma Bridge project, July 11, 2010.
[67] The World Bank, Statement of Loans and Credits, June 27, 2010.
[68] The World Bank, Taming Leviathan: Reforming Governance in Bangladesh: An Institutional Review, 1999.

Chapter 19

[69] Moisés Naim, "Fad and fashions in economic reforms: Washington Consensus or Washington Confusion?" Third World Quarterly (2000) 21:3, pp. 514.
[70] There is no readily available information on the funding the World Bank has provided for capacity building over the years. This estimate is derived from a sample of recently approved projects for which appraisal documents are publicly available. These indicate that technical assistance comprises 10-20 percent of the loan, which would make the estimate in the range of $80-160 billion. The Organization for Economic Cooperation and Development (OECD), which maintains statistics on aid flows, estimates technical assistance in the 36-40 percent range for all aid programs
[71] The World Bank, Capacity Building in Africa: An OED Evaluation of World Bank Support, 2005.
[72] As reported in Roger C. Riddell, Does Foreign Aid Really Work? (Oxford: Oxford University Press, 2007), pp. 211.

Chapter 20

[73] Sheherzade Jafari and Inder K. Sud, "Performance-Based Foreign Assistance Through Millennium Challenge Account: Sustained Economic Growth as the Objective Qualifying Criterion," International Public Management Journal (2004), 7(2), pp. 245-270.

Part III
Introduction

[74] Harinder Kohli and Anil Sood (eds.), India 2039: An Affluent Society in One Generation (Sage, 2009).
[75] Currently, LIBOR plus a spread of 60-115 basis points (or 0.60-1.15 percent), and repayment over 15-30 years, after up to 7 years of grace period.

Chapter 21

[76] As reported by David A. Phillips, Reforming the World Bank: Twenty Years of Trial-and Error (Cambridge University Press, 2009) pp. 242-243.

Chapter 22

[77] One exception was Barber Conable, who served from 1986 to 1990. Conable had been a Republican member of U.S. Congress, but enjoyed a bipartisan reputation. He was appointment by President George Bush at a time when there was a growing dissatisfaction with the bank in the U.S. Congress. Conable was expected to repair this relationship, and he was indeed successful in doing this.

Chapter 23

[78] A few years back, IEG imposed a restriction on its managers not being appointed in the bank. But this restriction was later removed in specific cases to get better-qualified managers from the operational side of the bank to apply.
[79] International Financial Institutions Advisory Commission, The Meltzer Commission Report, March 2000.
[80] Financial Times, March 12, 2002.
[81] Interested readers would find it instructive to read the 1-3-page summary of CODE review appended to major IEG reports before their release to appreciate my point about CODE's passive role.
[82] Report of the Blue Ribbon Commission chaired by Paul Volker and Jose Angel Gurria, April 26, 2001. Carnegie Endowment for International Peace.

Chapter 24

[83] http://www.oecd.org/dataoecd/57/60/36080258.pdf
[84] S. Lister, Evaluation of General Budget Support: Synthesis Report (University of Birmingham, 2006).

Chapter 25

[85] I consider the big jump in World Bank loans in 2009 and 2010, to $46.5 billion and $50.5 billion respectively, as an unusual one-time occurrence that was defensive borrowing by World Bank borrowers to cushion themselves against the financial crisis. This unusually high level of borrowing is not expected to be sustained.

Chapter 26

[86] "Multilateral Development Banking for this Century's Development Challenges: Five Recommendations to Shareholders of the Old and New Multilateral Development Banks," Nancy Birdsall and Scott Morris, October 5, 2016

Index

www.ingramcontent.com/pod-product-compliance
Lightning Source LLC
Chambersburg PA
CBHW030429290526
45786CB00001B/210